PRESIDENTS, KINGS AND CONVICTS

My Journey from the Tennessee Governor's Residence to the Halls of Congress

U.S. CONGRESSMAN
BOB CLEMENT, D-TN

FOREWORD BY COUNTRY MUSIC ARTIST
LEE GREENWOOD "GOD BLESS THE USA"

With Dava Guerin and Pete Weichlein

ARCHWAY PUBLISHING

Archway Publishing books may be ordered through booksellers or by contacting:

Archway Publishing
1663 Liberty Drive
Bloomington, IN 47403
www.archwaypublishing.com
1 (888) 242-5904

Because of the dynamic nature of the Internet, any web addresses or links contained in this book may have changed since publication and may no longer be valid. The views expressed in this work are solely those of the author and do not necessarily reflect the views of the publisher, and the publisher hereby disclaims any responsibility for them.

Any people depicted in stock imagery provided by Thinkstock are models, and such images are being used for illustrative purposes only. Certain stock imagery © Thinkstock.

ISBN: 978-1-4808-3443-9 (sc)
ISBN: 978-1-4808-3444-6 (hc)
ISBN: 978-1-4808-3445-3 (e)

Library of Congress Control Number: 2016948695

Print information available on the last page.

Archway Publishing rev. date: 10/19/2016

Contents

Foreword by Lee Greenwood vii

Endorsements... ix

Dedication..xiii

Acknowledgements xv

Introduction xix

Chapter 1 Don't Call it the Governor's Mansion 1

Chapter 2 Politics: The Family Passion 25

Chapter 3 Turning Point: You're in the Army Now................. 41

Chapter 4 Returning Home: Setting the Stage for My
Career in Politics... 57

Chapter 5 Saving Cumberland University 84

Chapter 6 From Nashville to Washington 132

Chapter 7 The World Before and After September 11.......... 163

Chapter 8 Country Music and Me: Tales from Music
City U.S.A 191

Chapter 9 The Rewards and Challenges of Lawmaking....... 213

Chapter 10 The Secrets of Great Leaders 241

Chapter 11 Why Can't We All Get Along?
Our Hyper-Partisan America................................... 259

Chapter 12 Life After Congress: Keeping the Spirit of
Service Alive 290

Chapter 13 Fixing America: My Prescription for Getting
the Country Back on Track................................... 305

Chapter 14 Behind-the-Scenes with Presidents, Kings
            and Convicts 321
Epilogue 349
About the Authors 353

Foreword

By Lee Greenwood

I believe your life's experiences mold your character.

In Bob Clement's book, *Presidents, Kings and Convicts*, he shows how his character was formed.

Standing shoulder to shoulder with leaders of our country from both parties, he helped shape decades of American life. Proudly reflecting his father's ideals, Bob has stood tall as a loyal southern gentleman, and one of our nations' brightest congressional leaders. A career soldier, a champion for Tennessee and a hero to his family, his handshake is his word, his smile infectious, and his humor disarming.

I met Bob at one of my shows in Tennessee at Mud Island in Memphis. It was a sold-out show featuring the Judd's as my opening act. Congressman Clement was in the audience and after the show he sent back an MIA bracelet. It somehow ended up on the bus with a wonderful note of gratitude for my show. I still wear it today!

During my first few years in Tennessee, I learned more about Bob and all that he had done for the state. Later that year, I agreed to do a fundraiser for him because I knew we needed a man like that to remain in Congress. That surprised a few of my conservative friends, but before long he won them over as well.

In this new book, Bob shares stories of life learned from the worst and the best. His life has been an amazing story and *Presidents, Kings and Convicts* will allow you to see the history he has lived through his eyes.

This book is an easy read and will capture your heart.

Lee Greenwood is a country music superstar, award-winning singer-songwriter, patriot and best-selling author.

ENDORSEMENTS

"Bob has written a wonderful book, and it captures the spirit of Music City U.S.A. It also will inspire readers anywhere in the country and hopefully encourage them to serve. The chapter on country music captures the magic of Nashville and its role as a world class city and the home of one of the greatest musical genres of the world. Thank you, Bob for writing it!"

—Steve Turner, chairman of the board of the Country Music Hall of Fame

"I've known Bob for almost my entire life, from when we were both teenagers in Tennessee to the days when we worked together in Washington, D.C. We share a deep love of country, a trait that was obvious in Bob's tireless work for the people of Tennessee and the United States. His autobiography, *Presidents, Kings and Convicts*, gives readers an inside look into Bob's remarkable life from Nashville to our nation's Capital."

—Former Vice President Al Gore

"Bob's book, *Presidents, Kings and Convicts,* is striking in that you feel like you are present though the various times in his life. His words are compelling and he takes you on a journey worth traveling. As a reader, you don't want to put it down. It is also a book that you want to read all the way through so you don't miss a thing. I've known Bob since we were in the ROTC program together at the University of Tennessee. Bob was in the Army and I was in the Air Force. He is a person who speaks with one voice and is as genuine a person as you will ever meet. I hope everyone will read his book, and learn and be inspired from his fascinating life."

—General Ken Jordan
Former Assistant Adjutant General
for the Tennessee Air National Guard

"Bob is a truly unique person and I am thankful to have had worked for him as his press secretary when he was in Congress. He was a great mentor to me, and I am not underestimating how he made me the person I am today. Bob's story is unique and needs to be told, and I am confident that anyone who reads it will come away a better and more educated person. I would hope every American reads this fabulous book!"

—Bart Herbison, executive director,
Nashville Songwriters Association

"I have known Bob for more than twenty years. We served together in Congress for five years, he as a moderate Southern Democrat and I as a moderate Republican. Despite our political differences, we had a great working relationship. Bob was always a bridge-builder attacking the issues never his fellow colleagues. In his new book, *Presidents, Kings and Convicts*, he gives readers a fascinating look at his life growing up with convicts, meeting with world leaders, U.S. Presidents, royalty and even, 'The King,' Elvis Presley. Anyone interested in politics should read this wonderful book, as well as those who want to be inspired to pursue a life of public service."

—Connie Morella, (R-MD)
former Congresswoman and Ambassador (ret.)

"If I were teaching political science, and I did at Cumberland, I would require it as reading in my class. It is a clear picture of politics and service and is very inspiring. It is a wonderful book!"

**—Dr. Charlene Kozy, former president,
Cumberland University**

"*Presidents, Kings and Convicts* is a fabulous book, and captures the country music scene here in Nashville. But it is so much more. It gives us a behind-the-scenes tour of politics here in Tennessee and on a national level and is a fun and interesting read."

—Jeannie Seely, Grand Ole Opry

"Bob's book is a tour de force of politics, from Tennessee to Washington. A must read, particularly in today's realm of partisan politics."

**—Terry Bivens, economics professor and former analyst,
J.P. Morgan Chase**

"I've known Bob most of my life and his book brings back so many memories for me. But it also shows his love of politics and his keen insights into how our government works and his role in shaping so many important issues the country has faced over the years. It inspired me and I know it will do the same for anyone fortunate enough to read it!"

**—Mike Hardwick, founder and chairman of
Churchill Mortgage Corporation**

DEDICATION

This book is dedicated to my partner in life, Mary Clement, my daughters Elizabeth (Trael Webb) and Rachel (Josh Raymond) my stepsons Greg, Jeff and his family, and my grandchildren, Tennysen, Selah Grace, Robert (Clement), Mary (Carson), and Savannah Burke, my parents Frank and Lucille Clement, for teaching me to be a good public servant and a compassionate human being, my brothers Frank and Gary, Mary's parents Noble and Maggie Carson for loving me like a son, Nelse and Verne Christianson and Robert and May Belle Clement for giving me the gifts of learning and love of the great outdoors, and all my extended family, including those who are no longer with us, my God parents, Bob and Gladys Lippner, Marshall and Mary Ledbetter, Sr. and Dr. Ray and Phyllis Phillips. All of these individuals have helped make me the man I am today.

Acknowledgements

Writing your life story is no easy feat and could not have been accomplished without a team of talented and dedicated professionals. Dava Guerin, the author of a wonderful and important book called, *Unbreakable Bonds: The Mighty Moms and Wounded Warriors of Walter Reed*, helped me organize my thoughts and put them down on paper in a clear and thought provoking manner. Pete Weichlein, CEO of the U.S. Association of Former Members of Congress, used his considerable political skills to help me recall and record some of the major historical events of our time, and added his thoughts and insights throughout the project. Of course my wife, Mary Clement was my own commander-in-chief, keeping me writing and thinking back on my thirty years in public service. Without her support, this book would never have been written. Bart Herbison's wise counsel and his own contributions to the book were invaluable. Dr. Charlene Kozy, Beth Prichard Geer, Roy Herron, Pamela Clements, Dr. Paul Stumb, Scot Danforth, Carolyn Waugh, Terry Bivens, Terri Dorsey and Tom Vickstrom took time out of their busy schedules to read the early book drafts and give me valuable insights which I hope they will see in the finished product. Our dear friends, Patsy Holt, Susan Lockhart and Lou Hughes, worked tirelessly with Mary the last couple of years to catalogue my stories and personal photos which helped set the stage for bringing it all together for this book. My agent, Lloyd

Remick Esq., guided me through the publishing process and gave valuable advice from his stellar career in entertainment law. Lee Greenwood was kind enough to write the forward, and I am most grateful. Al Gore, Dolly Parton, Justice Gary Wade, Gene Ward, Jeannie Seely, Steve Turner, Bud Wendell, and Mike Hardwick provided their valuable insights and for that I am eternally grateful. After leaving Congress to enter a new chapter in my life, I am also grateful for those who inspired and encouraged me as I embarked upon new challenges and opportunities. They include: Dell Crosslin and family, Henry and Sue McCall, Tom Simpson, Caroline Decker, Farzin Ferdowsi, Homey Aminmadani, Buddy Dukes, Charlie and Marie Cardwell, John McDowell, Dr. Jack Gayden, David Dumke, Barry Komisar, Bill Freeman, Jimmy Webb, Larry Woods, Jimmy Crossman, Kathy and Hugh Faust, Bob Tuke and Pam Slaton. I owe a debt of gratitude to my many friends and colleagues here in the State of Tennessee and around the country, especially those members of Congress with whom I was proud to serve. I would be remiss not to recognize the men and women who I served with in the U.S. Army, and the Tennessee Army National Guard, and for everyone who has served the nation with honor and distinction. Lastly, I want to thank those who supported me all along my political journey including the Tennessee Democrat Party and its current chairman, Mary Mancini, and past chairmen over the years. They have worked tirelessly on behalf of candidates like me. I also remain grateful to the thousands of voters who went to the polls to cast their vote for me, Democrats, Republicans, and Independents. The volunteers who worked hard on all my campaigns to get out the vote, helped put the needed structures in place that are necessary for positive outcomes. Also the donors who unselfishly supported my campaigns with their financial contributions, success could not have been possible. All these individuals became Mary and my dearest friends, and even though we don't see many of them on a daily basis we hope they will continue to know they are in our hearts. We truly became a family. Because of the closeness we shared and still do with many, it made it possible to love what we were called on to do during our political life.

Introduction

My life has been filled with ironic and unusual experiences. From growing up in the Tennessee governor's residence with prisoners who were convicted murderers, and meeting distinguished visitors including Presidents John F. Kennedy and Harry Truman, Billy Graham, and Elvis Presley—to having a heart-felt conversation with President Bill Clinton about how to deal with Iraq and its tyrannical leader at the time, Saddam Hussein, I've had a front-row seat to some of the most significant historical events in our nation's history. I've also had the distinct advantage of growing up with a famous political father and mentor.

My dad, Frank G. Clement, was elected governor of Tennessee for three terms. I spent my formative years under his tutelage, realizing at a very early age that I wanted a career in politics. It wasn't a picture-perfect fairy tale life as one might expect. Our family had upheavals as does every family. Dad endured death threats because of his unpopular, anti-segregationist policies in the deeply divided South of the 1950s and 1960s. We had Tennessee State Troopers guarding the perimeter of our home, and we often faced ridicule from some of the officials of the eight states that border Tennessee. But, still, I learned many valuable lessons from those experiences from a devoted mother and father who recognized my political prowess. They included me in all of their campaign activities, as well as their meetings with politicians, world leaders and country music superstars. Those experiences inspired me to pursue a career in public service spanning thirty years. I served in the U.S. military, was elected to the Tennessee Public Service Commission, appointed as director of the Tennessee Valley Authority by President Jimmy Carter was a college president, and I served eight-terms in the U.S. House of Representatives.

My new book, *Presidents, Kings and Convicts* tells the story of my colorful life as a moderate democrat growing up in the South in the 1950s. It also reveals many untold stories about famous and controversial people. Some of those encounters truly altered the course of U.S. history, though up to now has been locked away in my memory.

The book also shares my front-row seat to some of America's most significant events since WWII, including the desegregation of the South, Iran Contra, the liberation of Kuwait, and 9/11, among so many others. It offers my insights on the current crisis situations taking place in the Middle East and around the world. These include: the terrorist activities of ISIS (Islamic State in Iraq and Syria); the Russian invasion of Ukraine; and the continuing war between Israel and the Palestinians. I also addressed the dysfunction and lack of bi-partisanship among our nation's political leaders, as well as offered solutions for getting the country back on track. I hope my words will inspire the next generation to consider careers in public service and not view politics as a dirty word.

I hope it will also provide entertaining and captivating behind-the-scenes accounts of some of those memorable events and the people who shaped them. I will take readers with me to Nashville Tennessee, Music City U.S.A, and share many of my personal stories of country music greats including Eddy Arnold, Dolly Parton, Johnny and June Carter Cash, Lee Greenwood, Jeannie Seely and many others. I also explore the impact country music has had on American culture.

Readers will experience what it was like to be part of many major events in recent American history including: the bipartisan meeting with the exiled King of Afghanistan and leaders of the Northern Alliance at the king's home outside Rome Italy; intimate and personal moments with notable Americans such as, John Glenn, Al Gore and Elvis Presley; and encounters with Presidents Harry Truman, Dwight Eisenhower, John F. Kennedy, Lyndon Johnson, Ronald Reagan, Gerald Ford, Jimmy Carter, George H. W. Bush, George W. Bush, Bill Clinton and Barack Obama.

These diverse experiences, and my life-lessons learned from each, are summarized at the conclusion of each chapter. I call them Clement's Contemplations, and they include my thoughts and musings gleaned from a life filled with sacrifice, service and spirit.

With a generation lost in terms of wanting to pursue careers in politics, and many Americans without role models and mentors in their lives, I hope my book will inspire readers and offer them tangible life-lessons.

I hope that my life story will inspire young people and anyone interested in politics, business, entertainment or any other career. I pray that they can learn from my insights and the lessons I have internalized along my own life's journey. Things such as: overcoming life's inevitable disappointments; coping with trauma and tragedy; dealing with the challenges of political campaigns; or adjusting to the fact that everyone might not like you—especially when you grow up with a famous father, these are insights that I hope I can pass along to everyone who reads my life story. I hope they will also enjoy the inside and exclusive tales about famous people with whom I've had the privilege to get to know from growing up in the Tennessee governor's residence. They can experience along with me what it was like to be an eyewitness to history, and the remarkable people I've met who made it come alive.

Chapter 1

Don't Call it the Governor's Mansion

"The murderers were my best friends."—Bob Clement

Most people would run for the hills if they ever met up with a prisoner, especially if that prisoner was a murderer. But to me, they were my best friends. They cooked my meals and played basketball and football with me in the backyard. Some of them were the best pals a kid could ever have. I guess you could say that my childhood was a bit unusual. That is, if you think criminals are your friends, your father is famous, and the mansion you lived in was to be referred as a "residence." And add to those state troopers surrounding your home, receiving death threats, and oh yes, having a monkey living in your bathroom—well, that's just the beginning of my wonderfully colorful life.

I was nine-years-old when my father was first elected governor of Tennessee on November 4, 1952. He was the kind of person that you just couldn't ignore. To me, he was a giant, especially since I was so young when he took office. He was tall with thick wavy black hair piercing sky-blue eyes, and a voice that would mesmerize anyone lucky enough to hear him speak. He stood out among the crowd, and there were few in Tennessee who didn't know his name.

My mother, Lucille, was simply the most beautiful person inside and out. She could have been a movie star with Marilyn Monroe looks, and she might have gone on to Hollywood had she not met and married Dad when she was just nineteen years old. When Mother walked into a room, she took command of it, and not just because of her beauty. She had an elegance and grace that was truly unique. That resolve would be tested over the years, as she would be faced with the trials and tribulations of being a political spouse, suffering from post-partum depression, and losing her beloved son, my youngest brother, Gary, when he was just thirty-nine-years-old.

I was born in Nashville, Tennessee, a city that has grown so much since I was a child. It is now one of the most cosmopolitan cities in the country in terms of diversity of jobs and opportunities, not to mention being known as Music City U.S.A. When I was growing up, everyone knew one another and while it was a more innocent time, the 1950's in our Southern city was feeling the tensions of segregation, and was in great need of strong leadership. But, as a young boy, my thoughts were more focused on innocently mundane pursuits, like jumping into the lily pond or figuring out how to raise chickens and other farm animals.

During my dad's first race for governor of Tennessee in 1952 we moved from Dickson, Tennessee to the Hermitage Hotel in Nashville where we lived for six months during his campaign. The Hermitage Hotel was—and still is—Nashville's finest. Since Dad was such a fan of country music, residing in the heart of Nashville was like a dream come true.

During the campaign, Dad would have some of the biggest names in country music at the time help him get out the vote, and they would appear together at political rallies and events. Even as a young boy, I learned to love those heartfelt, gutsy songs, and the way people like Johnny Cash, Eddy Arnold, Roy Acuff, Minnie Pearl, Loretta Lynn, and Little Jimmy Dickens sang them.

But I knew I wasn't the average kid. After all, average kids wouldn't be about to move into a real-life mansion. I must admit, the place was very big and imposing to me at the time. It was originally built by Ridley Wills, the vice president of the National Life and Accident Insurance Company. He named it Far Hills, as a present to his wife. The house was situated on twelve acres of lush Tennessee land, and it had four floors, a winding staircase, and eight bathrooms. The Wills family moved in to Far Hills in 1931, and they lived there for eighteen years before they sold the property to the state of Tennessee for $120,000.

I will always remember my first visit to the residence. As a young boy I was particularly in awe of its size, and I especially remember being fascinated with the lily pond that was about three and a half feet deep. Once we were settled in, we removed all of the fish, and drained the water, and then painted it. My parents filled the pond back up with water and that became our little private swimming pool. I thought it was the greatest thing in the world!

Both of my parents wanted all three boys to grow up in a normal family environment, and they would always tell us that we were not the sons of a governor, but just kids like any others growing up in the south at the time. We were allowed to dress like average young boys our age, though most of my friends didn't live in a house with highway patrolmen stationed on the premises. Since I was the oldest son and the only child in the family for the first six years of my life, I had the advantage of having a great deal of attention from my parents as one might imagine. My parents named me after both my grandfather's--Robert and Nelson in an effort to honor them. Not knowing whether there would be any other children, they named me Robert Nelson Clement.

It was only my mom and me in the house most of the time since Dad had a grueling work schedule. Those were some of the best years of my life. I never remember even having a baby sitter until I was nine when we moved into the governor's residence. I can't even recall when my mother wasn't there at my school volunteering, or when she wasn't there cheering from the stands at my football and basketball games or other sports events. And she was as devoted a mother to my brothers too, wanting us to eat our meals together in the small dining room at the governor's residence as often as possible. She was always there for all of our school functions, even serving on the PTA to make sure we were receiving the best education possible.

Mother was the key to my future in many ways, because when I was twelve she enrolled me in speech classes that ultimately led to my joining the debate team in high school. That experience gave me the confidence to speak in front of groups both large and small, and would come in handy when I accompanied Dad on so many of his campaign stops. Mother allowed me to host many social events throughout the years we lived there, and she let us run around the house in blue jeans and tee shirts, not suits and ties or other formal attire that some people might expect of a public official's children at the time.

Since the property was so massive, we had plenty of room to cause endless mischief, but mostly I concentrated on more productive pursuits—like farming.

I always loved animals. Dr. Walter S. Davis, who was the president of Tennessee State University, would bring a fresh turkey as a gift every year for Thanksgiving and Christmas. At the time, the university had a substantial farm on its property, and Dr. Davis inspired me to create my own farm at the governor's residence. While I was nervous at first to ask my parents if I could set up my agricultural operation, I remembered what they said about us living normal lives, so I wasn't overly concerned that they would turn me down.

To my surprise, they really encouraged me. I started with hybrid chickens and some excellent laying hens and raised more than 150 of those white hybrid chickens—which are the best for laying eggs. Soon I had actual customers—enthusiastic people who came all the way to the governor's residence to pick up their farm-fresh eggs which I sold for sixty-five cents a dozen. Of course, looking back as an adult, I realized that it probably wasn't the quality of my eggs that kept them coming, but the probability of running into the state's chief executive. But whatever the stimulus, my sales were rather brisk!

Given my agricultural success, I decided to expand my farming operation to include many other animals. Besides the chickens, I added fifty turkeys—which I sold during Thanksgiving and Christmas—and three horses whose names were: Champ, a Tennessee walking horse; Thunder, a pinto pony; and Mr. Politics. I guess no one was surprised by my choice of names for my adorable, yet feisty, Shetland pony. Clearly, Mr. Politics was my favorite, but also he was my most feared. Why was I afraid? Mr. Politics had quite a temper, and if I ever turned my back on him he would come after me. Somehow that Shetland's contempt and lack of loyalty could be a metaphor for the state of politics today. More about that later, though.

Of course, any respectable farm operation needs more animals and people to help keep it going. Over time, I added many rabbits, dogs, two goats, and more than 150 guinea pigs. I was properly referred to as Farmer Bob, a moniker of which I was most proud. I even had my own form of transportation, thanks to a joint operation led by me and my two tenacious brothers—Frank and Gary. We devised a plan to use my goats as a way to move around the property by hitching them to our little red wagon. Those poor goats had the tedious job of taking us on many, many excursions all around our twelve-acre estate.

Friends of my parents also gave us a very lively monkey who had the potential to live like no other monkey could—in a luxury home with his own bathroom. I was so excited to have him around, and I couldn't wait to give him a creative name like I did for our ponies. Who knows? He might have been called, Monkey Business, or Mr. Monkey, but, sadly, we never got the chance to give him a proper identity. One day, we noticed that our monkey didn't look quite right, so my brother Frank had the novel idea that maybe he needed some extra food. Frank ran into the kitchen, grabbed a bag full of candy and fed it to him in one sitting; of course, he ate the entire bag. Sadly, our monkey eventually died. I jokingly always blamed my brother for killing our precious monkey.

Undertaking such an extensive farm operation, and having a relative degree of success, I got the bright idea to enlist some of the staff who worked at the governor's residence to help me with some of the daily chores.

Here's where the story of prisoners comes to life. But it does need some explanation at least for most people who would never dream of letting their children remotely near a convicted murderer.

To know Frank G. Clement the way I did, was to experience a daily infusion of actions that were designed to help others, or teach me valuable life-lessons—although as a young boy I was mostly unaware. He lived and breathed service rather than gaining power or wealth for himself. I believe Dad would have worked as governor for no pay at all because he loved people and wanted to make a difference in their lives. And also he had a special concern for those who didn't have a voice—the poor, the sick, or the displaced and he wanted them to know that their lives mattered just as much as his or ours.

One day he came up with an insightful idea to help those people who were disenfranchised, one that would mean the world to me and help me learn that all people—no matter what their lot in life—deserve a second-chance.

Enter the prisoners.

The state penitentiary was not that far away from the residence, and Dad thought he could give the inmates a chance to redeem themselves by putting them to work at the house. Every morning, as part of their trustee program, prisoners in bright white jumpsuits, would arrive, and get to work cleaning the house, cooking meals and doing many other chores. These were no ordinary prisoners but real-life murderers who were in prison for truly terrible crimes. So, Dad's theory was that the murderers would be better suited to work at the governor's residence as trustees. His reasoning for this was that he believed that some murderers commit a crime in a fit of anger but do have remorse and are sorry about it and would never do it again. Whereas, generally when thieves commit a crime, they typically only serve a short sentence and then as soon as they get out of jail they begin planning and scheming how they would get away with it the next time.

After I got to know the prisoners over a number of months, I relied on them for so many things. They were my friends, and I used to think that I was really special to them, too, and had a great influence on their lives.

One of the trustees who my father pardoned was a parolee convicted of murder over a domestic dispute. His name was John McCullough and he was the person who drove me to and from school every day. The prisoners also helped me tend to my farm, cooked our meals and were the ones I could turn to on a daily basis for almost anything. John and I were especially close. He would drive me and my buddies to the movies before I got my driver's license. In fact, John was such a good worker that Dad hired him as a state employee—working full time for us at the governor's residence.

During those days, and looking back, it was pretty incredible having both the highway patrolmen who were on duty twenty-four/

seven along with inmates working side-by-side at the governor's residence. It was a different time in our history where drugs, terrorism and the use of illegal assault weapons were not part of American culture.

Living with a famous and powerful father I guess rubbed off on me, too. When I was about twelve-years-old, I liked to think that I was the man in-charge especially when my parents were away. Even though there were highway patrolmen all around, I still found myself in the middle of the action, sometimes without knowing that I could be in danger. Like the time I broke up a knife fight in the kitchen between two murderers who were in a tussle. This was caused by one of the prisoners accusing the other of eating a whole hog in one afternoon. I don't know why the accused prisoner got so upset, but a struggle ensued between the two and I thought it was my duty to break it up! I felt really good about the experience and it laid the groundwork for quite an interesting adolescence.

One of the challenges of having prisoners working for your father is that sometimes they can stray from the straight and narrow. Here's an example of the kind of prisoner mischief that sometimes would occur at the governor's residence.

In my role as Farmer Bob I had a real knack for chickens, but absolutely no clue about cows. Back then, milk was delivered by a milkman, and instead of the cartons we use today, the milk was delivered to our doors in glass bottles. I sometimes wish I could have had a few cows at my farm, but I'm sure that would have not gone over too well with my dad.

Anyway, one day as I was tending to my animals, Dad clearly had a disgruntled look on his face. Knowing that I was a fairly good boy that day, I wondered what he could possibly be upset about. He gave me that look and said, "Son, have you been drinking all of the milk?" "No, Dad," I replied, "I just drink what I always do." He explained to me that our milk bill just kept getting bigger and bigger and he couldn't understand why that was happening. By the way, at the time Dad was making only $12,000 a year as governor, and he had to pay for all of the food for our family of five and our assorted brood of animals.

"Well, don't worry son, we'll figure it out," he said.

That's all I needed to hear; I was on the case. I decided to conduct my own investigation and get to the bottom of this milk mystery. Watching Dad over the years I fancied myself picking up some of his investigative skills that he learned during his tenure at the FBI. After a few weeks, and without much luck, I almost forgot the entire situation. That is until Dad discovered that one of the prisoners who worked in the kitchen made a deal with the devil. Here's what he did. Apparently, the milkman worked on a commission so the more milk we drank the more money he made. He convinced the prisoner to pour all of our milk down the drain in exchange for a smuggled half pint of whiskey. While Dad was the one who really solved the caper, I always liked to think that I helped foil the plot!

Another time one of my favorite inmates and our chief cook, William, wanted to visit his girlfriend, Floretta, who lived only a few miles away but, of course, as a prisoner he didn't have a car. By this time in my life, in the summer of 1958 when I was fifteen years old and had a limited license, I had my own ride—a fastback Mustang and that was my ticket to coolness. One day I noticed that my car was missing and so was William. I literally had everyone searching for him including the highway patrol. Somehow, the rascal managed to elude all of us. I was extremely upset, and with my parents away, I believed I had the full authority to take corrective action. When William finally returned three hours later, I was hopping mad. "William," I said, "Where have you been?" I went to see my girlfriend.

William apologized profusely, realizing that he could jeopardize his work release, as well as the friendship and trust we had built over the years. I thought, after I finally calmed down, "Gee, he's a great cook. I sure don't want to punish myself by giving him a hard time." After a few minutes I said, "William, if you ever get that urge again, please take Mother or Dad's car, not mine!"

It's hard to explain how the prisoners could become so much a part of our family life. But being around them made me realize they were just like everyone else—well, except for the fact that they were serving time at the state penitentiary. That camaraderie meant a lot to me as a youngster. Can you imagine playing pool, football or basketball with big burly men in white uniforms? By the way, one of the most famous pool players in the world, Willie Mosconi, came to the governor's residence when he was visiting Nashville. He holds the world record running 500 pool balls in the pocket without missing. It is incredible looking back at those tournaments that pitted the governor's sons, the highway patrolmen and the inmates together for literally hours playing pool. This may sound shocking but I am thankful for having the experience with the convicts, because it taught me many things, such as being tolerant of those who are different than me and not feeling uncomfortable in most all situations.

I vividly remember Dad once taking me to see Tennessee's death row at the main state prison where I first saw Tennessee's electric chair. It was a chilling and sobering experience. During Dad's first two terms in office, he did permit some executions in Tennessee. During his third term, though he had a change of heart, commuting the death sentences of six black inmates all from Memphis, to ninety-nine years. His feeling was that there was something wrong with the system if all of the prisoners on death row were black and from the same part of the state.

Dad was a regular visitor to the state prison. I'm guessing that came from his FBI training. He always wanted to meet personally with the inmates on death row. During a visit to deliver the message of their commuted sentence to ninety-nine years in lieu of the death penalty he would tell each prisoner, "I can save your life, but I cannot save your soul."

He said he commuted their sentences because many poor defendants couldn't afford the same access to lawyers as the wealthy. And, it was so clear to him that blacks were disproportionally sentenced to death than their white counterparts.

Dad's deep sense of justice and morality drove him to eventually question his role in directly making the decision of who was to live and who was to die. He would wake up in the middle of the night in a deep sweat constantly wrestling with his conscience. He knew that with one single phone call to the prison he could change the course of someone's destiny.

Every night before he went to sleep, no matter how tired he was, he got down on his knees beside the bed and prayed. He asked for guidance and direction, especially regarding capital punishment. He struggled with this as long as I can recall. I know that these times were the most heart wrenching and profound— intimate moments he reluctantly shared with his family and trusted advisors.

That could have been one of the many reasons Dad wanted to help people get back on their feet.

William, John, and the other prisoners were woven into the fabric of our family's lives in good times and bad. They were there to celebrate our birthdays and clean up our wounds when we fell down.

On another occasion, Colonel Tom Parker, whose office was on the outskirts of Nashville, brought a famous visitor to our house, none other than The King, Elvis Presley! Colonel Parker was one of the most celebrated and controversial entertainment promoters and master deal-makers in the music business at the time, and had a national reputation, primarily due to managing Elvis Presley's music career from the very beginning. Elvis regarded Parker as a surrogate father, and the Colonel thought of Elvis just like a son. Their relationship and the Colonel's business decisions and questionable past have been the subject of many books, newspaper and magazine articles over the years.

Parker wanted Dad to meet him because he knew that Elvis would become one of the most recognized superstars in the world.

I was thirteen at the time of Elvis' visit, and compared to the bombastic Colonel, Elvis was very shy and soft spoken. That was in 1956. Elvis was poised to become a famous star, but at the time, he was just a great guy who loved all types of music and relished their harmonies.

Before Elvis became so well-known as a music superstar he worked on the highway crew for the state of Tennessee. That fact wasn't lost on Dad. He asked Colonel Parker at one point during the evening, with a devilish smile on his face, "Tom, why couldn't I have discovered Elvis, not you?" Dad also had the prisoners from the state penitentiary, some of whom were really wonderful singers and were known as "The Prisonaires," join us for an impromptu concert; they couldn't have been happier to oblige. By the way, all of these prisoners had ninety-nine-year sentences, and the lead singer, Johnny Bragg, had six consecutive ninety-nine-year sentences. (I guess you could say that they all had plenty of time to practice their music behind prison walls.)

There we all were my mom and Dad, the colonel, me, my brothers and Elvis Presley. We moved upstairs to a small sitting room that had a piano, and of course, the Colonel wanted us to hear Elvis sing. As I looked around the room and saw such a diverse group of people—the prisoners, my father the governor, and the would-be King Elvis—I realized even at a young age I was learning important life lessons from all of them.

We certainly were a motley crew of southerners from all walks of life, gathering around the piano to hear the young Elvis sing a few songs. Just as he began his performance of Hound Dog, the Prisonaires started singing along too, each singer doing his own version of the tune in succession. Elvis would sing, and then the Prisonaires would do their own rendition of the song. And they were pretty good, too. You could see from the look on Elvis' face that he clearly enjoyed the experience; maybe even more than us. But, I sincerely doubt that!

The group sang well into the night in that small sitting room; that moment will forever be etched in my memory. Dad noticed how much the prisoners loved singing, and it was obvious that Johnny Bragg and the Prisonaires' performance clearly moved Dad.

About a week or so later, Dad suggested to the warden—Droopy Edwards—to utilize their musical talents in other ways, too. They began traveling around the state offering their testimonials and sharing their stories of how they repented for their crimes. The Prisonaires often spoke passionately about their transgressions, cautioning people against making the same mistakes they did.

Dad was the motivation for the Prisonaires' success, and they were thankful he treated them with respect and compassion. In fact, they even wrote a song about Dad called, "What about Frank Clement?" Meanwhile, Elvis was clearly on his way to becoming the most famous singer on the planet.

In addition to meeting Elvis, one of my other favorite experiences as a boy was meeting my childhood heroes—Roy and Dale Rogers. As kids, my brothers and I would watch them on television. We acted out the scenes just the way Roy did when he so gallantly fought off the outlaws. When I found out that Roy Rogers was coming to our house to meet Dad, well, Frank, Gary and I could hardly contain ourselves.

In he walks; larger than life. With his wide brimmed, white cowboy hat sitting on top of his head like a crown. He was the king of all cowboys. He brought along his wife, Dale Evans, and the two of them talked to Dad and Mom for what seemed like an eternity. They even gave us a very special gift—a German Weimaraner, a light tan dog with a short tail who could hunt for anything. Of course, we named him Roy. He was the smartest dog we ever had, and my parents decided that he was intelligent enough to have him specially trained. But, poor Roy, like my beloved monkey, met with an unexpected and tragic end. One day Roy wandered on to Curtiswood Lane and was hit by a car. The sudden death of two animals that I loved dearly, ironically, helped prepare me for what was to become the biggest loss in my life in the years to come.

Over the years at the governor's residence, many notable visitors impacted my life, but none more profoundly than Walt Disney. Even though listening to Elvis was a highlight, and receiving a coonskin cap from Fess Parker who played Daniel Boone on television made my day, meeting the legendary Walt Disney was my childhood dream come true.

So, we packed up our bags, and headed to California where we were the personal guests of Walt Disney for the opening day of Disneyland in Los Angeles. My brothers and I were speechless when we arrived. I will never forget feeling like I had just been transported to heaven. To this day one of my prized possessions is an original cartoon personally given to us and autographed by the great Walt Disney. Mine are original pieces featuring none other than Donald Duck and Mickey Mouse!

In fact, after we returned, we had another well-known visitor—Art Linkletter—who shared a fascinating story about Walt Disney. He told us that Mr. Disney had asked Art Linkletter if he would promote his new venture called Disneyland on his popular radio show at the time. Disney explained that he couldn't afford the huge fee that he would need to pay to get his promotion on the air, so he asked Art Linkletter if he might do a special favor for him and put it on the air less expensively. Mr. Linkletter told Disney that it was okay for him to just pay the union scale, then asked him who was going to sell the camera equipment and film at Disneyland. According to Art Linkletter Disney said to him: "Art, I haven't really addressed that vendor agreement yet." Linkletter asked him if he could have that franchise himself. Without signing a written agreement, Art Linkletter officially became the exclusive vendor selling cameras and film at Disneyland for many, many years. Like my Dad, Walt Disney was a man of his word.

With my coon skin cap, and memories of Disneyland, Elvis and Roy Rogers fresh in my mind, I couldn't imagine that life could get better than this. My farming business was going well, and I was having so much fun hanging out with my brothers and of course the prisoners.

Then one sunny spring morning, Dad said we were going to have another very special visitor at the residence. By this time I was a pro at the meet and greets, and was beginning to think that we were indeed very special people. Then, he informed me that our guest for the evening was none other than the former President of the United States—Harry Truman.

I only met one President before in my life—President Eisenhower—though through the years I have had the great honor to meet every President from President Truman to President Obama.

Before Former President Truman arrived, Dad told me, "This man will go down in history as one of the greatest American Presidents." Almost from the moment I shook his hand, President Truman impressed me with his gentlemanly manner and charm. But he caused quite a stir at our house, too!

Dad liked to get up early—around 5:30 AM, and so did President Truman. The President was sleeping in the bedroom next to my parents' master bedroom. When Dad awoke he went to check on President Truman. But he wasn't there. Dad was quite concerned and immediately went downstairs to find him. He asked the security staff if they had seen the President, and they had no clue where he was either. "How can you lose a President?" he anxiously chided the staff.

Everyone was in a panic, and Dad launched an all-out search on the residence grounds and throughout the neighborhood. Finally they found him! He was simply taking his daily morning walk and didn't think his absence would cause such a fuss. By the way, we never had a fence around the residence. Dad believed that our house should be open to all of the people of Tennessee.

I think back about that experience, and reflect on a more innocent time where even a President of the United States could take a long stroll all by himself. No Secret Service detail or aides at his beck and call.

Having such distinguished visitors at the governor's residence was a thrill for sure, but getting to attend a major national event in person—well that was the hallmark of my youth!

I accompanied Dad to the 1960 Democratic National Convention in Los Angeles when I was sixteen years old, which was the very first time I met John F. Kennedy and his brother Bobby. The 1960 Convention was by far the most exciting, because in those days the presidential nominee was usually not determined until the actual convention took place. Not like today, where political conventions are media extravaganzas and are merely a formality in terms of deciding the party's nominee. No matter, for me, attending a political convention was tantamount to the excitement of devouring my first chocolate ice cream cone, or selling a dozen of my farm-raised eggs to my very first customer.

Dad supported U.S. Senator Jack Kennedy for the 1960 nomination. Buford Ellington held the governor's office at the time, and most of the Tennessee delegates were committed to Lyndon Johnson, who was a southerner and the Majority Leader of the U.S. Senate. I was taking all of this in, and remember how important I felt being at a political convention with someone who could actually become President of the United States. I believe this experience sowed the seeds of my future career in politics. But here's where things get really interesting. With one phone call, history was changed!

Soon after Kennedy received the Democratic nomination for President, Dad got a call from JFK's father, his friend, Ambassador Joe Kennedy. He said that he understood that Dr. Billy Graham was going to endorse Richard Nixon for the presidency. Ambassador Kennedy knew that my parents and Billy and his wife, Ruth, were very close friends. Actually, they traveled together often, and Dad and Billy were even golfing buddies. At one point, Dad assisted Tennessee's Poet Laureate, Pek Gunn, in organizing a number of train excursions to attend Billy's crusades.

Dad and Dr. Graham were as close as brothers and had great respect for one another so Dad called him and said, "Billy, you know how much I love you. You are like a brother to me. But if it's true that you are going to endorse Richard Nixon, it could create a division between you and your ministry for millions of Americans. It doesn't mean that you don't have beliefs about certain political candidates, but many will see the endorsement as a personal expression of anti-Catholic sentiments." He asked Billy to pray about the situation, and said, "I know you will make a good decision." Dr. Graham's entire ministry has been about bringing people together rather than forming divisions among them politically because his goal was to reach people for Christ. The next day Dr. Graham called my dad and said he would remain neutral. At one point in time they had even discussed Dad leaving politics and joining Billy's ministry.

I was always amazed to think that if just one vote per precinct had changed in the election, Richard Nixon would have been elected President instead of John Fitzgerald Kennedy.

In 1963, Dad and I met President John F. Kennedy at the Nashville Airport after he arrived on Air Force One. He was gearing up for his presidential re-election campaign at the time, and was coming over to the governor's residence for a planned luncheon with a group of dignitaries.

He had just delivered a speech at Vanderbilt University and from there headed to our house for lunch. It was there that the President and Dad discussed his re-election chances in 1964 despite many racial and labor-related issues confronting his administration. He told Dad that he was also concerned that even if he were fortunate enough to survive politically and win re-election, he would still be a relatively young man when he would finally retire.

Right before lunch, the President, Dad and some others were mingling upstairs when President Kennedy asked Dad, "Frank, how does it feel to leave political office at such a young age?" Dad replied, "Mr. President; it is hell!"

After their conversation, and since he was a bit dusty from being outdoors, the President asked Dad if he could take a shower. Of course Dad would never turn down a request from the President of the United States. Surely if he let inmates use the facilities President Kennedy could, too!

As Dad showed him where the shower was, he thought it might be helpful for him to demonstrate to the President how to manipulate the shower knobs and make sure they worked. As the President was taking it all in, Dad by mistake turned on the faucet full-force dousing President Kennedy with a barrage of cold water, drenching the leader of the free world while he was still wearing his suit and tie. Eventually, the President did dry off. We all had a wonderful lunch. President Kennedy then headed out to Overton High School on Franklin Road where he took a helicopter to the Nashville Airport where Air Force One was waiting.

Later, Dad told me that a suspicious man was detained at the school after the security personnel discovered that he was holding a paper sack concealing a gun. Secret Service Agents suddenly appeared almost out of nowhere and took swift action. By the way, the Secret Service was originally founded in 1865 to suppress counterfeit currency, then assumed part-time protection of President Cleveland in 1894, and began full-time presidential protection in 1902. They rushed toward the suspect, grabbed him and confiscated his weapon. Once he was in custody the agents asked Dad to keep the matter top secret. They explained to him that every time incidents like that were publicized the number of threats to the President tripled! I was told later on by Dad that the man was eventually evaluated and released.

No publicity ever surfaced about the incident, which occurred only a few short months prior to President Kennedy's assassination in Dallas, Texas. Many years later, when I was in Congress, I related my memories of that event in a newspaper interview. While I have never suggested that there was any connection between what happened at Overton High School and the subsequent events in Dallas, I was criticized in some news reports that doubted the veracity of my account because there had been no coverage of the incident. One media report suggested that such an incident could not have happened so close to the events in Dallas without drawing coverage after the assassination. While I didn't personally witness the event, I knew that my dad had no reason to tell me anything other than what really happened during that historic trip to Nashville.

There were many other times that I accompanied Dad to campaign events where I met so many other great leaders who shaped American history and culture. To say that this was an exciting environment for a young person to grow up would be an understatement.

In 1962 when I was a senior in high school Dad was running again for governor. I had the bright idea to launch my own first political campaign which was for youth governor of the YMCA Youth Legislature. That year was one of my best. Dad and I both won our races!

With a big win under my belt, and almost near the end of my high school days, I decided to apply to college considering Northwestern University in Chicago and Southern Methodist University in Dallas, but decided upon the University of Tennessee in Knoxville where most of my buddies were going.

When I finally left for college in Knoxville, Tennessee, I was trying very hard to fit in and not be given special attention because I was the governor's son. As I was beginning to realize though, that was easier said than done.

Like some of the young men my age I went through fraternity rush week, and of course, continued to attract a lot of attention because of my family name. What I once considered a proud family moniker I was now beginning to think was becoming a liability. For example, I felt at times that I was living in a goldfish bowl, with everyone watching and observing me all of the time. At other times, I felt I had to be on guard and not totally be myself because of my father's political position. Regardless, joining a fraternity was among my top priorities.

My thought at the time was that I probably would be welcomed into a fraternity, primarily because all of the fraternity brothers were envisioning having rush parties at the governor's Residence. Little did they realize that we had inmates on the property and highway patrolmen around every corner.

I was seriously considering pledging Sigma Alpha Epsilon (SAE), because Dad had been a member. But, Bruce Conley, one of my good friends from Alamo, Tennessee was a senior member of ATO. He asked me to come to the ATO house on the final day of fraternity rush week. I arranged to meet him at the fraternity house. When I entered the large foyer, I was stunned to see my girlfriend who was still in high school. I couldn't believe it! How could this have happened, I wondered? It turned out that my buddies wanted me to join ATO so badly that they took up a collection to pay for my girlfriend's flight from Nashville to Knoxville to come and visit me. After I caught my breath, I noticed that all of the fraternity brothers lined up one-by-one and tried to convince me to be part of ATO. I couldn't help laughing to myself that the real reason they wanted me so badly was because of my "party mansion."

I was so taken back by what ATO had done that I decided to pledge.

At some point, though, I had a change of heart and began to feel guilty about breaking my promise to SAE. I went back and forth wondering what I should do, too. SAE put on the full-court press again, and even suggested flying a bank president from Nashville to Knoxville to meet with me to try to encourage me to join. Fraternities and sororities at that time had a great influence on college and university campuses. They would attract young men and women who would later go back home and become very involved in their communities. I was no different. Service was at my core and I wanted to make lifelong friends during my college days that would be with me throughout my life. I also knew that I would seek public office someday, and those same friends could help me in the future. Even though I felt some guilt for not joining SAE, I felt a strong urge to join ATO because of all the effort they put in encouraging me to become a member.

Shortly after re-pledging ATO, I ran for president of the freshman class. My "campaign staff" were UT college seniors including Franklin Haney, Jim Hall and Bruce Conley, all of whom have gone on to great success in life.

I was now officially part of the ATO fraternity, quite an esteemed social body!

I must say, though, I wasn't the best pledge. One day, some of my fraternity brothers decided to teach me a lesson and take me on what they called back then, a goat ride. I wasn't that worried, first because I fancied myself as an expert on goats, and second, I had connections.

The goat ride basically meant that the fraternity brothers would take the pledge to an unknown location far away from the fraternity house. There, the pledge would be left, sometimes with few clothes, and have to find his way back. Little did they know that being the governor's son would have another distinct advantage. I made my way to the first farmhouse I could find, talked my way inside and made a phone call. I immediately reached my friends at the Highway Patrol, who came in an instant, picked me up and got me back to the fraternity house. I made it back well before my brothers, and believe me, they were not happy campers!

But, I was never far away from the need to fit in and not be seen as different from the other students, which was now becoming more of an issue in college. There was one incident that reflected this, and has always stuck with me as a cautionary tale, of sorts.

When I ran for president of the freshman class at UT, and right in the middle of my campaign, I got into an elevator with a fellow student I didn't know but who seemed friendly enough. We entered into a conversation and of course the election was a topic of keen interest. I asked him, "Who are you going to support as president of the freshman class in the student government election?" He looked me right in the eyes and said with great purpose and certainty, "I'm sure not going to vote for that Bob Clement. You know he is the governor's son, and he thinks he's better than everyone else!"

For a moment my heart sank, but Dad would never show his emotions during times like this. I responded very calmly and firmly, "I don't think I ever properly introduced myself. I'm Bob Clement."

The look on his face was priceless! "I'm very sorry, I really don't know you at all, just that you are the governor's son. Hey, maybe I did pre-judge you." I tried to talk to him and be as friendly as I could, and that seemed to turn the tides. "You know, Bob, I think I *will* vote for you for President of the Freshman Class after all," he said enthusiastically.

I won my first big race by a whopping thirty-three votes!

Those relationships I formed as a young boy through my adolescence and in college are among the most precious to me to this day. Jack Gayden, Steve Hall, Steve Hewlett, Jimmy Duncan, Ken Jordan, John Tanner, Walter Bussart, Jess Campbell, Dave McDole, Ed Cary, Leon Stribling, Bill Acree, Jackson Downey, Carol Knox Frist, Joe Carr and his wife Carol Ann, Butch Garrett, and Tony Barrasso, among many others-have all gone on to do great things in life, business, law and politics.

To this day, I never refer to where we lived as a "mansion." It was and will forever be a "residence."

Clement's Contemplations:

"When in doubt, call the Highway Patrol"

"Never hitch a goat to your wagon"

"Believe in the power of the unexpected"

"The only real jail is in your head"

"Courage can be learned: decency is within"

"Shower a president with praise, not cold water"

"Every soul is worth saving"

"Animals exude love; people teach compassion"

"Open your doors to lives unknown"

"Keep your chickens close and your monkeys closer"

"Grudges are temporary. Forgiveness is forever."

Chapter 2

Politics: The Family Passion

"Youth was not wasted on me."—Bob Clement

George Bernard Shaw and Oscar Wilde have both been credited for the enduring and sure-fire quote, "Youth is wasted on the young." Now I'm not one to argue with great writers like the two of them, but in this particular case, I have to disagree. From the day I was born as I look back now at this age, I do believe that my life's purpose was to be in some form of public service. I have tried to make a difference with any and all gifts I have been given no matter where life led me. I didn't have a Pollyanna childhood at all, and yes, there were moments of youthful angst and disappointment.

It goes without saying that when you grow up with a famous and powerful father you have two choices. One, you rebel against him and want nothing to do with what he did for a living, or embrace the gifts you were given.

The Clement family had a long history of public service. In fact, if you read any of the Tennessee history books, you can trace it all the way back to the 1800's. Dad was born on June 2, 1920 into a family that was of modest means but rich in dreams and ambitions. He knew when he was a very young man, a country boy from Dickson County with no money or connections that he wanted to be in politics. Dad would tell people, "I am going to be governor of Tennessee." Everything he said and did from the age of sixteen to thirty-two was toward achieving that one singular goal.

Considering the environment in which he was raised, his political ambitions seemed perfectly natural. His parents—Robert Samuel Clement and May Belle Goad Clement—lived in a back bedroom of the Halbrook Hotel, which is in downtown Dickson Tennessee, forty miles west of Nashville. Back in those days, people got off of the train, then would stay overnight in the hotel right next to the track. My grandmother and great grandmother, Belle Goad, managed the hotel, which today is one of the few remaining authentic railroad hotels in the country. It is also the place where my father was born, and is currently the home of the Governor Frank G. Clement Railroad Hotel Museum.

The family moved for a short time to Vermont, then Scottsville, Kentucky where Dad's two sisters—Anna Belle and Emma Gene were born. While they had to stretch every dollar just to make ends-meet, you would never know it from the clean and well-pressed clothing they wore, or the fact that there was a hot meal on the table, day in and day out.

Dad and his sisters had a series of chores that they had to do each and every day, and the family regularly attended church on Sundays. It was an orderly and disciplined childhood for Dad and his sisters, but young Frank was not the stereotypical child growing up in the rural south of the 1920's.

My Great Aunt Dockie Weems would tell me stories about Dad's love of reading, and the thrill he got from writing and delivering speeches, even as a young boy. She noticed his unusual interests and decided she would encourage his talents by helping him hone in his public speaking skills, as well as teach him the art of debating. As he grew up, and entered Dickson County

High School, Dad would spend hours upon hours practicing the speeches he wrote in front of the mirror. He would ask anyone who was around at the time—and I mean anyone—to listen and critique him. Rather than get into boyhood mischief, Dad was concerned more about participating in high school speech tournaments. No one could have known at the time that these spellbinding soliloquies would catapult him into the national spotlight.

After my grandfather graduated from Cumberland University School of Law in Lebanon, Tennessee in his mid-30's he moved the family back to Dickson, Tennessee, and was the quintessential country lawyer. He eventually had a very successful law practice there, and was frequently involved with the movers and shakers of the time. In our household, Dad heard my grandfather and his guests discuss serious topics like how politics worked, or how to interpret the U.S. Constitution.

Eventually my grandfather became the Mayor of Dickson, and sometimes sat in as an acting member of the Tennessee Supreme Court. And, his father, my great-grandfather, James Archibald Clement, served as the Benton County Court Clerk and also in the State Senate. So, to say that politics is in my blood is certainly not an understatement!

Frank Clement was brilliant, talented and driven. He finished college and law school when he was barely twenty years old. Even more amazing to me was that he passed the bar exam before he even graduated Vanderbilt University School of Law, where he was an exceptional student. After law school he became a G-Man and worked for the Federal Bureau of Investigation. He became an FBI agent at the age of twenty-one. He was the youngest FBI agent in America at the time, and one of the youngest in Bureau history under then FBI Director, J. Edgar Hoover.

One of the first cases he worked was that of the infamous gangster, Roger Touhy in Chicago, Illinois. Touhy supposedly was the only man Al Capone ever feared when they were rival faction mobsters in Chicago's organized crime network. Because he was so young, Dad was assigned to work as an undercover agent posing as a college student. The FBI had him observe Touhy's comings and goings, and detail his organized crime operations prior to his arrest. The crime boss was in jail for many years, all relating to his racketeering empire. When he finally got out, he was murdered, gunned down only days after being released from prison.

Dad loved being a G-Man, but when World War II erupted, he made it clear to the local Dickson Draft Board that he wanted to serve in the military. At the time, FBI agents were getting direct commissions without going through Reserved Officer Training Corps (ROTC) or Officer Candidate's School (OCS). FBI Director J. Edgar Hoover was uncomfortable with the practice of using FBI influence in that way and so was Dad. He enlisted in the U.S. Army as a buck private, without any influence peddling or special favors. It was no surprise to me that Dad had risen through the ranks solely on his own merit and attended OCS. When he graduated he was commissioned as a Second Lieutenant in the U.S. Army and was stationed at Ft. Sam Houston in San Antonio, Texas, Ft. Custer in Kalamazoo, Michigan, and Ft. Gordon in Augusta, Georgia.

When World War II was over, he began practicing law in his hometown of Dickson, and revisited his dream of a career in politics. Shortly after that, the three public service commissioners appointed him General Counsel for the Tennessee Railroad and Public Utilities Commission; he was only twenty-six years old at the time. He was called up again for military service during the Korean War and served another sixteen months. Then, in 1952, when he was only thirty two years old, he won his first race for governor of Tennessee. The reason he was in a position to take on such a challenge was that he made a name for himself by being in the FBI at twenty-one, then in the U.S. Army, then State

Commander of the American Legion, the Tennessee Jaycees, Young Democrats and so much more. People all across Tennessee encouraged him to take the next step and enter politics. He impressed everyone he met with his command of the English language and his amazing oratorical ability.

I was nine-years-old when I made my first campaign trip with my Dad. What a thrill it was. With my freshly-pressed white tee shirt that read, Vote for my Daddy on the front, and on the back his name in big, bold letters, Frank G. Clement, I knew I was part of something really special. When we would step onto a stage, or appear before a large crowd of supporters, I always noticed that people would be spellbound. Dad was one of the greatest orators this country has ever produced.

Not only were there strong and powerful men who shaped my life, but the women in my life were equally significant. They played a great role in helping me develop my confidence and self-esteem.

Believe it or not, I was shy as a very young boy, and Mother knew that I had the potential to come out of my shell so she exposed me to speech and forensics. We would work on many things together such as reading book reports aloud and writing small speeches. She listened to me present them, and generally helped me develop a skill that would take me on a road I had not even imagined yet. I am grateful that mother had the insight to recognize how beneficial this exposure would mean at such a young age.

Being on the campaign trail almost all of my youth, I learned a thing or two about life on the road, and much more about human nature—warts and all. After all, we literally visited all ninety-five counties of Tennessee—and probably shook over a million hands. Or at least it seemed that way to me at the time.

By the time I was eighteen, I went from being a little boy to having my own opinions. I was growing and maturing, so much so that Dad would hand over the microphone to me during most of his stump speeches and say to the crowd, I am the candidate not my son. In fact, I had prepared remarks myself, and depending upon the county we were visiting at the time, I would tailor my speeches to highlight what Dad had done to help the people of that county in the two terms he served as governor.

There is a thread that runs throughout the Clement genealogy as it relates to public service. My Dad's sister, Anna Belle Clement O'Brien, worked on my father's campaigns and also was an administrative assistant to my father and Governor Buford Ellington. Eventually, she was elected to public office, winning her own campaign for the Tennessee House of Representatives and later the State Senate. My cousin, Sara Kyle, was elected to the Public Service Commission and the State Senate, and was only the second woman ever to be elected to statewide office in Tennessee. My middle brother, Frank, Jr. was elected chancellor and then appointed to the state court of appeals in Tennessee, and has been re-elected several times.

Like Dad, and his father before him, I was inspired not just by the power of words but the actions that went along with them. I felt I could discern who was genuine and who was not, and had the benefit of learning from Dad that even though some people may not support you this time they may support you next time. My father was always looking ahead. Being gracious to people who opposed him was one of Dad's greatest gifts.

I remember in high school accompanying him on a campaign rally where thousands of people were there, most of them, cheering and shouting, "Clement, Clement, Clement!" The feeling was electric, and I was caught up in the thrill and excitement of being in the moment, witnessing first-hand the energy and passion of a southern-style campaign rally. That is until I heard that voice.

It seemed to come out of nowhere, like a summer thunderstorm, and I will never forget her words and Dad's stunning response.

"Frank Clement, you drink alcohol and I hope you go to hell a mile a minute," she screamed, not caring anything at all about who was there, or Dad's response. He stood there serenely and let her go on and rant. Finally, after about three minutes or so, he looked her straight in the eye, smiled broadly and said, "Ma'am, you'll pray for me won't you?" You could have heard a pin drop! I couldn't believe what he had said, but that was Dad. He respected everyone's opinion, and even when someone like this woman insulted him, he wouldn't be ugly back. In fact, after the speech had ended that same woman came right over to Dad and apologized for her nasty remarks. He was a true Southern gentleman with a heart of gold and had a comeback for any and all situations. All of those years practicing his speeches in front of the mirror really paid off. Maybe that's why his political opponents would often say about him, "Don't ever go hear that SOB speak, because if you do, you WILL vote for him."

In the Clement family, we have looked at the word politics as a positive not a negative. In the United Kingdom, for example, when you ask a student, "What is your major," they do not respond, "I major in political science," they say instead, "I major in politics." I consider politics an honorable profession. I have heard all of my life, "Politics changes lives for the better, helps those who are disadvantaged and need representation, and makes a difference in the lives and dreams of American citizens." I saw Dad exhibit political courage, honesty and loyalty so many times that I have lost count. It was in those moments that made an impression on me so much so, that by the age of eleven I knew that I, too, wanted to be a politician.

I was the oldest of three children. My brother Frank, Jr., was born on August 1, 1949, and my youngest brother Gary, was born on November 28, 1952. We all had the advantage of being alive during Dad's public service years. I think Dad wanted us to serve our fellow man one way or the other. He and Mother were always insistent that we never take our privilege for granted. He would always tell us, "Be kind to the people you meet as you climb the ladder of success because you'll be meeting the same people on your way back down." The real truth was that our family was never really comfortable with all of the fancy stuff.

As busy as Dad was during those early political years, he never missed a day of teaching his Sunday school class. Mother kept the family together and picked up the slack when he couldn't be around during those times he was on the campaign trail.

I must admit, that much of my political education came during a very tumultuous time in American history. The social and moral fabric of our country was drastically changing. We were dealing with issues like the space race, the Cold War, labor unrest and the integration of our public schools. In the South at the time we felt a particular feeling of unrest. Dad was a key player in the integration effort in Tennessee, and he took the bold and risky position that Tennessee would uphold the law of the land when it came to integrating the public schools. While other governor's would stand at the school house door, refusing blacks and whites from going to school together, Dad took the opposite position. He was a champion of racial equality and equal opportunities for everyone regardless of the color of their skin.

As a young man watching Dad exhibit such moral courage and fortitude, and seeing how he was sometimes ridiculed for it, taught me so many lessons that I have carried with me throughout my life.

But they were not easy pills to swallow, for sure. One of the more frightening experiences for me as a young boy was a situation that arose in 1956 in one of the toughest counties in Tennessee—Benton, which is in Polk County. Apparently, some very angry people from Benton, Tennessee, killed the local sheriff there, and as you can imagine, law and order broke down almost immediately. Dad decided he had to go there right away to deal with the crisis and spoke at the courthouse to try and restore law and order. With people in the audience carrying loaded guns the tension was palpable. I was twelve or thirteen at the time, and I marveled at how Dad had the political and personal courage to do what he felt was right regardless of the consequences.

He also showed that same courage in 1956 when Clinton High School was to become the first public school in the South to integrate. Anti-segregationists blew up the school with dynamite to prevent black students from going to school with white students. Dad had to call out the National Guard and dispatch the highway patrol to make sure law and order prevailed. There were many angry protestors and other agitators, one of whom was John Casper. Casper was a far-right activist from out of state and was a member of the Ku Klux Klan. He was also a militant who used violence to protest his segregationist beliefs. He hated my father and would make derogatory comments such as, "I'm going to stay here in Tennessee until I kill Frank Clement." Dad had him locked up. Casper came to the realization that he couldn't get anywhere with his agitating tactics, so after he got out of jail he left Tennessee for good. No one was happier to have him gone than Dad.

These were the toughest and roughest times that Dad experienced as governor; tensions were high on both sides. But, I learned from his moral courage, and his belief that the law of the land must be always upheld, that politics does certainly matter.

Even though Dad was called horrible names at the time, and some claimed that he sold out the South, he was such a great communicator that he was able to get people to think sensibly about fairness and upholding the law. He did not allow their emotions to run over their best judgment. He was able to calm the waters. That was his greatest gift, and quite an accomplishment given the South's segregationist views at the time. It was so tense that Dad could not travel to some parts of the state because there were so many threats on his life. It was a time of great anger and emotion and that made a huge impression on me. As time passed that hysteria became history and the South changed dramatically.

In those early years when I was a fly on the wall, that helped me understand how to be an emerging politician and a better young man. It didn't shatter my feelings towards Dad when people criticized or taunted him.

However, there was no question that being the son of one of the most popular politicians in Tennessee there were times that I did have a few tough moments. One of which was the time that Dad raised taxes in 1963, which of course wasn't very popular with Tennessee voters. Nearly every time I would walk into the local market or grocery store, people would lash out not knowing I was the governor's son. They would say, "That damn Frank Clement. Every time you buy something here it's more tax money for Clement." It was only a penny sales tax, but you would think it was the end of the world. While it bothered me, I understood that the man behind the counter, nevertheless, had a right to his opinion not knowing that eighty percent of the increase was for education which was one of Dad's main priorities.

Still, politics is not for the faint of heart, and over time I was beginning to understand how to handle criticism and stand up for what I think is right. Some of a person's most unpopular decisions are the right decisions and ultimately become popular over time. I remember one incident when Dad ran against the incumbent governor, Gordon Browning, and beat him two times in 1952 and 1954. I'll never forget the ugly things he said about Dad--even accusing him of recklessly building a swimming pool at the governor's residence. What he never said was that the so-called swimming pool was actually a small Lilly pond. We took the fish out, painted it blue and jumped in. That was the extent of it! And, in Mother's home county in1954, Browning said: "Frank Clement is so crooked that if he died today you could not bury him like a normal person. You would have to screw him into the ground and couldn't track him even with an elephant in a six-foot snow storm." In Dad's typical acerbic way he replied, "Who would want to?" Despite the differences between Dad and Governor Browning, I got to know him personally after Dad died. He supported me for the Tennessee Public Service Commission and he served the state well as governor. His negative comments were made in the middle of a heated, competitive political campaign. He was surely a great governor, but, unfortunately, just happened to face a young whipper-snapper by the name of Frank G. Clement.

Political campaigns in my youth were colorful, full of drama and for sure more personal and different than they are today. And there are clear reasons for that. Everyone got entrenched in campaigns and spent endless hours working for the candidate they favored. One of the main reasons was that Civil Service wasn't created yet, and a person's job literally was dependent upon who won and who lost. If you worked hard on a political campaign you were most likely to get a state job.

Political rallies in the south at the time were theatrical productions. Motorcades went from one end of the state to the other and people would hold signs and posters. Cars would be replete with bumper stickers and anything else to attract attention. There were even people who would announce the details of the rally on loud speakers, mentioning when the candidate would arrive and all of the country music entertainers coming to town for the political rally.

Literally, thousands of people would come out to hear Dad. He spoke with great command of the English language, used humor in his speeches, and he didn't mind making fun of himself either. I remember after one of his speeches in East Tennessee, Eddy Arnold, a country music superstar, was campaigning with Dad. After Dad's speech was over the woman approached the stage. Dad assumed she was coming over to meet him or get his autograph. Instead, she walked up to Eddy, threw her arms around him and hugged him like there was no tomorrow. She said, "Eddy, I love you; you are the greatest!" Dad gently touched her on the shoulder and said, "What about me?" She replied, "Who are you?" Dad just laughed and told her, "I'm Frank Clement and I'm running for governor of Tennessee." Then she gave him a big hug, too. Dad often used to tell people in his speeches that, "Your greatest applause is making fun of yourself. If you can tell something on yourself that's all you need."

Recently, a man came up to me and said, "I know you." The fact that he recognized me made me feel good, especially since I have been out of politics for thirteen years. "You work at Wendy's, don't you?" he said. "That's where I know you from." I had to roar at that. I really thought he remembered me from my past Congressional service. Some politicians would be offended by that, but it gave me a great laugh on the way home.

That incident made me think about all of the characters I observed at so many of Dad's campaign events and rallies. I thought about those old fashion rallies—almost like religious revivals—that had all of the intense emotions at their core. Dad was such a great speaker because he was able to capture and stir people's emotions, use powerful biblical references and get their adrenaline going at a fever pitch. While we had our share of protestors they were generally peaceful and always passionate.

The enthusiasm generated by the people who attended Dad's political events, was a clear example of unabashed political loyalty. Not like today where people are not as personally involved as they were back then. Loyalty was one of Dad's most important core values. Over the years, I saw it time and time again. And it wasn't disingenuous either. He would treat people the way he wanted to be treated-whether you were the President of the United States or a janitor.

An example of this was the story of the late Leslie Young. Leslie was a man who worked at the Tennessee state capitol building giving guided tours to visitors. Leslie Young worked for governor Browning, and when Dad became governor, he interviewed Leslie to see if he would fit in his new administration. He asked him during the interview one simple question, and Dad made up his mind that if he lied he would fire him on the spot. The question was this: "Mr. Young, who did you vote for governor?" Young replied, "Governor Clement, I worked for Governor Browning and I was loyal and voted for him." Dad replied, "Well Leslie, I planned on firing you, but you told me the truth and you did what was right. As long as I'm here you have a job."

The one great attribute I did develop, and most of the young people my age did not, was the love of public speaking. Studies have revealed that next to death, public speaking evokes the greatest fear among all human beings. But I just loved it! While I was comfortable in front of a crowd, still I was nervous but I used that nervousness to keep me focused. I wanted my audience to judge me for myself. It bothered me more than anything that my peers would prejudge me before they ever met me. I hear Dad's words back then and they ring true today. He said: "People vote for you for a thousand reasons, and they vote against you for a thousand reasons."

While Dad's words and deeds shaped my young political life, he was not one to offer a critique of my speeches or campaign strategies. He was wise to let others assume that role. Matter of fact, he didn't know 'till he ran for governor for the third time that I could deliver a rousing speech. Mother, after coming to my high school when I was President of the debate club, told Dad that she heard my speeches, and they were wonderful. My father never actually heard me give a speech. But when Jack Kennedy ran for President in 1960, I was the speaker at Hillsboro High School's mock-election. Mother was in the audience, and though

Kennedy lost the mock-election, because our high school was mainly Republican, she was still so proud of my speaking ability. That was, for me, my transition from being the young son at the campaign rally to the adult with a voice of his own. I can still remember Dad turning the microphone over to me in1962 at one of his rallies. He did that because of Mother's encouragement.

After he witnessed the positive reaction from the crowd and saw how well I did on my own, he was beaming. His piercing blue eyes were ablaze with fatherly pride and affection. Also, he knew he needed a jolt in his campaign, and having a father and son duo was just the ticket. It excited me knowing that it made Dad feel so good. Together, we spoke at campaign events at every county in the state, which was unheard of at the time. He just bragged about what a great job I did and how proud he was. I guess he liked my performance because he kept using me. And his campaign staff thought our father/son duo was highly effective in endearing him to the crowd. On election night, Dad was victorious again winning his third term, and it was a thrill to be part of yet another high point in our family's political life.

When I was a young man I never experienced the pain of losing, only the elation of winning. As the years went on, though, I sure learned the difference between those polar opposite experiences. When you win you feel like everything you've done in the campaign was right, and when you lose, everything was wrong; but neither scenario is actually correct.

Growing up in a prominent political family was the best experience of my life regardless of the ups and downs, the joy of winning or the despair of losing. Among some of the most valuable life-lessons I've embraced are: you can be tough but fair; if you can't help someone, tell them, don't just write them off as casualties; recognize all people, even if you can't help them; don't brag on yourself, just listen to others; always keep your mind active and try to learn, regardless of whether you think you are the expert; enemies today can be friends tomorrow; and always give people a second chance and never hold a grudge.

I still cherish that tee shirt that Mother often wore at home while she was pregnant with my brother, Gary. It read: Vote for my Daddy. It is a constant reminder that fathers and sons have a special place in this world. Frank G. Clement is always with me. While Tennesseans remember him as a caring and charismatic governor, I just remember him as Dad.

Clement's Contemplations

"Laugh at yourself often and with gusto."

"If they vote for you, great; if they don't vote for you, maybe next time."

"If Ebola doesn't get you, don't fret about public speaking."

"When campaigning, bring out the celebrities. At least they'll get noticed!"

"Loyalty is measured by trust; trust is measured by honesty. All of them matter."

"Everyone's kids need to learn respect; famous peoples' kids--humility."

"Youth is only wasted if you discard the learning curve."

Chapter 3

Turning Point: You're in the Army Now

"You never know when that call will come."—Bob Clement

I will never forget that day. It was a cool November morning, and after completing college and graduate school, I was now in the U.S. Army, stationed at the Civil Affairs School as personnel officer at Ft. Gordon, Georgia. Dad had finished three terms as governor but he was still in the Tennessee National Guard. He pulled his two-week National Guard duty in October at Ft. Gordon which gave us some quality father/son time together. We had a terrific couple of weeks. Matter of fact; it brought back so many memories for Dad because he was stationed at Ft. Gordon when he served in the Army during World War II and the Korean crisis. We spent time touring around the base where he was assigned to the military police (MP) school; we even had a few pretty good meals at the officers club, as well.

Since Dad loved to play golf and was quite good at it, we naturally had to visit the prestigious Augusta Country Club where the Master's Golf Tournament is held every year. Dad had played with some of the golf greats of his time like the legendary players including Ben Hogan and Sam Snead. Those two weeks with my father were so precious to me. Aside from all of our extracurricular activities we also had many deep conversations that lasted well into the night. Mostly, as one can imagine, the subject turned to politics, but religion came up a lot, too, since Dad was a Sunday school teacher, knew the Bible through and through and Billy Graham was his best friend. Towards the end of his visit, I wanted to bring up some of the concerns I had with Dad considering his run for a fourth term as governor of Tennessee. I watched him all of my life never taking time for himself and running ragged in his role as governor, teacher, husband and father. I always thought of him as a high-spirited race horse, one that would push and push to get to the finish line. I was seriously worried that going through the rigors of yet another campaign would literally kill him. I was also worried what it would do to his health, and as well as him being able to hold up with the ridicule and criticisms that go with the territory. But he wanted no part of my anxiety at all. Matter of fact, he kind of brushed me aside, and I could feel his annoyance the more I pushed the conversation forward.

The day that I took Dad to the airport to return home to Tennessee was a day I wish I could take back. On the way we had more words, and I was so angry and frustrated with him that I said, "Dad, I never want to talk to you again!" Right away I knew it was a stupid statement and I really didn't mean it anyway. Now most fathers and sons have moments just like this, and over time they make up with each other and the whole incident is forgotten. At least that's what I figured would happen. But we parted ways, and I went back to the base knowing that eventually things would calm down and we would be back to our old selves.

A few days later the telephone rang. It was November 4, 1969. I picked up the telephone thinking that it would be Dad. I was really looking forward to hearing his booming voice again, especially after not talking to him since we left on somewhat difficult terms. "Hello," I said, one hundred percent sure it was him. It was my grandfather. "I have some bad news," he said. "Your father was in a terrible traffic accident, and he didn't make it." I almost fell to the floor. It was the last thing I ever expected to hear. All I could think about were the last eight words I ever said to my father, "I never want to talk to you again."

My entire life flashed before my eyes. Every moment, every conversation I replayed over and over in my head. In my gut I never thought Dad would live a long life because of his endless drive and energy. But the fact remains that the phone call devastated me. As an Army officer I tried to be strong. As a young man who just lost his father and mentor, I was lost. Those ironic and powerful words would haunt me to this day. Our military experience at Fort Gordon would be our last memory together.

Military service was a tradition in the Clement family. My uncles, cousins and brother Frank were all veterans. Dad served proudly in the U.S. Army, the Tennessee Army National Guard and the Tennessee Air National Guard. As governor, he joined the Guard to help to strengthen the organization's public image and also stimulate recruiting. At the time, the Tennessee National Guard had a reputation for being weak and inept, and not fulfilling their mission of protecting the citizens of the state. It was a time of great civil unrest in the South, and segregation of the public schools had just been outlawed. By enlisting in the Guard himself, Dad wanted to illustrate Tennessee's strength as a state that can take care of its own people and their security. That is one of the main reasons that as governor my father declared, "I'll never let Federal Marshall's or troops march in Tennessee as long as I am governor. We will solve our problems as Tennesseans." (The governor of Tennessee is also the commander-in-chief of the Tennessee National Guard.)

It was natural for me to serve. Even as a young man I always admired our great military leaders, but I must admit, the influence of my father's service in WWII and the Korean War, as well as serving in the FBI were my main inspirations.

Coming out of high school, I had a low draft number just as I was turning eighteen. Today, we have an all-volunteer military, but back then during the Vietnam War the draft was what most young men my age feared. When you turned eighteen, every male was required to sign up for selective service knowing that they might be called up for military duty. I asked myself, how could I serve my country and also enter the military as an officer and not a buck private? I decided to enroll in the ROTC program at the University of Tennessee, which gave me a real sense of independence, pride and patriotism. Like many young men at the time, I kept asking myself what was the real reason for the Vietnam War. Were we fighting a war of containment, or a war to win?

It seemed to me at the time that we fought a purely defensive war, taking territory, then giving it up, then fighting again to move the Vietcong back. And even as a young man, I could see how our warfighters were being treated by some Americans; this made me very uncomfortable. Why? Because when you grow up with family members who believed that service is a proud and noble pursuit, then that heroism is taken for granted, and in the case of the Vietnam veterans even mocked, well, that really alarmed me. My first two years in basic ROTC (Reserve Officer Training Program) was mandatory. But, the experience, though intense and very difficult, made me even more determined to serve my country. I committed myself to the U.S. Army by completing my last two years of advanced Army ROTC training, and upon graduation, I was commissioned as a second lieutenant. For the first time in my life I felt like I was able to step out of my father's shadow and finally become my own man.

But, you could say I was far from being a mature, self-sufficient man during my four years in the ROTC at the University of Tennessee.

One of my first weekend training experiences almost ended my military career even before it really got started. We were participating in some ROTC military exercises in the rugged East Tennessee Mountains, the perfect place for practicing maneuvers and routine drills. During one of our breaks, I rested my M-1 rifle against an old oak tree deep in the Appalachian hills miles away from the nearest town. Most people who visualize settings like that usually equate it with the film *Deliverance,* and that is certainly understandable. Anyway, when I came back to retrieve my rifle, it was gone. I almost had a heart attack! At first I thought that it was just a joke that my buddies had played on me, but after a few minutes it was clear to me that this was serious. My commanding officer was very upset, and I must say that was an understatement. He was livid. We did some investigating and someone had said that they had seen a mountain man in the area, and maybe he was the one who stole my rifle. I called a friend at the Tennessee Highway Patrol and told him what happened. They immediately were on the case, combing the hills in search of the mystery man who might have taken my gun. What was even worse than just losing my rifle was the fact that I visualized having kitchen patrol duty or latrine duty if that weapon wasn't found.

Over the next few hours, with the help of the highway patrol, we managed to finally track down the mountain man. He was dirty, unshaven, and to me it looked like he hadn't bathed for weeks. Though I was taken aback by his demeanor, I went right over to him and said with great determination, "Hey, you can't just walk off with government property." He looked at me as though I was speaking Greek, and then I continued, "Taking a weapon is a Federal offense and the U.S. government will prosecute you."

He replied, in a very odd way, "What is the U.S. government?" I couldn't believe what I had just heard, but I realized this man probably never traveled more than a mile from his back woods home and lived in a way you or I could never imagine. "Please, sir," I said. "You really need to give me back my rifle. It won't do you any good anyway, because you would never be able to find any ammunition for it." With a quizzical look on his face, the mountain man reluctantly handed me back my M-1 rifle and all was back to normal. But I must say, my buddies wouldn't let me live it down, and more than one time over the next year, they would chide me by saying, "Clement, do you know where your gun is?"

I would distinguish myself once again with my marching skills, which my friend Ken Jordan from South Pittsburg, Tennessee, who was in ROTC with me, and who served in Governor Ned McWherter's administration and in the Tennessee Air National Guard, would never let me forget.

Since I was placed in charge of conducting routine marching drills with my squad, I was always working hard to perfect those skills and pass them along to the young soldiers under my temporary command. On one occasion, I gave them the order, "Forward March." Everything was going along just as I had planned, and as the sun was setting along the rolling Tennessee hills, I apparently forgot to issue a very important command in this process—halt or about face. The platoon kept marching and marching, eventually marching straight over a hill. Thankfully, it wasn't steep, and the worst that happened was that I was really embarrassed. After that embarrassing situation during my ROTC training, I was hoping that I could put it all behind me. Matter of fact, after my platoon almost fell off of that hill, Ken came over to me and said: "Bob, I think you are in serious trouble! How could you forget to tell them to halt?" I replied, "Ken, I have no idea!" That was the beginning of a friendship that has lasted for more than fifty years. Ken went on to having a distinguished military and civilian career after graduating Vanderbilt Law School.

But that was child's play compared to what happened next during my officer basic training at Ft. Bragg, North Carolina.

This was by far the toughest and most rigorous military training I had ever experienced. It was no secret that I was the son of the governor and like other times before in my life, I was the target of ridicule just for that reason alone. We had a very nasty drill sergeant at the time, who I soon realized was trying to make me the private that had to be made an example, and so he did everything in his power to humiliate and bully me. He had just returned from active duty in Vietnam, and most likely had PTSD, but we didn't know it at the time. As part of our supposed training, he stood right in front of me and pulled out a string that had many grey colored human ears attached to it. It was horrifying to say the least. He said he took them from the bodies of dead Vietnamese soldiers who were killed in battle. Looking back on that experience, I wish I had reported him to his command. But that incident reminded me about some atrocities that happened during those tumultuous years, not the least of which was the My Lai massacre.

After I completed my training and graduated from the University of Tennessee, and before I was to fulfill my active duty Army commitment, I asked for and was granted a one-year educational deferment so I could get my MBA Degree from Memphis State University. I was determined to get my degree in one year, and it was a real challenge to study full-time and also work part-time for a local car dealership and the Bureau of Business Research.

The mid-1960s were a time of political upheaval in America. The civil rights movement was in full swing, and Dr. Martin Luther King, Jr. was preaching peaceful civil disobedience in pursuit of equal rights for African Americans. Early in the evening on April 4, 1968, life would never be the same. Time seemed to stand still in Memphis on that day, when shots fired by

James Earl Ray from a high-power rifle rang out from a boarding house located across the street from the Lorraine Motel, killing Dr. King. He had been viciously assassinated, and with that one bullet, the social consciousness of our nation would be forever changed.

Sitting in my room at Memphis State, I heard the tragic news over the radio. Emotions were running high on the campus among both white and black students. Dr. King was the personification of non-violence, and his death gave us all a feeling of hopelessness and loss. Hopelessness, because many people fought so hard to give African Americans equal rights, and it seemed like those dreams just died, and loss because Dr. King was an icon and a leader who could not be replaced. It was also particularly painful for me. He, like Dad, was a man of unparalleled principle and sense of justice; we were all in a prolonged state of shock.

A curfew was declared in Memphis and on campus, and literally nothing or no one moved in or out after 5:00 PM. Memphis felt like a ghost town. What was once a vibrant and energized city now felt like a morgue--the place where the greatest civil rights leader of our time was gunned down by a madman. We all were glued to our television sets like the rest of the country. For days, America was suspended in disbelief. Riots and unrest broke out in many of the urban areas and Memphis was no exception. As a resident of Memphis and a student at Memphis State University, I was very proud of the black and white communities rallying together to keep peace and stability rather than burning the city to the ground. Half of the population of Memphis was black; we all had a stake in the city's future.

In January 1969, after graduating from Memphis State University Graduate School where I received my MBA, I reported for active duty at the Adjutant General School, at Fort Benjamin Harrison in Indianapolis, Indiana, and went through three months of specialized administrative training. After completion of Adjutant General School, my new military orders took me to Ft. Gordon in Augusta, Georgia, where I was the new personnel officer at the Civil Affairs School.

As part of one of my first assignments, I was given the fiscally responsible job of making sure seventy-five reservists received their pay. I had a total of $17,500 to dole out among the reservists, and I meticulously asked each one to sign the middle of the form saying that they agreed that the amount was correct. I handed in the forms to my command and was very proud of my achievement. All seventy-five of the reservists left with the cash payments; all was well in my world. That is until the finance officer said, "Lt. Clement, you owe the Army $17,500." I couldn't believe what I was hearing. I thought to myself that I've only been in the Army a couple of months and I'm already $17,500 in debt to the U.S. government. I replied, "Are you serious, how could that be? I did everything you told me to do, Sir." He turned to me and said with an accusatory tone, "You forgot to have them sign the bottom of the form that acknowledges that they received the money. Lt. Clement, you owe the government the money unless you can get me all of those forms signed." Obviously, he was very serious. I knew I was in deep trouble and I couldn't have Dad or the highway patrol get me out of this one. Over the next six months, I had to find each and every one of those reservists, who lived all across the U.S., and ask them to sign the bottom of the form so I could get out of this mess. Fortunately, though it seemed to take forever, I was able to track them all down and had every form signed, sealed and delivered. I grew up very quickly after that experience for sure, and it taught me to be more careful and consistent, and most of all, realize that the devil is truly in the details!

As personnel officer at the Civil Affairs School, I was part of the pacification program. Our mission was to work with the soldiers who were going to South Vietnam and help them learn how to understand and communicate with the villagers. Among other things, I had to break the news to soldiers when they received orders that they were going to Vietnam, which one might imagine was not an easy task. By 1969, the war was not popular, and warfighters knew there was a great chance that they would not make it back alive, or would come back physically and mentally broken.

On September 24, 1969, as I was coming back from lunch at the mess hall, I heard Sergeant Perkins call out to me in a very calm, discreet manner. He said: "Lt. Clement, I have something to tell you." I replied right away, "What is it Sarge?" He looked me straight in the eye and said, "Lieutenant, you've just received your orders for Vietnam." I thought he was joking, so I said with a tone of disbelief, "Don't joke with me, Sarge." Then he looked at me very intently and told me that he wasn't joking and that I was going to Vietnam. Now, to be fair, anyone who was in the military at the time knew there was a possibility they would be deployed. That is what we train for each and every day. The reason I didn't believe him at first was because that was what my job was, and surely, I would have known first about my own potential deployment. Over the next few days I learned that I was going to be working as a courier, carrying top secret information, which did sound intriguing to me. I was scheduled to leave for Vietnam on January 4, 1970.

It was a tough time to be in the military, due to the anti-Vietnam feeling throughout the land, and while I did understand the sentiments of those who opposed the war, still, I wanted to serve my country. There were things, of course, that I didn't agree with at the time, and I was frustrated with some of our military strategy, such as layers of needless bureaucracy, and the incessant infusion of politics in making military decisions. Nevertheless, you learn in the military to obey orders and that is precisely what I did.

Anyone who has been to war will tell you that it is an emotionally and physically tough way to make a living. But thank goodness there are brave men and women in this great country who sacrifice so much to keep all of us safe. But the truth is, war is ugly and it hurts, especially when you lose one of your buddies, who become like family when you spend so much time together away from your own loved ones. I lost friends in that war— my ATO fraternity brother, Stanley Sullivan, from Fayetteville, Tennessee, who was killed in action in Vietnam, and one of my ROTC comrades, Charles Ayers, from Greeneville, Tennessee, who died in a military training accident just before he was to be deployed.

Today, as a result of the wars in Iraq and Afghanistan, more than 4,000 brave men and women have made the ultimate sacrifice; hundreds of thousands have sustained serious physical injuries; and 250,000 suffered from non-visible injuries such as Post Traumatic Stress Disorder and Traumatic Brain injuries. In addition, sadly, twenty-two service members and veterans commit suicide every day. But if you ask these American heroes, like Cpl. Christian Brown of Munford, Tennessee, who is a Silver Star recipient after he ran into enemy fire to save his buddies and lost both of his legs after he stepped on an IED (improvised explosive device) he would do it all over again. This is the American spirit I treasure.

I believe that every young person of legal age should have some type of public service whether it is in the military, or some form of mandatory service like Job Corps., Domestic Corps., or the Peace Corps., which I strongly support. These experiences can help young people feel like they own a piece of the rock. It is something I wish every young person at some point in their lives would take part. In Israel, military service is mandatory, and though here in the U.S. it is voluntary, still, I think it is one of the best experiences a young person could have. I also believe that it teaches you discipline and responsibility and something even more important—an intrinsic love of country. When you serve in any capacity you become part of the rich American experience, and know first-hand what the word freedom truly means. Very few current members of Congress have served in the military, and it is estimated that less than one percent of the American population serves. Perhaps even fewer people know someone in the military personally. I am hopeful that every young person will be engaged in some meaningful service to this great nation of ours.

Now that I knew I would for sure be going to Vietnam, I naturally told my parents and grandparents the news. While they of course were concerned about my safety, they knew that my military service was a source of great pride for the family. I must say I was proud, too, knowing that I was going to continue the Clement legacy of patriotism and service. January wasn't that far away—only three short months, so I spent a good part of my time at Ft. Gordon training for my assignment as a civil affairs officer. I had my Vietnam orientation course and series of shots to plan for deployment. I had made peace with the decision to go to Vietnam.

Then the phone rang. Most military families fear the knock on the door. A Casualty Affairs Officer is the one person no one ever wants to meet. They are specially trained military members whose sole job is to notify families in the event of the death of their children, husbands, wives, brothers or sisters. It is a job no one ever wants to do, but getting it right can mean all the difference for family members who will be notified in-person if their loved one has died in the line of duty.

A phone call was the last thing I ever expected, especially from my grandfather bearing the worst news anyone could ever imagine—by telephone no less.

I kept thinking about my last conversation with my father after hearing the news of his death. Was I too hard on him? I told him that I didn't want to talk to him anymore, and those terrible words that I kept hearing in my ears haunted me. Why did I say that? I didn't mean it. I remembered I also qualified those remarks to him by saying that I didn't want to talk to him anymore if he was going to spend the next year deliberating about running for governor. The reason I was so upset was because I was worried that if Dad lost another election, it would be devastating since he had three successful terms as governor. And with the surge of Republicans in Tennessee, I was just trying to protect his legacy. Then, I realized that Dad was always civil to me and rarely got mad; he was the most unselfish person I have ever known.

The next day, I flew home to say goodbye to Dad, to a man born for public service, whose life abruptly and tragically ended at the tender age of forty-nine. The funeral was planned and was attended by at least 10,000 people. They came from all across Tennessee and the country. There were politicians, business leaders, clergy and others who just wanted to come and pay their respects. Mother was ill at the time, and the loss of her beloved husband was a burden almost too difficult to bear. I, too, felt a deep sense of grief and responsibility that haunted me for a long time. I lost my best friend. I wanted to tell him so many things. The first was that I was so sorry for my harsh words, for not being able to apologize. It really hurt. But I got to thinking that Dad would often talk to me about death, and he would say that it was something he didn't fear. So I tried to be strong for him and for all of my family.

My Dad's funeral was held at the First United Methodist Church in Dickson, Tennessee, where Dad was born. Johnny Bragg, the leader of the Prisonaires sang a song in his honor, and a gospel quartet performed Dad's favorite song, "Precious Lord, Take my Hand," which was written by Thomas A. Dorsey. Here are some of those moving lyrics: *"Precious Lord, take my hand, lead me on; let me stand. I'm tired and weak, I'm alone. Through the storm, through the night lead me on to the light. Take my hand precious Lord, lead me home. I'm tired and weak, I'm alone through the storm, through the night, lead me on to the light. Take my hand precious Lord, lead me home."*

Dad also had a few favorite poems, and this one he would recite over and over. It gave me comfort during his service and throughout my life. To this day, I'm not sure who wrote it, but whoever did, had a huge impact on our family's spiritual life. Here's what the poem said:

"I have a house inside of me; a house that people never see; it has a door through which none pass, and windows, but they're not of glass. "Where do you live?" Ask folks I meet, and then I say, "On such a street," but still I know what's really me, lives in a house folks never see.

Sometimes I like to go inside, and hide and hide, and hide and hide, and 'doctor up' my wounded pride when I have been treated rough outside. Sometimes, when I have been to blame, I go indoors and blush for shame; and I get my mind in better frame, and get my tongue and temper tame.

I meet my Heavenly Father there, for He stoops down to hear my prayer, to smooth my brow and cure my care, and make me brave to do and dare. Then, after I have been made strong, and have things right that were all wrong, I come outside where I belong, to sing a new and happy song."

There is an old saying, "You can tell a lot about a man by the size of his funeral." Or as Governor Ned Ray McWherter of Tennessee would often say in his speeches, "The number of people attending your funeral has a lot to do with the weather." Both of those comments were apropos during my father's service. The overwhelming size of the crowd on that day, spoke volumes about who Dad was as a man.

In a strange way, his death saved my life. After leaving the Army I joined the Tennessee National Guard, where I spent twenty-nine years and retired as a Colonel. Had I stayed in the Army I would have certainly gone to Vietnam, and perhaps Dad would have been the one to receive the telephone call or what's worse, a knock on the door.

Through every dark cloud there is a rainbow waiting to appear. I know that his passing has given me even greater resolve to not just be my own man, but to celebrate his legacy as an integral part of who I am as a husband, father and friend. I continued to soldier on.

Clement's Contemplations

"Never underestimate a mountain man."

"Military service brings you closer to God and country."

"Words have power beyond compare; use them wisely and without anger."

"March along in life, but don't forget to 'halt' at times."

"If you owe the government money—pay it back as fast as you can."

"Fathers and sons may disagree, but they are bound forever."

"Answer every phone call from a loved one, for it may be the last."

"An M1 rifle, like a prisoner with a Mustang, should never be left alone."

"The dark clouds in life are waiting for rainbows to appear."

"Some people march to a different drummer; some just march over a hill."

Chapter 4

RETURNING HOME: SETTING THE STAGE FOR MY CAREER IN POLITICS

"Someone once said some people might not remember
what you say in speeches but sure do remember
how you make them feel."—Mary Clement

After I returned home from the U.S. Army, with a very uncertain future, I was fortunate to land a job with the University of Tennessee Center for Government Training. I was hired by Eugene Upshaw to work with city, county and state officials on training programs designed to improve effectiveness and efficiency for their employees.

I worked for UT before I enlisted in the military. I was able to return to a university where I had a history that I treasured.

But the political itch was beginning to take hold; I couldn't ignore the pull and influence.

I was always impressed with the Tennessee Public Service Commission (PSC). The Commission, at the time was made up of three elected officials who were responsible for regulating private and investor-owned utilities, such as telephone companies, railroads and trucking firms in the State of Tennessee. In fact, I even wanted to buy a small independent telephone company of my own when I was in college. I eventually decided not to pursue that idea because it would be too difficult to raise the funds I would need. Nevertheless, I still had an interest in the agency and the regulatory industry, so before I was discharged from the U.S. Army, I called then PSC chairman, Hammond Fowler, to discuss my working for him. Fowler was one of three PSC commissioners and he had served in that capacity for twenty-three years. I was very excited about meeting with him and talking about how I could get a job with the PSC.

"Bob, we will be in touch with you," chairman Fowler told me during our telephone conversation, and I had the definite impression that he was going to try to help me. After waiting and waiting, but hearing nothing from chairman Fowler, I finally called him again, only to be given the run-around by a junior staff member who thanked me for calling, but gave me no additional information or encouragement; I was deeply hurt by that incident.

While I was still working at UT in Nashville, I decided to return to Knoxville to pursue my doctorate degree in education administration and public finance full-time. About halfway through my course work, I just couldn't stop thinking about the cold shoulder I had received from my dad's close friend, Commissioner Fowler. Perhaps, I was more sensitive considering the tragedy I had just experienced, but felt surely I would receive a returned phone call. When we all go through tragedy or heartache we most often turn to those we feel will help us. I realize today that a call not being returned or a door shut in your face is usually a blessing in disguise because life will lead you in another direction. That is exactly what put me on a path that I otherwise would never have traveled.

In the meantime, I was receiving calls from across the state encouraging me to run for the PSC. As a result, I decided to make the race and challenge the chairman who would be seeking re-election for his fifth term in 1972. One week before I announced my candidacy, I got a call from the PSC offering me a job, but

I had already made up my mind. Tennessee author, Criswell Freeman, says in his book *When Life Throws you a Curve Ball*, "Hit it." That's exactly what I decided to do.

Loyalty is very important to me, and in fact, if I had gone to work for the PSC I would have never run against Commissioner Fowler. But destiny had created an opportunity for me to seek office after my father's death, and for the first time I felt a fire within me to run my inaugural political race.

When I publicly announced my intent to run for the PSC, it was exhilarating. The campaign took me to each of Tennessee's ninety-five counties, and I won a landslide primary victory.

The race was full of interesting contrasts between me and Fowler. He was seventy-one years old, and I was twenty-eight. Blatantly attacking his advancing age would have been a tactical campaign mistake. Still, I knew that somehow I needed to get the point across that my opponent, who used to refer to me as, that young whipper-snapper, was off-base because while I was young, I was still eager and energetic and ready for the challenge. He would be seventy-seven-years-old if he completed another six-year term. My way of getting that message across was to say, "I sure hope that my opponent, Mr. Fowler, won't criticize me for being only twenty-eight years old; I sure won't criticize him for being seventy-one!"

The substantial vote I received in the Democrat Primary gave me the much needed momentum for the general election race against Republican State Senator Tom Garland of Greenville, who served as senate minority leader of the Tennessee Republican Party, and was an outstanding public servant. The campaign was a very clean one. One of the main issues revolved around Southern Bell's effort to seek a significant increase on the rates they could charge customers for installing a telephone. When I voiced strong opposition to the rate increase, Senator Garland criticized me for pre-judging the issue. My response was that the voters had a right to know our position on these matters prior to the election, not afterwards.

The race was complicated by the fact that I was running on a ticket with the unpopular Democratic nominee for President, George McGovern, as well as Democratic U.S. Senate nominee, Ray Blanton. Garland, on the other hand, was running on a ticket with the very popular Republican combination of Presidential nominee Richard Nixon and incumbent U.S. Senator Howard Baker, who had defeated my father in a bid for the Senate six years earlier. The other two Republican candidates won, but voters crossed party lines in the PSC race and gave me a great victory. I was the second non-attorney to serve on the commission and the first non-attorney to be elected.

In January 1973, my grandfather, Judge Robert S. Clement, administered the oath of office and swore me in as the new PSC commissioner. He was so proud of me, but was initially hesitant about me running because of Dad's last two election losses. Still, he supported me, giving me one hundred percent of his love and backing. This was a momentous time for both of us.

After my swearing in, and as I began my new career, many people viewed me as a populist. I was extremely outspoken and often voted against a number of proposed utility rate increases because I really wanted to make sure the consumer's interests were represented. My passion for public service developed as a young man, and was based on addressing the needs of people in their day-to-day lives. It became the basis for the way I approached my job at the PSC. During my tenure at the commission, I established a reputation that would follow me into my future political campaigns. Being commissioner really amounted to acting as a consumer advocate, and for the next six years of my life, I would serve as the people's representative. I was a watchdog and the voice for the average consumer. My position was not accompanied by lots of perks, privileges and patronage, which is almost impossible to fathom today. At the PSC we did not control big budgets or thousands of jobs. Making the choice early in my career not to become part of the so-called political machine allowed me to make decisions based on what I believed was best for the people. When I was later elected to higher office, I continued to view myself as an advocate for working people and not as a power broker. I never catered to the powerful political leaders or special interest groups. Sometimes my pro-consumer stance cost me in my political career, but serving the interests of the people is to me the most rewarding aspect of public service.

During my term, the agency considered many important issues, such as telephone rates and service, trucking authority, railroad and gas pipeline safety and more. To this day, I am most pleased that we really helped Tennessee consumers. We eliminated 55,000 eight party-line phones that were reminiscent of an Andy Griffith television episode. Believe it or not, with that antiquated system, people had to literally ask their neighbors to clear the phone line if there were an emergency, or they really needed to make a call. Neighbors could also listen to everyone else's conversations. We also provided the first telephone service to areas such as the Stinking Creek community in Campbell County where residents had no telephone service at all. It was amazing to me that we could send a man to the moon but had communities in our state without telephone service.

We also instituted the first drug enforcement program to ensure that truck drivers were substance-free when transporting freight along our state's highways. We increased the number of motor carrier and railroad enforcement personnel within the agency and dramatically improved truck and rail safety.

Many of the people I met, and the staff I inherited during my six years as a commissioner, became part of my extended political family. Those relationships continue to be a part of my professional and personal life to this day. Dottie Moore, even though she openly worked for my opponent, Hammond Fowler, became my confidant and assistant at the commission. I met her after I won the election and was immediately impressed. She was very open and honest about her loyalty to my opponent during the race, and admitted that she had campaigned and voted for Hammond Fowler. I liked her candor so I asked her to remain on my staff. I still jokingly say, "Since Dottie once worked and voted for my opponent, she had to work for me for over thirty-years to redeem herself."

After serving six years on the Public Service Commission, speculation was mounting as to whether I would run for governor of Tennessee in 1978. Frankly, serving on the PSC was fulfilling. "Why," I asked myself, "should I risk running for governor?" Yet, at the same time, I had higher political ambitions. At the PSC, the scope of the issues we confronted was limited. I had hopes to one day run for another political office where I could serve the people of Tennessee on a broader front.

When I was considering my options, I was haunted by the memories of my father leaving office as a relatively young man and watching him struggle without a clear direction. I thought to myself at the time, "What will I do if I win and have to leave office after only four years?" I asked myself this question over and over.

At that time, the governor could serve only one four-year term, and I would not learn until March, 1978 whether a state Constitutional Amendment would be approved to allow the governor to serve two consecutive four-year terms. The Democratic Primary election would be held in August and the general election in November, which left a scant amount of time to execute a successful campaign.

If I decided to enter the race, I would face Jake Butcher and other candidates in the Democratic Primary. Jake was a well-known figure all across East Tennessee, and I knew him both personally and professionally. He was a very successful banker and businessman and was extremely wealthy and well connected. Jake was also the major promoter of the 1982 World's Fair in Knoxville, Tennessee. The Butcher and Clement families were close friends and political allies for many years. As we each considered our candidacies, Jake told me that he only wanted to serve one term.

Butcher showed up in Johnson City, Tennessee, in a meeting brokered by a mutual friend of ours who was hoping we could resolve our differences. Despite the mounting scrutiny on our potential candidacies, very few people knew about the meeting that was held in a small hotel room with no one else in attendance. Jake appeared nervous, or at least more nervous than I was. He began by emphatically stating, "I'm going to run for governor, Bob." We were sitting in small wooden chairs, and Jake was fidgeting around so much so that his chair collapsed! While it gave us some brief comic relief, the moment quickly faded, and the atmosphere once again reflected the somberness of the meeting's purpose. It seemed that each of us was waiting for the other one to blink.

"Jake," I said, "I feel strongly that I can win the primary. But even if you beat me, according to my professional polls and some of the best political wisdom, you can't win the general election." I offered to share the polling data that I had with me. He refused to even look at it, but I suppose the encounter had some impact on him anyway.

I heard from some credible sources after we both left the meeting that Jake met with some of his family and friends in Maynardsdville, Tennessee. Jake shared the details of our conversation, and then said to them, "I don't think I am going to run for governor." Everyone there couldn't believe what they were hearing. Someone said to Jake, "In 1974 you didn't have a chance of winning, yet you ran and missed the Democratic nomination by only a few votes. Now, with everything you have going for you, why wouldn't you step up to the plate and run?" I guess Jake was influenced by their encouragement and boldly declared, "I *am* running for governor!" And from that moment on, he was a committed candidate in the 1978 Tennessee governor's race.

Pondering my decision about the 1978 governor's race, I kept checking with Tennessee's Speaker of the House, Ned McWherter, because I did not want to run if Ned decided to become a candidate. But McWherter was also hesitating to make a decision about his candidacy. I often wondered if it was just a big waiting game. Was McWherter waiting on decisions by Butcher and me before determining his own political course? I kept waiting for an answer and finally, in March of 1978, after learning the state constitution would be amended to allow the governor to serve two, four-year terms, I informed McWherter, who still had not declared his intentions, that I would be seeking the office of governor. Looking back I am sure McWherter felt the composition of the race was not good for him at the time and I am sure he was right. When he later ran for governor and was successful, his timing could not have been better. He served Tennessee well, and will be remembered for his many accomplishments, but especially his ability to connect with people.

Delaying my decision whether to enter the race proved a huge strategic error. When I finally committed to run for governor in April 1978, I was far behind in practically every phase of organizing a campaign and raising the money to fund a state-wide race. I waited to establish the campaign organization that would be required for me to run successfully for the office of governor. I waited to compile my list of supporters and contact people to make sure they would remain uncommitted. And, I waited to raise money. I was still trying to bring back more personalized politics that I had witnessed growing up.

Former Lt. Governor Frank Gorrell came to my assistance and we managed to raise $1.4 million, even though his support came with a touch of irony. Years earlier, Gorrell had aligned himself with the independent faction in the Tennessee legislature when he ran for lieutenant governor, and my father supported his opponent, State Senator Jared Maddux. Maddux won that race by one vote that was determined by ballots cast by members of the State Senate.

Securing the support of one of the most capable and respected political advisers in the state was a real coup. Frank never criticized anyone. People trusted him, and he always told the truth and never played political games. His voice, echoing our message throughout the Tennessee political community, brought excitement and momentum to my campaign, and fueled the perception in political circles that the Bob Clement campaign was putting the pieces of a viable organization together. His eternal optimism provided our staff and me an emotional lift on a daily basis. Whenever he was asked how he was doing, he'd always reply, "Magnificent!"

The Finance Committee was one of the strongest parts of our organization. We knew that Jake Butcher would have a generous campaign budget, so in order to compete we had to focus on fundraising. Between April and August we raised $1.4 million, an adequate amount of money to get our message across to the voters, even though we were outspent by a margin of three-to-one.

I called on many life-long friends during the campaign and named Steve Hewlett, a Nashville builder who would later be elected to the Tennessee Public Service Commission, my state coordinator. I've known Steve since our high school days when he attended Antioch High School in Nashville. John Tanner, my ATO brother, served as my West Tennessee coordinator. He and I later became colleagues in the U.S. House of Representatives when he was elected to the 8th Congressional District House seat in West Tennessee. Jerry Wyatt, who was director of the motor carrier division when I served at the PSC, played a key role in West Tennessee. He later served as chief of police in his hometown of Brownsville, Tennessee, and eventually became adjutant general of the Tennessee National Guard where I served under his command as a lieutenant colonel. Walter Bussart and Bart Gordon were Middle Tennessee coordinators. Bart was elected to Congress and they would be instrumental in my election to the U.S. House of Representatives.

I met Bart through his work on behalf of the Tennessee Democratic Party and when he served as state party chairman. My life-long friend Jess Campbell, a Knoxville attorney, served as east Tennessee coordinator in the governor's race. Tom Griscom, a former reporter for the *Chattanooga News Free Press*, was my press secretary during the campaign. He later served as press secretary for Howard Baker in the United States Senate, and accompanied the Senator to the White House when Baker agreed to serve as Ronald Reagan's chief-of-staff. Griscom himself eventually became President Reagan's chief-of-staff. The late Tom Seigenthaler, who headed a successful public relations firm in Nashville, was appointed as my director of communications. Irby Simpkins, who would become publisher of the *Nashville Banner*, served as my campaign treasurer. I've known Irby since high school. Kent Syler, Jeff Whorley, Mike Williams and Tim Thompson started their political careers with me, driving around in a sound truck with loudspeakers encouraging people to vote.

The campaign was a learning experience for all of us as we paved the way for future careers in business and politics. I'll always remember the campaign's opening day. I needed a good start, but that is not what happened. *The Tennessean* newspaper interviewed a dear family friend, Marshall Ledbetter, Sr., an activist and well-known political operative who is now deceased. He was asked, "How do you feel about Bob Clement running for governor, particularly since you were so close to his father Governor Frank G. Clement?"

"We're back in the saddle again," my friend responded. I cringed when I read the interview. I knew his comments would infuriate my father's enemies. A few days later, another reporter asked one of my relatives, my Aunt Anna Belle Clement O'Brien, who held political office, a similar question. "If you vote for Bob, you get two for one," she responded. I knew for sure that statement would reinforce some people's impression that I wouldn't be totally in charge. That was the furthest thing from the truth and would give my opposition fodder for trying to discredit me.

I knew both of these comments would not be helpful, and the other side would twist them for their own political gain. Butcher's campaign suffered from the same sort of media faux pas when his brother, C.H., was asked how Jake, who was living a rather expensive lifestyle, could support himself on the governor's pay which was paltry compared to the millions he was earning as a businessman. C.H. replied that he personally would subsidize Jake's income while he was governor.

The positive response we received from the public when I made my formal announcement was amazing. Entering the race late, we did not have the infrastructure in place to manage the large number of people who volunteered to work on my behalf. We were simply overwhelmed and needed a more organized team in order to have a successful campaign.

Our television advertising was marginal at best. Our commercials were not effective in positioning me to the public, and we didn't spend enough money on TV advertising either. Our political strategy was lacking, too. We should have been more confrontational with Butcher on a variety of critical issues, such as insisting he disclose funding sources for his campaign, and stressing his apparent business-related conflicts of interest. But I had a number of people who for one reason or another kept telling me to back off of the criticisms fearful that it would hurt us in the general election. Unfortunately, I listened to the whiners rather than the winners.

We spent so much time during the primary campaign in East Tennessee trying to build momentum for a battle against Republican opponent Lamar Alexander, who would be very formidable in that part of the state in the fall general election, that we shortchanged our Democratic strongholds in Middle and West Tennessee. We should have put more focus on defeating Democrat Jake Butcher in the primary. Hindsight, as they say, is twenty-twenty, and in retrospect, the lesson I learned was to concentrate on the primary rather than the general election.

The Memphis vote is essential in a Democratic primary and critically important for Democrats in the general election. Memphis is tough campaign territory in a statewide race, especially for someone who is not a native, which at the time was Tennessee's most populated city. Still, I had graduated with an MBA degree from Memphis State University and felt my chances for strong support in Memphis were good.

The black vote in Memphis was solidly behind Butcher, mainly due to the backing of Congressman Harold Ford, Sr. and his political organization. My strategy had been to attempt to split the loyalties of the Ford family. I knew Harold would endorse Butcher. He even named one of his sons, Jake Butcher Ford. Harold and Jake had joined forces during the 1974 governor's race when Ford was reported backing candidate Franklin Haney, but in mid-campaign switched his support to Buthcher. In 1978, Harold was solidly for Butcher and so was his brother, State Senator John Ford. I solicited the endorsement of another brother, Emmet Ford, who was a state representative. My efforts initially appeared to be working, but eventually the entire Ford family stuck together behind the Butcher candidacy.

Next to the Ford political machine, the strongest black political organization in Memphis was the American Federation of State, County and Municipal Employees (AFSCME), the union that represents government workers. The local union, led by Reverend James Smith, officially joined my effort with a formal endorsement of my candidacy. We worked together throughout the city to solicit support from blue collar workers.

It was obvious the Butcher organization had neutralized or somehow won over many of my potential AFSCME supporters. As the results filtered in from across the state on election night, I was leading before the votes from Memphis were tallied. But, I was defeated by such a wide margin in the black precincts of Memphis that I lost the governor's race. The black vote was split in many other parts of Tennessee, but in Memphis, Butcher received sixty-nine percent of the black vote; I received twenty-five percent; and Dick Fulton, even though as a member of Congress he had shown political courage by supporting civil rights and open housing legislation, only tallied six percent.

Ironically, Fulton, the most liberal candidate in the primary race, ended up with most of the white vote in Memphis, in part because Jake Butcher and I were both trying to win the black vote. Fulton and the other primary candidates; Roger Murray, William Jackson, Willie Jacox, Ben Miller and Shelley Stiles drew enough support from me to make a difference in the primary election. Those candidates tallied more than 174,000 votes with Fulton gaining more than 122,000 votes and Roger Murray more than 40,000. Fulton pulled much of his vote from Nashville and Middle Tennessee, both areas where I would fare very well against Butcher if those candidates had not been in the race. Butcher finished with 320,329 votes to my 288,577.

I was crushed when it became evident that Jake Butcher would win. I knew the race would be close, but when the outcome was apparent, I felt my whole life begin to unravel.

I didn't blame anyone else for my defeat. I congratulated Jake on his nomination and pledged my full support. A room full of my backers at our election night headquarters at the Opryland Hotel hissed and booed when I made positive comments about Butcher.

Politics can be very emotional. I've never seen as many people in tears in one room, not even at a funeral. The Clement organization had become a very close-knit family, and some supporters were extremely unhappy because they felt Butcher had bought the election rather than by earning it. It was obvious on election night he had much work to do within the Democratic Party in order to win the general election.

I was only thirty-four years old when I ran for governor and looked even younger. My boyish appearance was an enormous detriment during the campaign. Even my grandmother May Belle Clement said, "Bob, you are older than your father when he ran for governor, but you look so much younger." After the race, narrowly losing the primary by less than 32,000 of the more than 800,000 total votes cast, I conducted a survey. It indicated that while the voters agreed with me on the issues, and believed we had an effective organization, however, my youthful appearance was a negative.

I surprised myself, hitting the streets the very next day after my loss, knowing that I couldn't let any grass grow under my feet. I've seen too many people over the years fail to immediately attack their campaign debts and was later unable to eliminate them. I knew if I ever wanted to run for another political office I had to pay back my creditors. I also knew that whether I decided to go into business or any other professional endeavor that I couldn't allow a campaign debt to remain an obstacle. I immediately contacted my creditors, asking for additional time and made them aware I intended to meet my obligations. Every single creditor cooperated with me.

Following his primary victory, Jake Butcher took some time off, which proved to be a terrible mistake. Perhaps he believed that he should let the emotions of my supporters cool before hitting the campaign trail, but he actually needed to reach out to Clement loyalists to heal those wounds as soon as possible making them feel a part of his campaign. That did not happen, and the bitter emotions lingered, contributing to his eventual defeat in the fall of 1978. Lamar Alexander, on the other hand, had television commercials running the day after the Democratic primary appealing to my supporters with the message, "I know that many of you feel Jake Butcher bought this election and didn't earn it. I want you to know that if you voted for Bob Clement, we have room for you in the Lamar Alexander political camp." Alexander's strategy worked. During his own primary campaign, he had actually visited with many of my supporters soliciting their help. When they would tell him that they were committed to Bob, his response was to ask them, "Well, if Bob Clement doesn't win the primary, will you support me in the fall?" In fact, he did get a number of commitments after the primary by using that novel approach.

Butcher came to see me after the primary and we visited at my home in Nashville. He had aired many TV ads that portrayed him as a farm boy who grew up the hard way. To remind me of my childhood farm at the governor's residence, I still kept one chicken in the back yard of my Nashville home. During our visit, Butcher looked out of my window and saw the chicken. "Jake," I said, "That chicken lays one egg a day. You wouldn't believe how many people think a hen needs a rooster to lay an egg!"

After my defeat, Lamar Alexander also called me, and we exchanged pleasantries. He asked to meet with me personally. I thanked him, but said that we really didn't have anything to discuss. I wished him well in the governor's race, but made it clear that I had run as a Democrat, lost as a Democrat, and would support the Democratic nominee. He still wanted to sit down and talk, but I told him that would send the wrong message to potential Democratic voters, and again made it clear that I was not in a position to offer him any help.

Jake met with me again, several weeks later and he wanted us to appear together on various campaign stops. I told him I would do everything I could to help and certainly intended to vote for him, but added that my number one priority was to retire my campaign debt. He offered to host a fundraising event for me after the general election. I thanked him but made it clear that I could not afford to wait and had already scheduled a fundraiser. His disappointment was evident because he knew my efforts would siphon funding from his own campaign.

"I understand your feelings," I said to Butcher, "but I have to think about my family," concerned that if he lost the general election, his promise would be meaningless. The fundraiser I organized worked perfectly. Lamar Alexander and Jake Butcher attended and so did many of their supporters. J.D. Sumner and the Stamps Quartet, who on many occasions toured as backup singers for Elvis Presley, provided the entertainment for the event which was a huge success. I didn't care whether those who attended were Democrats, Republicans, or Independents. I just focused on erasing my campaign debt. I was able to pay off all my creditors, and the huge turnout indicated that I still had a great amount of political support despite my loss in the primary.

In 1978, Lamar Alexander was victorious. Like Butcher, Alexander had also run in 1974 and was defeated in the general election by Ray Blanton. But Alexander had kept his political organization intact and ran an excellent campaign in 1978. He hit Jake hard on the issues, particularly joining the media's focus on the Butcher financial empire and his personal finances. The final vote count in the general election was Alexander 661,959; Butcher 523,495.

The raucous campaign season was finally over, and having erased my political debt, I started to focus on the future. It's hard to regroup after such a disappointment, but I've always considered myself an optimist and a survivor. At times, I would feel sorry for myself or dwell on the past, but I didn't give up. As one chapter closes in your life, another one always opens. But my anxiety could not be denied. After my loss, the headlines read, "The Clement era is over." But that only made me more determined; I was ready to move on.

Following the loss in the governor's race, I focused on finding work and providing for my family. A future in the political arena was not something that occupied my thoughts. In January 1979, I started a marketing and management firm called Bob Clement Consulting. With training and experience in marketing and management, I knew I would enjoy working in that field for a while. It would also give our family an opportunity to regroup following the election loss.

Almost immediately, however, Tennessee Speaker of the House, Ned Ray McWherter and U.S. Senator, Jim Sasser, asked if they could submit my name to President Jimmy Carter for a possible appointment to fill a vacancy on the Tennessee Valley Authority Board of Directors, created when Bill Jenkins resigned. I agreed to allow my name to be submitted for consideration for the appointment. (Years later, I would serve with Jenkins in the U.S. House of Representatives.)

I was honored about the possible appointment as TVA director. My work at the Public Service Commission had come to the attention of President Carter who had named me to a national committee in 1976. Little did I know that my work at the PSC would lead to an ideal opportunity at such a perfect time in my life. The position, if I were appointed and confirmed, would be similar in many respects to serving on the PSC. Like the Public Service Commission, the TVA board had three members.

Since the TVA was the largest electric utility in the nation, it served parts of seven states, with 55,000 employees and a six billion dollar budget. My expertise from the PSC helped me immensely for the upcoming job. President Carter, I learned, was inclined to appoint me. The President, however, was also very close to Jake Butcher who had helped him in his election campaign. Butcher, according to my sources, was opposed to my nomination. The President finally told Butcher that he was going to do one of two things either appoint me as TVA director, or give the appointment to someone from outside Tennessee. After learning the President's position Butcher dropped his opposition to my appointment, and he called to tell me that he was one hundred percent behind me. Within hours of speaking with Butcher, I received a call from the White House offering me the TVA appointment, and asking me to schedule a time for Mary and me to come to Washington to personally meet with President Carter. It was quite an experience traveling to the nation's capital to meet with the President and witness his official announcement of my nomination for the vacancy. I filled out a number of papers required for a mandatory background investigation. The FBI, as part of the process, checked with my neighbors, friends, relatives, and even with my political enemies regarding my past. While the White House was still processing the necessary red tape, one reporter after another called me for comments regarding the prospective appointment. During one of the interviews, I made some remarks that definitely slowed up the confirmation process and probably caused the White House some trepidation.

Hal Heflin was a newly elected U.S. Senator from Muscle Shoals, Alabama, which housed some TVA facilities and was a very important region for the utility. A reporter asked me a question about my views on moving the TVA's main office from Knoxville, Tennessee, to Muscle Shoals, Alabama. Alabama residents would have obviously liked the TVA headquarters in their home state. TVA's executive offices, since the agencies' creation under the administration of President Franklin D. Roosevelt in the 1930s, has always been based in Knoxville, while the administrative offices for TVA's power operations were located in Chattanooga. Many of TVA's agricultural activities were centered near Muscle Shoals.

"TVA's executive offices have always been in Tennessee. It would be expensive to move the headquarters, and we needed to be sensitive to the ratepayers," was my response to the reporter. I didn't believe it would serve any useful purpose for TVA to move its headquarters from Tennessee to Alabama.

My remarks outraged Senator Heflin. A former State Supreme Court Judge in Alabama, the senator was adamant that TVA's main office should relocate to his home state. It was a popular political issue for him. Heflin responded, in turn, by announcing that he would use his position on the Senate's Committee for Environment and Public Works, the committee that would consider my confirmation, to block my appointment. Heflin also said he wanted someone from Alabama to fill the vacancy on the TVA Board. He added that he would ensure that the CIA, FBI and every other appropriate authority thoroughly investigate me prior to my confirmation hearing. Heflin personally told me that if I would agree to recuse myself when the issue of moving the TVA headquarters from Tennessee to Alabama came to a vote, that he would not fight my confirmation. I told him that if confirmed, I felt compelled to vote on any and all issues that came before the TVA board. At that point, Heflin made it very clear that he would oppose my nomination to the bitter end. And that is exactly what he did.

It seemed to take forever for the White House to finally complete the required FBI background check and forward my nomination to the Senate Committee for Environment and

Public Works. I was already frustrated because the prospective appointment was for a very short period. Normally the term of a TVA director is nine years. My term would be brief because director Bill Jenkins had resigned with less than two years remaining on his nine-year term. I finally notified the White House that if they did not send my name to the Senate for an expeditious vote, I would withdraw my name from consideration for the appointment. Apparently, my tactic worked because the U.S. Senate proceeded with the nomination.

During the confirmation hearings, Senator Jim Sasser of Tennessee championed my nomination. He managed to keep the hearings moving smoothly despite Senator Heflin's persistent and steadfast opposition. Tennessee's senior U.S. Senator, Howard Baker, attended the hearings. Baker and Sasser wielded great clout and were very helpful in support of my nomination. Senator Lloyd Benson of Texas, who was the committee chairman, also supported me and provided great assistance in my effort to secure the TVA appointment. When the final vote for confirmation occurred, Senator Heflin cast the only dissenting vote.

Several weeks passed and emotions had quieted to a certain degree. My first meeting with Heflin as the newly appointed TVA director took place in his Senate office. "Bob," he told me, "I want you to know that it really helped me in Alabama to oppose your nomination. And Senator Sasser said it really helped him in Tennessee to support you." "Senator Heflin," I responded, "I am pleased both of you came out so well at my expense." That seemed to break the ice between Heflin and myself. We both chuckled; our working relationship was outstanding during the rest of my TVA term.

My swearing-in as the new director happened in Knoxville in front of the imposing TVA Towers. Retired Federal Judge Charles Neese, who was hearing matters regarding the controversial case against Tennessee Governor Ray Blanton in Nashville, traveled to Knoxville to perform the ceremony. I had known Judge Neese for a number of years and had gone to school with his sons, Chuck and Gary. While returning home from the swearing-in ceremonies, Judge Neese suffered a serious heart attack and had to recuse himself from the Blanton case.

As I began my new job, the national economic climate and the international political landscape had forced Americans to place a great focus on energy-related issues. The Shah of Iran had recently been overthrown and the Ayatollah Khomeini had become the new ruler. The U.S. Embassy in Teheran was seized by student-revolutionaries who took fifty Americans hostage. Instability and anti-American sentiments in the Persian Gulf region had brought great attention to our country's dependence on foreign oil supplies. In the United States, a near disaster occurred at the Three Mile Island facility outside Harrisburg, Pennsylvania, when the plant's containment building was flooded to avert a release of nuclear contaminants into the atmosphere. The national economy was in the doldrums. Inflation and unemployment were up. The foreign trade deficit rose by thirty-three percent, the largest increase in thirty-three years. U.S. Steel had announced the closing of thirteen plants which would idle 13,000 steelworkers and impact employment in other sectors of the nation's manufacturing industries. The worry over oil supplies, concern over energy costs and the slumping economy made our job at TVA more important than ever. Energy-related issues filled the news while consumers had less disposable income and could not afford increases in their utility bills.

In most political jobs you enjoy at least a brief honeymoon period, a time to get your feet wet in the new position. But that was not the case for me at TVA. I had participated in a number of tough battles in rate cases over issues that came before the Public Service Commission, but from the outset, it was evident that the TVA would be a much more difficult arena. TVA chairman,

David Freeman, made no bones that I was not his first choice for the new appointment on the board. Director Dick Freeman was the other member. Although they had the same last name, the Freemans were not related. Chairman Freeman had helped persuade the Carter Administration to appoint Dick Freeman, which had, in effect, created a buddy system on the TVA board. Due to their philosophical loyalty to one another, I was the odd man out, and the Freemans, it seemed, would find reasons to oppose me on nearly every issue. In a short time, it became apparent that I couldn't look to my colleagues on the board for any support. I decided to take my case directly to the people.

Soliciting public support and airing TVA's dirty laundry in the media was something that had never been done before. I suppose the Freemans expected that I would simply coast through my brief term and keep my mouth shut. But I wasn't willing to take that approach. Public service means more to me than quietly filling a chair in a boardroom and drawing a paycheck. If the public would side with me on the issues, I reasoned, the vote would be two-to-two. With congressional support it would be three-to-two. Congress has oversight authority over the operations of TVA. After all, the utility was created by the Federal Government and received government funding.

Rates were also skyrocketing. The utility was losing its competitive advantage, and much of it had to do with the commitment to build seventeen nuclear reactors. The reactors were ordered during the tenure of TVA chairman Red Wagner, prior to the time the Freeman's and I were appointed on the board.

I strongly believed that the utility was placing too much emphasis on the nuclear option and needed to change course. My view was that construction of at least some of the reactors should be canceled and others should be delayed because the cost was driving up TVA electricity rates at an alarming speed.

Many customers could not afford the higher utility bills they were being forced to pay. TVA's rates were becoming less and less competitive compared to utility rates outside the TVA region. I knew that higher rates would also have a negative impact when it came to recruitment of industry and economic development for the TVA region.

I have never been part of an organization that had more depth of knowledge and expertise than TVA, but at times, in my opinion, it was headed in the wrong direction. The original price tag of TVA's nuclear construction program for seventeen reactors, projected to be six billion dollars, had soared to more than thirty billion! Rather than risk the utility's entire future solely on the nuclear option, I believed that we needed to balance our future energy needs with coal, solar, hydro, nuclear, alternate energy sources as well as placing a much greater emphasis on conservation. My effort to discuss these matters with the other two board members fell on deaf ears. I discovered that the best way to draw public attention to TVA's nuclear gamble was to vote no on each and every electric rate increase, and then explain my position. Dave and Dick Freeman became angry when I voted against an electric rate increase and they portrayed me as totally irresponsible. During one board meeting chairman Freeman proposed giving merit bonuses to reward TVA's top managers for doing an outstanding job. Director Freeman agreed, but I voted against the proposal. I was disappointed and was quoted as saying that, "Rewarding top managers for the inefficiencies at TVA was outrageous." I added that the management team bore part of the responsibility for ordering seventeen reactors when the utility didn't possess resources to undertake such a massive nuclear construction program. On another occasion, I proposed that any expenditure of more than $100,000 require the approval of the TVA board. Existing policy allowed expenditures up to two million without board approval. This practice gave middle managers too much authority. I did some homework and learned that some projects with cost estimates often hundreds of millions of dollars were often broken down into individual contracts of less than two million dollars! My proposal must have caught the TVA board by surprise. Chairman Freeman and director Freeman initially voted in favor of the new policy, but reversed their votes at the next board meeting. Chairman Freeman explained that approving new expenditures in excess of $100,000 would require the board to meet more frequently and would slow down the contract process.

One day a reporter called me and asked me whom I was going to vote for President of the United States. Jimmy Carter, who had appointed all three TVA directors, was seeking re-election. The fight at the convention, it appeared at the time, would be between President Carter and Senator Edward (Ted) Kennedy. My response to the reporter was, "I would vote for President Carter." The next day the newspaper headline read: "Bob Clement Endorses Jimmy Carter for President." I promptly received a call from the White House informing me to stay out of political matters. I listened politely to the caller but had no overt response. As a TVA board member, I was, by law, already quite limited from engaging in political activities.

Ronald Reagan defeated President Carter in 1980, and I knew full well that my days were numbered at TVA. My term would expire in May 1981. Some wanted me to start jockeying for the re-appointment to a full nine-year term. It was clear that my loyalties had been with President Jimmy Carter. I was a Democrat and certain that President Reagan would appoint a qualified Republican to take my place. Had I been in his shoes, that's precisely what I would have done. I did not seek re-nomination and my term ended in May, 1981. I am proud to say that the TVA board ultimately changed directions concerning the nuclear building program and canceled and deferred some of the nuclear reactors. I was never opposed to the nuclear option but felt that we were over-building and over-projecting the demand for energy.

The Freemans' and I did have our differences on the TVA board, but we accomplished so much as well. We were able to come to an agreement between TVA and the white water rafters to divert water from the Ocoee River which was generating hydro power. By doing that, TVA was able to set aside a specific number of days for recreation and economic purposes. The TVA board also approved construction of a magnificent building in downtown Chattanooga that was solar powered and energy efficient.

In addition, our working together helped forge an agreement between Israel and TVA on research and development of solar power. Finally, we created energy conservation programs to reduce the amount of wasted energy in the Tennessee Valley area. TVA was a growing and learning experience for me. Through the years, I was proud of the fact that I could sit down with someone as bright and talented as Chairman David Freeman, now one of my good friends, with whom at times I didn't agree, yet still joke about our differences. The lessons I learned from my public services experiences were immeasurably important.

Once again it was time for me to prepare for a return to life in the private sector. Among the options I considered was going into business with Doug Horne who had worked for TVA for fourteen years. He had become my confidant and good friend. Doug and I left TVA on the very same day. Although he had one of the best jobs at the agency, he felt it was time to seek other opportunities. Doug had decided to enter the real estate development business to build shopping centers. We discussed starting a business to be called Clement-Horne Properties. Doug eventually became an extremely successful businessman and served as chairman of the Tennessee Democratic Party. Another option was to form a company called Charter Equities, a real estate investment business with Steve Hall, a life-long friend from Nashville, who had been in the real estate field for many years, and Bill White, a CPA and accountant from Murfreesboro, Tennessee. My role as general partner would be to bring in investors to purchase apartments and shopping centers. I decided to move back to Nashville and work with Charter Equities. I had a degree in Real Estate and Public Finance from the University of Tennessee, but hadn't yet worked in the real estate business. Initially, I was very excited about the new possibilities, and while I found Charter Equities to be interesting, ultimately, this business didn't prove as personally satisfying or challenging as I had hoped. We were very successful in acquiring properties including four apartment complexes and one shopping center. But, my thoughts kept returning to some form of public service which I knew, deep down, had always been my true calling.

Clement's Contemplations

"Politics at its core is not about who lays the egg, but who gets the hen."

"Tennessee politics is like politics everywhere, except for the charm."

"Sometimes life takes you in unexpected directions. Embrace the space in between."

"Political courage is being able to take a blow without injuring your ego."

"A political opponent may be against you for the moment, but there's always another day."

"Campaigns may break the bank, but will never silence the true reformers."

"Caring about those you serve is the prize."

"Being governor of Tennessee would have been a dream come true. Being a Congressman from Tennessee made all the difference."

Chapter 5

SAVING CUMBERLAND UNIVERSITY

"They call me Mr. President"—Bob Clement

As drivers make their way toward Nashville, Tennessee on Interstate 40 westbound, there is a large sign for exit 238, U.S.-231 toward Lebanon, Tennessee. And there is another one that directs them to take that exit to get to Cumberland University. Now to most people, a simple sign on a highway means very little, but to me it means the world.

Lebanon, Tennessee, specifically, South Cumberland Street, eases visitors away from the busy twentieth century highway into a time gone by. Antebellum-style homes and streets lined with aging live oak trees flourish there. A city of about 28,000 citizens, Lebanon was founded in 1801. Its name is derived from the biblical Cedars of Lebanon. The popular restaurant chain, Cracker Barrel, was founded in Lebanon, and many of the local residents work at the company's headquarters.

Just off of South Cumberland Street, and within a couple of short blocks, is University Avenue, the main access road to the campus of Cumberland University. Today, the school has a student population of more than 1,500, the vast majority from the State of Tennessee. A faculty of nearly one hundred professionals provides a small teacher/student ratio of about sixteen students for every professor. Students can attain degrees in a variety of programs, with the emphasis still– as it was when founded in 1842– on liberal arts. It has regained the academic standing and accreditation that originally made it one of the most revered institutions of higher learning in the entire South. But the story of Cumberland University wasn't always so rosy.

The graduates of Cumberland University include more than eighty members of Congress, several justices of the United States Supreme Court, thirteen governors, a number of U.S. ambassadors, and dozens of college and university professors. Some of the universities' graduates include: WWII Secretary of State Cordell Hull, who won the Nobel Peace Prize in 1945; and Senator Al Gore, Sr. More importantly to me, five members of my own family attended Cumberland, including my grandfather and my father. I remember Dad reminiscing many, many times about his college days. Our family, for many generations, believed that education was the key to success in life and Cumberland was a big part of that equation.

My father graduated from the college, and my grandfather graduated from the Cumberland University School of Law. When it was founded in 1847, there were only eleven law schools in the entire country, and Cumberland Law quickly became one of the most respected and largest law schools in the nation, alongside Harvard and the University of Virginia. The Civil War almost destroyed the school, and many of its students and graduates died on the battlefield, mostly on the Confederate side, but also some fighting for the Union. In 1866, Cumberland was rebuilt from the destruction of the Civil War and adopted the image of the Phoenix as well as the motto, I rise from the ashes. In 1901, Cumberland became one of the first law schools to admit women, and even prior to that, a member of the Choctaw Nation had been enrolled. In the 1930s, 40s, and 50s, graduates of Cumberland Law held leadership positions all over the South, whether as judges, CEOs, or elected officials like my father. It was, for sure, the school of choice for young people who wanted to accomplish great things and make a difference in the world.

Sadly, even the success and reputation of the law school couldn't prevent the downward spiral of Cumberland. In 1961, this decline culminated in the sale of the law school from Cumberland University to Samford University in Birmingham, Alabama. As far as I recall, the law school was sold for just $155,000! In my opinion, selling the law school, and for such a ridiculous price, was the biggest mistake the administration of Cumberland ever made; instead of preventing the demise of this iconic Southern academic institution, it actually accelerated it. At the same time, Cumberland became a two-year junior college, and was no longer known as Cumberland University, but now Cumberland College of Tennessee. It was heartbreaking for our loyal college family to know that even as a two-year school, Cumberland had a hard time competing with the more established and better run community colleges in the South.

There are so many reasons for the school's decline. Like many other small private colleges at the time, Cumberland was recovering from the Great Depression and WWII. And, there was no doubt in my mind that the school's leadership lacked vision and energy. And what's worse was that the budgetary shortfalls were not compensated by outside fundraising, but rather by drastic moves such as selling the law school. Even though Cumberland could always claim an impressive group of alumni, the school never reached out to them to ask for help which was surely a mystery to me.

The Cumberland University of old, and the Cumberland University of today, is very different from what I inherited as its twentieth president back in 1983. By the time I walked through the door, the school was in dire financial straits and its future uncertain. I, too, was at a crossroads in my life, with an uncertain future and some tough experiences in my recent past. In a way Cumberland College and I were destined to find each other, and become each other's stepping-stone into happier days ahead.

Here's why that happened. I had made an unsuccessful run for the Tennessee governorship in 1978, coming in second in the Democratic primary. In 1982, I ran for the seventh Congressional District, a seat that was being vacated by Robin Beard, so he could run for U.S. Senator. The seat had always been a strong Republican district. While I won the Democrat primary, I lost to Don Sundquist, the Republican candidate from Memphis. The Congressional district ran from outside of Nashville to the suburbs of Memphis. My involvement with Cumberland might not have ever happened had I won that election. In fact, on election night of the general election, CNN and other major television networks projected us the winner at approximately 8:30 in the evening. But then we needed to wait to receive the remaining votes in Memphis. When the votes finally were tallied around midnight, we were short nearly 1,500 votes. Certainly, there was much disappointment after thinking we had won the election, but turned out it was a blessing in disguise for so many reasons. (I did, however, have a very good showing, and was the first Democrat who had a real shot at switching the seat.) Nevertheless, that made the loss even more painful, because we fought such an uphill battle and we almost pulled it off. What was so heartbreaking at the time actually paved the way for me fulfilling my dream to become a college president and the father of another beautiful daughter, Rachel.

After that loss, I kicked the dust off of my shoes, and returned into the business world, mostly doing real estate, and probably would have been quite content making a living that way. But shortly after that congressional loss, and completely out of the blue, my phone rang. Sam Hatcher who was editor of the *Lebanon Democrat* newspaper where Cumberland College is located and a close friend called to say that the board of directors was looking for a new president. Though the job opening was not widely circulated, I couldn't have been more excited to learn that people on the board thought highly enough of me to consider my application for the job of president of Cumberland.

As Mary and I considered the opportunity and challenges facing Cumberland, I became more excited about what could be accomplished as the leader of this wonderful school with its rich history – a history that was important not just to the South, but to me and my family. Second, I became more and more aware of a feeling inside of me that I was ready for a new challenge, ready to try my hands at something I had never done before. In my career I have worked in many professions, so, obviously, I have an attraction to the unknown and have no problem completely switching gears if the challenge is right. As I thought about the opportunity to lead Cumberland, a strategy began to form in my mind on how to turn the school around. I could feel the energy and was excited to put my ideas to the test!

I had told my classmates at the University of Tennessee that one day I wanted to be a college president. Here, now, was my opportunity, and once I had decided to pursue it, I became more enthusiastic about the prospect. However, this was by no means a done deal. Just because the search committee had reached out to me didn't mean the job was mine.

Over the next few weeks, the board of directors expanded its search and publicized an official position announcement. To my surprise the posting led to about sixty serious candidates who were applying for the job. My challenge as part of this candidate pool was always going to be that people thought of me as a politician first and foremost, and certainly not as an academic or an administrator. Rather than fighting against that perception, I embraced it. To prepare for the interviewing process, I formulated a rather detailed plan that spelled out my clear objectives, with the number-one goal being to move the school from a two-year institution back to a four-year university. I also described my management and leadership experience. I made the board aware that I was a proven decision maker who could move quickly and decisively, and that my organizational skills, and, most importantly, fundraising prowess were evident during my gubernatorial and congressional campaigns.

Walking into the interview and the review process I had clear and well-thought out vision for the immediate future that showed the board that I was a planner and perhaps turned some no votes into supporters. In addition, there were a number of good friends on the board on whose support I knew I could count. But I was also keenly aware that there were other board members who possibly wouldn't vote for me. Perhaps those who felt I wasn't the best choice, had their reasons. But I figured there was nothing I could do other than to deliver the best application possible. Instead of lobbying for the job, I let my plan and my vision speak for itself. My vision was to modernize Cumberland, and elevate the academic standards and overall reputation in an effort to make it a leader in liberal arts education with an emphasis in business. Some of the challenges the board was facing was the college's deteriorating reputation, physical neglect, and weakening enrollment. It was moved from a four-year accredited university to a two-year college. It had lost its law school and the student enrollment was at a very low level. In addition, the campus infrastructure was not properly maintained and the overall climate was one of desperation and despair. My proposal to the board included specific recommendations. They included: moving it back to a four-year accredited college; changing its name from Cumberland College of Tennessee to Cumberland University; increasing enrollment and major gifts; making the physical changes needed to improve the campus; and helping create a culture of optimism and excellence.

The process eventually reduced the number of candidates from sixty to just three. The other two each had doctorates and vast experience in academia, while I, clearly, did not. With about a week to go before the board's vote, my name appeared in the local newspapers as one of the three finalists. I never really knew who leaked my candidacy to the press, but I sure made the headlines. While the positive press was appreciated, it also caused some uneasy feelings about the selection process because they mentioned me as the front runner, adding new pressure as to whom would be the next president. My aunt, who was always such an astute politician, cautioned me that since I had become a target, I would need to proceed with caution. That one little leak resulted in some Republican activists across the state campaigning against me. I think one concern they had was that I would use the Cumberland presidency as a stepping stone back into politics, and translate any success I had into a winning run for elected office. I wasn't thinking about another election. My philosophy has always been and still is today that if I can make things better where I am, other doors of opportunity would lead me elsewhere.

While I knew that a large number of board members were Republicans, I still knew that a number of them would vote for me. I didn't realize at the time, however, that others' opposition to me was real. On the morning of the vote, I was optimistic, but a bit nervous as well. To my delight, I managed to become the next president by a single vote!

The selection method and the final vote were a dignified and professional process, for sure. Despite the public opposition by some Republicans, this was not a race for political office but a decision that the board made to do what was best for the school. I am convinced that the votes that were cast against me were based not on my politics, but because those board members strongly believed someone with a more academic background was the better choice. In the end, I think my fundraising abilities probably made the difference, plus the fact that I had a proven track record of managing people and resources. After a fairly evenly divided outcome that was decided by one vote, the chairman of the board, Dr. Robert Carver Bone, asked whether the board could take a second vote that would elect me unanimously. He wanted to show that during this difficult time in the school's history, the board was completely united behind its new leader. I really appreciated that gesture, and to this day regard it as an act of political courage. And over the years, as many of the changes I had put in place were beginning to bear fruit, I always enjoyed a very good working relationship with the board of trust. Even the ones who had voted against me were pleased with the progress and were supportive of my initiatives.

But, the school I inherited was a sad version of its former self. Cumberland's financial difficulties had taken its toll. The facilities were run down and in need of repair. There wasn't a single building on campus that didn't require immediate attention. The grass looked like it hadn't been cut in a month and there were brown bald spots where green grass should have been. All over the walkways there were weeds—some as tall as a mountain lion. We even had a furnace simply die on us within my first week on campus. The mail system was in disarray! It was located in a small room in the main building, and there was a large table where the mailman literally dumped the mail each day. After he would throw the mail down, the faculty, staff and students, on their way to class, would stop by the room and sift through the pile to see whether they had received any mail that day. Modern technology, let alone computers, was nowhere to be found on campus. By the early 1980s, personal and commercial computers were still new technologies, but they were none-the-less found only in larger businesses, and very few in academia. At our small, struggling school, believe it or not, we were still relying on typewriters and notecards. That meant that our alumni records were horribly out of date, denying us the opportunity to truly engage our alumni in rebuilding the school. I knew I had so much to do, but realized that to get things done, I needed to work fast. I never looked at these challenges as negative, but as an opportunity to let the Phoenix once again rise at Cumberland.

What was my very first order of business? Of course, it was rallying the troops.

The student body was over 500 at that time. They were incredibly supportive and eager to help bring about change. The faculty also realized the gravity of the situation and backed me up on a number of very difficult decisions that went against their own interests. For example, as he was exiting his post, my predecessor, Dr. Ernest L. Stockton, Jr., was going to offer all staff and faculty members a one-year contract. I heard about this offer and immediately went to see him. I told him, "I hope you will reconsider the one-year contract for each faculty member because I'm trying to implement changes and need to make decisions." There had not been contracts before and I knew that it would critically limit my ability to move forward and move fast. The faculty knew about Dr. Stockton and my conversation before I officially arrived on campus. But they understood, too, that I was making the changes I felt were important to move the school forward, and they came to trust that I was implementing sound policy for the greater good. Thankfully, Dr. Stockton withdrew his support for this proposal. That was a great help to me by not tying my hands and I was very grateful. That trust was really put to the test again when I asked the faculty to abolish tenure. Like implementing term limits; the public loves the idea, but the politicians hate it! I argued that we could never become a credible four-year institution with a tenured faculty meant for only a two-year school. I have spent years advocating on education issues, later founding the education caucus in Congress. While I believed in the concept of tenure, I also realized that I had to get Cumberland accredited for a four-year institution first. The reason that tenure was an issue for me was that because some of the tenured professors at the time were not academically qualified to teach at a four-year university. I needed more flexibility and freedom to make sure I had faculty and staff that were qualified, and who would be up to the standards to teach with proper credentials. I knew how incredibly difficult a vote like this would be, and that I was asking the faculty to vote against what would appear to be in their best interest. But they trusted me once again and decided to abolish tenure anyway.

Incidentally, President Stockton handed the mantel over to me with great professionalism, cooperation and courtesy. I really appreciated how he let me be my own man from the very outset, and did not try to exert any undue influence. Because of that, I felt comfortable going to him for advice and counsel over the years and I came to respect his opinion a great deal. I promised myself to play that same supportive role when it came time for me to move on. I thought it best to be a good soldier and let the next leader of the school shape the place according to his or her vision. Later, I learned that my successor, M. Walker Buckalew, may have heard one too many times, "Bob Clement did this," and "Bob Clement did that." Then when one of the school's largest benefactors asked him, "How's Bob Clement doing?" He replied, "I don't know anyone who misses him!" That benefactor never gave another dime to the school.

But during my first days on the job, my immediate and pressing needs were so easy to identify. We had to spruce up our campus, make the facilities safe and visually appealing, put new roofs on the buildings, cut the grass and get rid of the weeds. The Women's Club came to our rescue and made Cumberland's campus beautiful once again. I am so very grateful for their support and help because they truly made a huge difference in the school's physical appearance. Everyone knows that first impressions count, and I didn't want our dilapidated campus to be the first impression for potential funders or students. I had some initial success raising money so that we could invest in our external environment and make it a much more pleasant and appealing place. Also, while I knew my strengths, I recognized some of my weaknesses as well, which in this case was my lack of experience in academia. I decided I needed to find a right-hand person who could focus on the academic challenges of full accreditation and move us toward a four-year institution. I would focus on fundraising which became ninety percent of my job. That right-hand person turned out to be one of the most important and productive professional relationships I ever had.

Dr. Ray Philips had just concluded a long and distinguished academic career at Auburn University. Born and raised in Tennessee, he and his wife, Dr. Phyllis Philips, relocated back to Wilson County, which was her hometown, and were enjoying the rewards of retirement. They had a beautiful farm, and one day I decided to visit Ray and try to talk to him about coming out of retirement to work with me at the college. I wasn't going to take no for an answer! While it took some convincing, Ray and I became a fabulous team. Matter of fact, I teased with him after he accepted the job that Cumberland was in trouble now that we have a politician and a farmer running the college. I appointed him to the position of vice president of academic affairs. I was most pleased that Ray accepted the job. (After I left, he joined the board of trust, Cumberland University's name for what is more commonly called a board of trustees, and in 1991, Dr. Ray Philips became the twenty-third President of Cumberland University.)

Making Ray the first vice president of academic affairs was a sign to the faculty, the student body and the community, that

Cumberland was moving from a two-year school mindset into a four-year one. Ray's advice was always sound, well-reasoned and often compassionate. One example of that compassion was when I received a phone call from a distraught mother whose son had some difficulties at two previous universities. Let's just say he wasn't as focused on academics as his mother would have liked. Ray and I met with her son, and he promised us that he was ready and even mature enough to work hard and become one of our standout students. As we chatted with him, Ray's words echoed in my mind: "Bob, we're here to mold and build young lives, not to destroy them." I decided to give the kid a chance and admitted him on probation. He sure did make us all proud! His name was Ed Labry, and after graduating from Cumberland University he later became one of the nation's most successful businessmen becoming president of First Data North America, a global leader in electronic commerce and payment processing.

Years later, President Dr. Charlene Kozy, whom I had hired when I was president, called upon Ed to help fund a new business school at Cumberland. The hope was that he would contribute a sizeable sum and inspire others to also step up to the plate. He asked what the new business school renovation would cost, and Dr. Kozy said: "Ed, we want to refurbish an historical building that will house the new Labry School of Business, and the projected cost is four million." Without one iota of hesitation he replied, "I'll do that." Then, Ed Labry wrote a check for the entire amount! He told Dr. Kozy, "If it wasn't for Bob Clement, I would have never finished college. He gave me a chance and this check will give others a chance, too." That really sums up what I hope my legacy will be as Cumberland's president; giving all young people, regardless of their limitations, an opportunity to be their very best.

Over the years, I had developed a crystal-clear vision for the school, and my latest challenge was to sell that vision and make it a reality. One of the things I learned early on was that a successful fundraiser doesn't ask for money because something is so bleak and it needs to be fixed. Not at all, a successful fundraiser paints a picture of the future and focuses on how great things could be. That's what gets people excited and makes them willing to support you, either with money or by volunteering. That, to me, was an incredibly valuable lesson, and I tried very hard to run my later political campaigns the same way. I wanted to be the candidate with vision and optimism. I didn't want to ask people for their votes because things were bad and I was going to fix them. I wanted people to vote for me because they shared my vision for the great things that could be accomplished; simply the power of positive thinking.

In the case of Cumberland, what could be accomplished depended on our ability to move the school from a two-year program to a four-year institution and achieve full academic accreditation. I surrounded myself with as many competent and intelligent people as I could find, whether in the administration or on the faculty. In those transition years we found a great number of excellent professors who ended up coming to Cumberland and staying for many, many years. We also strengthened our liberal arts degrees by inserting more business courses into the curriculum and raising the requirements for graduation. In addition, we made our student selection process more competitive and raised the standards for admission.

As we implemented these changes and got the school on more solid footing I wanted to let everyone know that Cumberland was back. Originally, when the school was founded in 1842, it was called Cumberland University. Now, finally, I had everything in place—so much hard work and energy went into getting the school ship-shape. I was so confident that we had made such great strides that I went to Nashville to the secretary of state's office – that's the state agency that incorporates businesses and regulates names of organizations – and filled out an application for us to call ourselves Cumberland University once again. I was so excited to fill out those forms, but couldn't believe my eyes when the application was questioned. It turned out there was another group that had trademarked the name and called itself Cumberland University of Nashville. After we did some research, we discovered they had just reserved the name, but never had actually used it, so I knew we had a chance to take our good name back where it belonged. I asked the Secretary of State, Gentry Crowell, "Since the other organization isn't using the name, let Cumberland have it, and if they raise any objections, we'll argue our case at that time." That seemed to satisfy the regulators and we were back in business as our beloved moniker, Cumberland University.

And as quick as the wind, word got out that Cumberland University's name was restored, and the school soon began attracting new faculty members with doctorates and teaching experience; we were receiving more student applications. One night, after a long meeting in Nashville with a potential donor, I drove back to campus and realized that there were no signs on the Interstate giving any directions to the school. People just used to say, "We know where Cumberland is, and you'll know it when you see it," I responded with a laugh. "What about everyone else?" I thought, "What good was it to be a top-notch university when no one can find you?" We asked the State Department of Transportation to help us get new signs approved and placed on the interstate—40 East and West.

Over time, I must say, we became very creative and professional in our school's fundraising efforts. Initially, this was a one-person job, my job, until I had the resources to create a development office that could help in this massive effort. I hired Bill Fletcher to be my vice president of development. One pressing need was identifying and researching potential sponsors, cultivating a relationship with potential donors and soliciting their support. In my outreach efforts, I always tried to paint a picture: this is how great this place could be because of your help. Alumni were one group we reached out to, but actually more money came from non-alumni. I called them friends of Cumberland who wanted to help us for a variety of reasons. For example, some gave because they strongly believed that small, private independent colleges needed to remain as an alternative to the larger state-funded universities. The others gave because we met with them personally and they were moved by our rags-to-riches story.

Friends of Cumberland came from the local community. One benefactor, Tommy Lowe, the co-founder of Cracker Barrel, lived in the heart of Lebanon where its corporate headquarters is located. It didn't take too much digging to find a phone number for him, and so I called and asked him whether I could pay him a visit. We ended up meeting on his boat, enjoying the beauty of Old Hickory Lake and chatting about my plans for the school. To my astonishment, no one had ever asked him to become a benefactor of Cumberland. Here we have one of the most successful businessmen in the South right in our backyard, and no one ever thought of seeing whether he would like to be supportive of the school. Amazing!

We agreed that a better local university would translate into a more qualified labor pool, which in turn would benefit a business as robust as Cracker Barrel. I thought I had scored a home run and took the bull by the horns: "Tommy," I said, "The school sure would appreciate a $250,000 donation from you." He almost fell off the boat! "Well, Bob," he answered, "That's fine and dandy, but my problem is that I really don't get paid all that much by Cracker Barrel. Instead of a big salary, I have stock options, so I can't really write you that kind of check, but I could give you some stock. Would that help?" I gladly accepted his offer, and he signed over to the university $50,000 worth of Cracker Barrel stock.

And about a year and a half later, we sold the stock for $125,000 and used it to make some much needed upgrades to our campus facilities. One steadfast rule in business, politics or academia—always keep an open mind and imagine the possibilities.

The real lesson is that success in almost any field is based on a person's ability to build, maintain and cultivate relationships. The worst that can happen if you ask someone for help is that person says no. But if you never ask, then there is zero chance of ever hearing a yes.

As I continued on my relationship building tour, I was really surprised how uninvolved the alumni were, and how few people in Wilson County even knew about the school and the great strides we were making. It became my main mission to get to know as many people as possible, get them excited about Cumberland and its future and find ways to garner their support. I worked that way with our board of trust, too. I made it a point to get to know as many of them as possible on a very close and personal basis, so that there was a foundation of trust. Based on those relationships, it became much easier to get the board to approve something, or even have board members take an active part in fundraising. Ironically, my political background was a huge advantage because of knowing how to manage people and resources, being a good decision maker, being able to raise money and having a solid business strategy to keep the college afloat. In addition, I already had my MBA Degree and was halfway finishing my doctorate in education administration and public finance from the University of Tennessee. Ultimately, the fact that I was a politician, once I got the job, was actually very positive.

The joy of success came with a steep emotional price for me. To get accredited as a four-year institution meant that some on our faculty who did not have doctorates, and who were qualified for only teaching in a two-year school, had to be let go. (I appointed Dean Bill McKee as my liaison between the college and the Southern Association of Colleges and Schools. He was my key person to get our accreditation as a four year institution.) I tried to move them around as much as I could, but in the end there was no avoiding having to terminate the employment of some very fine faculty members and staff. I tried to be as professional and as compassionate as possible when having these incredibly difficult conversations. Those affected understood that my hands were tied if I wanted to move the school forward. But that didn't make it any easier, either for me or for them.

My first two years at Cumberland flew by. My entire staff and I worked incredibly hard and in a very short time laid the groundwork for a really bright future. By the time I left Cumberland in 1987, we had achieved full accreditation as a four-year institution of higher learning. We tripled the amount of private gifts to the university, and we doubled the educational income from tuition and research grants. We also expanded the curriculum and increased the number of majors we were able to offer. Through a much more focused marketing and public relations campaign throughout the South, we communicated loudly and clearly the Phoenix was rising once again at Cumberland University. This resulted in almost doubling the number of students and attracting higher quality applicants. At the same time, we changed the profile of the student population and added more diversity to the student body.

By the time I left Cumberland, in my heart, I felt that I was leaving the school a much better place than it was when I arrived. I considered my mission accomplished, though there were some other initiatives I didn't have time to realize. For example, I had always wanted to create a second campus. We were on the east side of Nashville, and having a campus on the west side would have opened us up to a whole new group of potential students. During my time at Cumberland, the board wasn't quite ready for such a radical expansion and didn't think we needed to explore it further at the time. I also had thought about finding a more appropriate home for the president off campus. This would have been something I would have liked to present my successor with: a more stately and representative home for the university president where he or she can entertain and court potential benefactors. In addition, although we had great success fundraising, I would have loved to get the school into a position where a large endowment could serve as a rainy day safety net and to give out scholarships. Lastly, if fundraising hadn't taken up so much of my time, I would have devoted more energy to establishing Cumberland as the premier school in the South for public service. Given our rich history of over eighty alumni who served in the House of Representatives or the Senate, thirteen governors, as well as U.S. Supreme Court justices, and U.S. ambassadors, I would have liked to have made a real push for us to capture a public service niche for the college.

Looking back now at my time as university president, it is rewarding for me to quantify the accomplishments and add up the successes. It also is obvious to me where I could have done more or could have done better. But in addition to this very goal-oriented analysis, a review of the Cumberland years is incomplete without thinking about the impact that part of my life had on my family.

Mary and I were young parents when we first went to Cumberland. While my schedule was as hectic as when I had been a candidate for office, we also were more settled and there was a little bit more time to spend with the kids. Almost every day my two young daughters, Elizabeth and Rachel, would mount their tricycles and pedal from our on-campus house to my office, swerving to avoid hitting undergraduates on their way to class. Most nights when I came home I would hear about the adventures of the day, many of which involved the huge tree house we built for the girl's right in our back yard.

Mary was outstanding in her role as (FLOCU) or first lady of Cumberland University. One of Cumberland's most sought after programs today is in the Jeanette C. Rudy School of Nursing, which has an excellent reputation nationwide. In recent years, it has become Cumberland University's number one revenue generator. Mary, Dr. Kozy and I introduced Jeannette Rudy, a registered nurse, whose husband was one of the founders of Rudy's Farm Sausage, to Cumberland University. This relationship grew and prospered over the years, and Jeanette became one of one of the school's top donors. On one occasion Mary and Jeanette were having lunch, and by the end of the lunch Mary had a check in hand from Jeanette to restore one of our buildings. Matter of fact, Sam Hatcher, vice chairman of the board of trust, and Mary, were the driving force behind the Phoenix Ball, which has become one of the premier fundraising events in Tennessee. It is a black tie gala benefitting Cumberland University, and it brings together hundreds of prominent individuals to raise money for the school.

I loved my time at Cumberland. I cherished the academic environment and being around young people every day. It was electric. I also relished meeting the challenges of fundraising head-on and putting the school on solid financial footing. And then there were the diverse groups of people I got to meet. Many alumni have gone on to wonderful careers in their chosen professions and returned to the university as visiting speakers sharing their experiences and expertise with the students.

Quite a few politicians, as well, came to speak at Cumberland during my time, including prominent members of the U.S. House and U.S. Senate such as, Congressman Joe Kennedy, Governor Lamar Alexander, Congressman Tom Lantos, and House Speaker Jim Wright, as well as NASA Astronaut Margaret Rhea Seddon, a Tennessee native. We even had T. Boone Pickens, the oil magnate from Texas speak at the university because his father was a Cumberland grad. (Incidentally, I landed him as our speaker because of a bet. A friend of mine said he'd donate $100,000 to the university if I could get T. Boone Pickens to give a speech on campus. That's how badly he wanted to meet him. It did take a while, but eventually I succeeded, and when T. Boone spoke on campus, I put my friend at the head table. Following the event, my friend stopped returning my phone calls, and I never did get that $100,000 he had promised.) I heard he eventually moved out of the state, so I guess he must have felt real bad about having gone back on his word.

To this day I run into former students who think of me as Cumberland's president first and Congressman Clement second. The students certainly were one of the main reasons why leaving Cumberland University was so difficult. Being on campus and surrounded by the energy and enthusiasm of these young women and men was inspiring.

These days I serve on the board of the U.S. Association of Former Members of Congress. One of that non-profit organization's premier outreach efforts is called the Congress to Campus program. It sends bipartisan teams of former members of Congress to about thirty college campuses across the nation, where the former members spend on average three days on campus. They have a full schedule, meeting with different classes, student organizations and campus leadership. I try to participate as often as my schedule allows, because for those three days I'm emotionally back on Cumberland University's campus. I get to interact with students, hear about their ideas and their worries, encourage them to become active and involved, and share with them some of the experiences I have had over the years. I am sure I learn more from them than they learn from me. What is so enjoyable about visiting a college campus with a Republican former colleague is we can showcase how people with different political ideas and points of view can have a productive and respectful debate.

I spent almost five years at Cumberland and the school was showing incredible improvement. While there were certainly a number of challenges still ahead, my main goal – accreditation as a four-year academic institution – had been achieved. There definitely was a large part of me that could envision continuing life in academia, but there was also a nagging voice in my head that kept telling me that I wasn't quite done with politics yet.

In 1987, Congressman Bill Boner announced his candidacy for mayor of Nashville. Once I heard that, it piqued my interest because it would mean another opportunity for me to run for Congress. I also appreciated the history of the Hermitage area and the fact that it had produced political giants who represented Tennessee in Congress including Andrew Jackson and Sam Houston. Again, Mary and I had some long conversations and soul searching to determine what would be best for our family. I felt that I had accomplished what I had set out to do at Cumberland, and I knew in my heart of hearts that I was ready for a new challenge. Cumberland University was finally on solid footing, both academically and financially, and an open seat that so clearly favored democrats wasn't going to come around again anytime soon. Mary, as always, was a great counselor and partner, and once we had reached a decision she was one hundred percent behind me.

Once I make a decision, I tend to move forward quickly and decisively. This was no different, and as soon as I had resigned from Cumberland we moved to Nashville where I was born and lived most of my life. I wanted to get a head start on other democrats exploring a primary run, so I immediately put my energy into setting up my organization to run for Congress. Having that head start paid off mightily because the primary was much more competitive than I had anticipated. It turned out to be a hard race and once or twice I did question my decision because of an uncertain future. But while having a head start paid off in the end, it almost bit me in the rear end, because Bill Boner ended up in a very competitive race, but he finally prevailed and resigned his Congressional seat.

Even though I had largely stayed out of politics while at Cumberland, getting back into the swing of things took no time at all. Also, many I met, and knew while running Cumberland were supportive of my Congressional ambitions and helped me both financially and as volunteers. And it certainly helped to have a well-known and very public track record of saving Cumberland University. People knew that Cumberland was doing much better and that I had laid the foundation for the school's resurgence.

I'll never forget my last visit with John Seigenthaler, publisher of the *Nashville Tennessean* and one of the founders of the Newseum in Washington, D.C.. I had driven him to Dickson, Tennessee—now the home of the Governor Frank G. Clement Railroad Hotel Museum—to give me some ideas about the museum's future. In that conversation John said to me, "Bob, if I were writing your obituary today, I would say that Cumberland University was one of your greatest accomplishments." Coming from a journalism genius and legend of his time, it was really touching; his words still resonate with me to this day.

Truth be told, I couldn't have accomplished all that I did without the support of the board of trust, who were outstanding leaders in their own right, and had the vision to move ahead during what was a very difficult time. Because of them, Cumberland continues to fulfill its destiny.

Clement's Contemplations

"Success in almost any field is built on the ability to create and cultivate relationships."

"You can have a difference of opinion without a difference of principle."

"Be nice to the people you meet on the way up, because you're surely going to meet them again on the way back down."

"When asking for big money, don't bet on it."

"They say the grass is always greener. That is, unless you don't have any."

"Take stock of your life; buy stock in Cracker Barrel."

"Finish your PhD. Your job depends on it."

"U.S. Presidents inspire; college presidents beg for bucks!"

"Champ" and me; Our Tennessee walking horse 1954

Governor Frank G. Clement, and my mother, Lucille, with the boys' favorite form of transportation at the Governor's Residence – their goats and cart.

My younger brothers,
Gary Clement and Frank Clement, Jr.

Our dog (Roy) that was given to us by Roy Rogers
and Dale Evans, TV cowboys in 1955.

*My Reeves kindergarten friends and me (third from left)
next to Centennial Park near our home on 31st Avenue
at the Parthenon Apartments in Nashville, Tennessee.*

*President Eisenhower, Mom,
Dad and me at age nine, 1953.*

Elvis Presley (The King) performed at the governor's residence, along with the Prisonnaires. (Second from left) me, seated (far right) my brother Gary.

First Inauguration for Frank G. Clement when he was sworn in as Governor of Tennessee in January 15, 1953. He was 32 years old.

Dad and I speaking in Jackson, TN in the summer
of 1962; we campaigned in all 95 counties
during the Tennessee Governor's race.

Robert S. Clement, President Harry Truman, MayBelle
Clement, and Governor Frank G. Clement.

President Kennedy's motorcade traveling from Vanderbilt
University to the Governor's Residence for a luncheon hosted
by Governor Frank G. Clement
May 18, 1963 – Nashville, TN

Dr. Billy Graham, seated center; flanked by Vice President Al Gore on left, me and George Beverly Shay on the right, during the 1996 ceremony when Dr. Graham and his wife, Ruth were awarded Congressional Medals of Honor.

My campaign poster during my successful run as Governor of the Tennessee Y.M.C.A. Youth & Government Assembly – 1962

National Guard Camp (Hattiesburg, Mississippi)
Bob Clement, Commissioner Cayce Pentecost and
Tennessee Governor Ned Ray McWherter.

Tennessee National Guard Adjutant General Carl Wallace.

*Congressman Harold Ford, Jr. who represented Memphis,
General Ken Jordan and me at the U. S. Capitol.*

*My promotion to Colonel. Mary and the State Adjutant
General of the Tennessee National Guard,
General Dan Wood.*

*General John Pickler-retired three-star General
from Chattanooga, TN congratulating me
for my military service and retirement.*

*I was sworn in as Tennessee's Public Service Commissioner
by my grandfather, Judge Robert S. Clement. Judge
Clement presented me with a picture of the late
Governor of Tennessee, my father, Frank G. Clement.*

Bob and Mary's wedding reception, November 6, 1976

Announcing my race for governor on the steps of the War Memorial Building in Nashville, Tennessee, April, 1978 with my communications team, Tom Seigenthaler and Tom Griscom in the background.

My nomination to the TVA Board by President Jimmy Carter in 1979 with Senator Jim Sasser, and my wife, Mary.

Bob, Mary and Federal Judge Charles Neese – when Bob was sworn in as the new TVA director.

Chairman Freeman and director Richard Freeman congratulating me on becoming a new member of the TVA Board of Directors.

Our guide, Larry Guy, takes my daughters, Elizabeth and Rachel, my brother, Frank, Jr., and his daughter, Jennifer and me down the Ocoee River in Tennessee.

President Ernest Stockton, Jr. turns over the reign of Cumberland University. I became President of Cumberland in 1983. I served from 1983 until 1987 when I resigned to run for U.S. Congress.

Congressman and Mrs. Joe Kennedy with Mary and me when they visited Lebanon, Tennessee when Congressman Kennedy spoke at Cumberland University during my tenure as president.

U. S. House Speaker, Jim Wright, and Congressman Bart Gordon during a trip to Cumberland University where they addressed the "friends of Cumberland" and students.

Dr. Rhea Seddon, an astronaut, and Congressman Bart Gordon with Mary, Elizabeth, Rachel and me.

Mary and I attending "The Phoenix Ball" in
2013 – nearly 30 years after she founded the fundraising
dinner to benefit Cumberland University.

*Mary's Mother and Dad at their fiftieth anniversary
with their children-(top left) Ruth, Montelle
and Ray and (bottom left) Mary and Joe.*

*Mary's entire family at her home in Nashville for
their annual Christmas dinner, December, 2014*

FROM OUR FAMILY TO YOURS IN 2016
BOB, MARY, MARY CARSON,
TENNYSEN, SELAH GRACE AND CLEMENT

Our grandchildren (left to right) Tennysen, Selah
Grace, Clement, and Carson in Mary's arms.

Jeff's children Lyndsey, Brandon and Todd.

My stepsons, Greg and Jeff with daughters,
Rachel and Elizabeth.

Mary's sister, Ruth, and her late husband,
Herbert, on the lake with Mary and Bob.

My daughter, Elizabeth, at the funeral of Mary's mother where Elizabeth played the 200-year-old violin that belonged to my grandmother, Vern Christianson.

On the historic Omaha Beach in Normandy, France. (Left to right) Mike Hardwick, Steve and Polly Hardwick, Mary and me.

Bob and Mary with their children, Elizabeth and Rachel and their husbands, Trael and Josh.

Mary and I at the beach with our girls, Elizabeth and Rachel.

Trael, our daughter, Elizabeth and their children, Tennysen, Clement and Savannah on the way.

Our daughter, Rachel, and her husband, Josh, with their daughters, Selah Grace and Carson.

Our daughters, their husbands,
and our grandchildren

Chapter 6

From Nashville to Washington

"Any man worth his salt will stick up for what he believes right, but it takes a slightly better man to acknowledge instantly and without reservation that he is in error." —Andrew Jackson

The 665 mile drive from Nashville, Tennessee to Washington, D.C. can be long and tedious, especially in the days before the automobile. I have driven that route many times as a member of Congress from the 5th Congressional district of Tennessee. Often during that eleven hour ride I thought about the first person to ever hold that Congressional seat, the seventh President of the United States--Andrew Jackson. The founder of the Democratic Party and a man known for supporting Americans' individual liberty, Jackson was a man of the people, and I wanted to be the same. While his journey to the nation's capital was fraught with cold nights and bumpy travels on horseback, mine was much more palatable, at least the traveling part. Regardless, I knew from my past political experience, that I would make mistakes. But Jackson's words gave me comfort. After all, politics is not for the faint of heart. But, those who can admit their errors and still stick up for what they believe have a shot of making a real difference. Those words would be tested for sure during my first run for the 5th Congressional District, a race filled with nail-biting drama, tension, and uncertainty. The 5th Congressional District when I ran was primarily an urban district, with about ninety-five percent of the constituents living within the metropolitan area. It included Davidson and Robertson counties. Obviously the district lines have changed over the years because of congressional redistricting. This process takes place every ten years or so and the history of the district and its representatives is always a colorful one.

Today, more than 700,000 people live within the district lines, mostly in metropolitan Nashville, though growth into the suburbs already had begun and many people were moving their families into nearby neighborhoods outside the city limits. The backbone of this district was a strong and viable middle class, well educated, hardworking, and very diverse and with very little racial tension. I give a lot of credit to Tennessee State University, Meharry Medical College and Fisk University (all historically Black educational institutions) for bringing Nashville a strong Black middle class that has made the city what it is today and that separates Nashville from many other cities.

Any candidate running for political office needs to realize that sometimes you learn your most important lessons after defeat and adversity. That fact was not lost on me, and I took away from my previous campaign losses that I had to pick myself up and not lose confidence in my abilities and vision.

When I made my decision to run for the 5th Congressional seat, I thought about the great men who were my predecessors – Andrew Jackson and Sam Houston, and how they must have felt when they decided to run for Congress. Jackson once said, "One man with courage is the majority." I knew that I would have to channel his words, muster up my own political courage, and just go for it!

As a result, I started planning my campaign earlier than ever before. One of the things I realized was that I had to clearly articulate my vision and message. In addition, having a top-notch campaign staff was essential, as well as setting up my fundraising mechanism, and a host of supporters. I also reviewed my strengths and weaknesses and conducted my own interpersonal analysis. What I discovered in that process and what might have played a part of my earlier losses, was that I was very young and looked even younger. When I won the Tennessee Public Service Commission race, I was only twenty-nine, which made me the youngest person ever elected to statewide office in Tennessee history. I remember one of my political campaigns stops in Jackson, Tennessee. The *Jackson Sun* newspaper published an article about me, and they had a lot of fun commenting on my youthful appearance and how young I looked running for political office. They said that I had a baby face and commented, "Of course, all babies look like Bob." But this time around, father time had taken care of the being-too-young problem, and I entered the race for the 5th District as a forty four-year-old professional with a few gray hairs starting to come through, I must admit. I was hoping the good people of the 5th District would now see me as someone who combined that youthful energy with a resume of experience and accomplishments.

My team for the campaign included one of my very good friends in and outside of politics as well as my close advisor, Bart Gordon, a former Democrat member of the House of Representatives. He was kind enough to let me borrow his capable, Chief of Staff, Kent Syler. Kent took a leave of absence to become my campaign manager. He is one of the country's most respected political strategists and knows Tennessee politics like few others. Having him run my campaign gave me the boost I needed and proved to be one of the best decisions I made at the time.

The 5th Congressional District of Tennessee has been a Democrat stronghold for generations. The last Republican representative elected in that district was Horace Harrison who served one term from 1873–1875. Since then, nineteen democrats have held the seat and I was number eighteen. Number nineteen, Jim Cooper, succeeded me in 2003, and has been easily reelected every two years.

While I had no intention of taking the general election lightly, my focus was squarely on the December 1987, Democratic primary, period! With Bill Boner not officially resigning until October fifth after he was elected mayor of Nashville; this made the primary campaign both very short and immensely trying. It was difficult to openly campaign for a seat that was not even officially open! By the way, in cases like this where you have a vacant Congressional seat for any reason, the governor of Tennessee by law has to call for a special election within sixty days. No one has ever served in the U.S. House of Representatives without being elected by the people in their Congressional District, unlike the U.S. Senate where one can be appointed.

My campaign was in full swing with an incredibly short timeline, but I was up to the challenge. It was also a blessing in a way, because Nashville is my home, and knowing I left my job as the president of Cumberland University while bittersweet, was a chance for me and my family to finally come back home. The years Mary and I spent at Cumberland were truly blessed both from a professional as well as personal point of view. But Nashville was the place we both called home. We were both born in Nashville at the same hospital, Vanderbilt, and were even delivered by the same doctor—Dr. Scott Bayer. You can't get much more connected than that. As I've said before, both of our families lived in the same neighborhood even though our parents did not know one another personally.

It became an all-out family affair, with Mary as well as the kids attending campaign events and playing a very active role. Elizabeth and Rachel were six and four, and I must say were as cute as buttons. They didn't realize what a political campaign really was at the time, but they were just happy to be with their

Mom and Dad, and get lots of attention that young children always do in situations just like this. Even though we had a very short timeline for the campaign, we still conducted a traditional grass roots effort, with lots of neighborhood meetings, attending community events, giving speeches, along with conducting media interviews and running numerous campaign advertising.

I must say I really enjoyed campaigning for office. I love meeting people and hearing their stories, as well as sharing my vision. Throughout my life, my biggest asset and secret weapon was Mary, or as her friends and close family called her, "Witsie." She had been politically active and engaged her entire life and campaigning came naturally to her. Of course, before our marriage, she could usually be found in the Republican camp, and some of our friends at times even compared us to James Carville and Mary Matalin. Witsie was great in front of a crowd, too, and could deliver a speech with passion and conviction, and capture the audience from the second she spoke her first words. She was also great at reading a room full of people and connecting with each person on an emotional level—much better than me. My strength was on the issues and addressing the concerns of the people—education, healthcare, transportation and job security, for example—and hers was giving them a personal reason for viewing me as an effective voice in Washington.

One main difference from my earlier campaigns was the amount of money that now is involved in politics, and the incessant amount of time a candidate needs to spend fundraising. No one likes to fundraise, but since the late 1980s each and every year the stakes are higher. In 2012, it is estimated that a House of Representatives race on average costs one and a half million, a Senate race on average ten million (the most expensive Senate race in 2012 was between Scott Brown and Elizabeth Warren in Massachusetts, where the two candidates plus outside PAC dollars combined for a eighty-five million dollar Senate race), and

Mitt Romney and Barack Obama broke the two billion milestone in their combined fundraising efforts in 2012. This is outrageous, but a necessary evil for anyone seeking a national political office. This time I had to up my game, reach out to friends and neighbors asking them for campaign contributions. I simply had to do it, because the danger of being outspent by my opponents was very real. And it doesn't matter how good your message is when no one can hear it, especially if you can't afford buying television and radio time and being drowned out by the other camp. Fundraising had become a necessary evil, and unfortunately, has become much worse since my 1987 primary. These days, campaigns are almost all about fundraising, and I am concerned that candidates way too often buy elections rather than earn them.

One of the positives of my 1987 Democratic primary race for the 5th Congressional District was that it was filled with some exceptional candidates and in my opinion was unique. Here's why.

Phil Bredesen, for example, had been a successful businessman with a very impressive corporate track record. He had run against Bill Boner for Mayor of Nashville and lost the election. Then he changed his focus from the mayoral to the congressional race. I was surprised how quickly he was able to do this; he became a formidable opponent right off the bat. (He would go on to be elected mayor of Nashville and then serve as governor of Tennessee from 2003 until 2011.) Another one of my primary opponents was Jane Eskind, former chair of the Tennessee Public Service Commission. She was the first woman in Tennessee to win a statewide election, and in 1994, she became the first woman to chair the Tennessee Democratic Party. In addition, the field included Walter Searcy, who had been active in both the Tennessee Democratic Party and the NAACP for years.

All in all there were thirteen candidates in the primary and most of them were talented and serious contenders. While it was both an honor and a challenge to run against these fine men and women, the race was, nevertheless, emotionally and politically charged. Mostly, we all ran positive and respectful campaigns, focusing on the issues instead of spending time and money on smearing one another. I think that's why people like Bredesen, Eskind and Searcy, really tried their best not to stir the pot and they took the process seriously. That is not to say that we didn't have tested moments. Like the time when I attacked Bredesen because of his obscene campaign spending. Naturally he attacked me back by saying I had a rich name, and because he didn't have the name recognition like I did, he would have to spend more money. The barbs went back and forth between the candidates, but were generally still respectful. I must say, I have always enjoyed serving in office more than the hot and often divisive rhetoric that occurs during campaigns, when often times the candidate is put down in order for another to look good.

The night of my primary election was about as tense as it gets. I don't care how positive a campaign you run, or how far you think you are ahead, election nights are anxiety-filled, nail-biting moments, not just for the candidate, but for the entire team of volunteers and supporters. We all gathered at the Opryland Hotel, next to the historic Grand Ole Opry in Nashville, a place I frequent and love. I brought together all my campaign staff, family, our volunteers and our supporters to watch the election returns. Of course we had a private area where the family gathered, and I could feel the tension in the room as we watched the results come in. Mary tried to keep all of us humored, as only she could do, and inside I felt a combination of elation and fear.

As the evening wore on a huge crowd assembled and filled the entire ballroom. After the polls closed at 8:00 PM, I made my way to the ballroom, and felt relieved that the moment of reckoning was finally here. All of a sudden the crowd erupted into deafening cheers, as the news media projected the primary winner as early as 8:30 PM.

That winner was me! In fact, the media said that I had won the primary race by three percent. After I hugged all of my family and supporters, of course I was thrilled, but I have to admit that over the next hour or so I started thinking about the general election that was still ahead – right around the corner as a matter of fact. In only thirty days, I had to run a campaign in a general election; it was daunting. Why? Because, first of all, I sure didn't want to be the first Democrat in more than one hundred years who was unable to win the 5th District, and also because I was wondering whether I would be able to unify the party after a contested primary with a great number of different candidates and platforms. Would those voters now stay home for the general election because their candidate was not on the ballot? Could I stimulate my own supporters a second time so close after the primary since the general election was only thirty days away? Finally, the general election was to take place in January, the coldest month of the year, and I knew it would be tough for me to persuade voters to come out and vote when it was so cold outside.

My path became crystal clear: I needed to replicate all the hard work of the primary and build upon the grassroots effort of getting out the vote. I knew I had to stay in contact with not just those voters who had elected me, but with all the voters who had come out for the Democratic primary regardless of whom they supported. One thing that was a huge help in this process was that all my primary opponents endorsed me for the general election, and I was most appreciative of that kind gesture and show of party unity. The one silver lining, about the short time between the primary and the general election, was that there really wasn't any time for my staff and campaign team to miss a beat, lose their focus, or fall apart. The day after the primary was the first day of the general election, and all of the issues I had focused on to become the party's candidate were the same issues I talked about to become the 5th District's

Representative in Washington. My campaign was about jobs, education, transportation, national defense, social security, healthcare and the plight of America's small business owner (all issues, by the way, my father had focused on thirty years earlier when he addressed the Democratic National Convention). In fact, if I closed my eyes and listened to his speech back then, I would think that he could be speaking about the same issues that affect people today. I asked myself, has anything really changed?

Aside from jobs, education and healthcare, there was one issue that emerged during the campaign as something that Nashville voters were very concerned about: the level of airplane noise around Nashville's airport. I felt strongly that the federal government should do a better job of protecting those living near and around airports from the incredible noise that could wreak havoc on their lives, not just in Nashville, but across the country.

We didn't spend much time celebrating the primary win, because the general election was in just a few weeks. My Republican opponent was Terry Holcomb, one of the nicest and most interesting candidates I've ever faced. His background was in education, but he had also spent a lot of time as an activist and consultant in Tennessee Republican politics. I genuinely liked Terry, but obviously I was not going to become his pal until well after election day. Terry and I had much in common, including a very strong work ethic and a conviction that a campaign should be positive, respectful and productive. We had only one televised debate during which Terry stated vehemently that he would never vote for a tax increase, no matter what. I replied that I thought such a blanket pledge was irresponsible, and that while I certainly didn't want to raise taxes on anyone, I also couldn't rule out the possibility that there might be situations where a tax increase was unavoidable, such as in war or a financial crisis. People respected my sincerity and thought I came across as aboveboard and reasonable, and I believe that our debate had a lot to do with showing that side of me.

Terry ran a very good campaign and I appreciate the opportunity to have had an honest and respectful discussion about the issues that concerned our constituents. But he had an uphill battle from day one, and being the Republican candidate for the 5th Congressional District of Tennessee was certainly no easy task. I think the Republican Party abandoned him somewhat during our campaign because the seat was so clearly a Democratic stronghold. He ended up with some pretty significant debt following the race, too. Since I really liked him, and because of his burden and subsequent debt load, I helped him raise funds to pay off his campaign debt. Incidentally, his last position, before he passed away much too young in 2011, was teaching at Cumberland University.

Now that the election was finally over, it was beginning to sink in that I was just elected to Congress, following in the footsteps of two of my heroes. It was a moment that I will always cherish, but I couldn't bask in the glow of victory for too long. I had to get ready to go to Washington.

One of the first major moves I made was putting together my team who would accompany me to Washington. Among my first hires was Dr. Tom Stenger. Tom received his doctorate from Southern Illinois University and he was a professor with the University of Tennessee at Martin. I hired him at Cumberland University where he dutifully served as assistant to the president and professor of political science. He resigned at Cumberland the same time I did to help in my campaign, and became one of my trusted advisors. He was a bright, young and exceptionally gifted person who came into my life at a time when I could not have managed without him. Tom had earned his doctorate at a very young age and simply lived and breathed politics like few others I had ever met. He became one of my most important campaign aides and was so dedicated that he often slept at our campaign headquarters. I remember one late night, when I was about to pass out from exhaustion, I noticed that Tom was still working, ruminating over a speech I was to deliver the next day. "Tom," I said, "What's keeping you going like this when all I want to do is go home and get some sleep?" His answer simply was: "I want nothing else than to be the chief of staff to a U.S. Congressman and that's been my life-long dream. I want you to win, Bob, and I want to go to Washington with you and help you represent our home state." Tom had the enthusiasm and conviction that few could match, and I was delighted to have Tom Stenger on my team. I'm not sure I would have been elected without him. And his wish came true; I hired him to be my chief of staff. Then the unthinkable happened. My trusted friend and now chief of staff was diagnosed with cancer at age thirty-five, which I knew before I brought him on board. That is how much I valued him. Tragically, I was heartbroken when Tom died during my very first year in office. This was a very sad moment in my life and to this day I miss hearing Tom's voice. I'm not sure it is appropriate to dedicate an election win to someone, the way a football player would dedicate a touchdown. I'm guessing not too many people would fault me for dedicating my first Congressional election victory to my dear friend, Dr. Tom Stenger. I'm sure if he were alive today he would himself have been elected to public office and would have made an outstanding elected official.

During my first year in Congress I had many great moments and some that were totally unexpected. I was feeling tired from the campaign and suffered from a shortness of breath. I was urged to go see a doctor, and I finally gave in to only learn that I needed an angioplasty procedure to open one of my arteries. I can't believe, looking back, that I went through my entire campaign with shortness of breath, chest pain, and pain up and down my left arm. After receiving the news about having to have the procedure my good friend, Kent Syler, said, "Bob, don't worry if anything happens to you we've already starting printing the 'Mary Clement for Congress' bumper stickers." We all had a good laugh!

After receiving a successful balloon angioplasty, I was good to go. All of my symptoms disappeared and I felt one hundred percent again.

I worked very hard to make my constituents proud of having me represent them in Congress. During my first year after arriving in Washington, I sponsored the Noise Reduction Reimbursement Act of 1989, which President George H. W. Bush signed into law on August 4, 1989. It is almost unheard of for a House freshman – a rookie – to introduce and get major legislation passed during a first full term in Congress. This was a promise I had made during the campaign and I knew my constituents expected me to live up to that promise. By the way, my colleague in the Senate to get the bill passed was then U.S. Senator Al Gore, Jr. This was the first of many instances of us working together in the Congress.

Years later, in 2000 during Al Gore's presidential campaign, Alex Haught, my chief of staff decided that he would like to take a leave of absence to work in the campaign. Alex was one of the most gifted people to ever work for me. His talents as well as insider's knowledge of Tennessee politics were well known. Alex was barely thirty-five, and just one month after moving to Nashville to work in the campaign his life was tragically cut short. He was driving his car in Nashville and a drunk driver, who had been arrested more than seventy times for drunk driving, ran through a red light and hit Alex's car. The force was so intense that it smashed into the glass plate window of Amerigo's Restaurant which is located on West End Avenue in Nashville. This was another major and tragic loss for me, almost too much to bear with the sudden death of my second chief of staff. Alex Haught was thirty-five years old and already had accomplished much at a young age. Both Al and I spoke at Alex's funeral; it is an emotional moment in time that I will never forget.

I was very excited to be in Washington. Obviously, the nation's capital has emerged in modern history as one of the most important and powerful cities in the world. But in addition to this incredible status as a seat of global power, Washington is also one of the most beautiful cities in the world, rivaling others such as London or Paris. I had been to Washington on a number of occasions, but now I was finally arriving as a newly elected member of Congress.

To be a freshman member of Congress is very much like starting your first day of high school. It was that quintessential awkward moment when you can't find your office, the cafeteria, or even the restroom. Everything is new. You are a freshman when you enter Congress after your first election, and your freshman year lasts two years until the next election. Then, all the new members become the freshman class of the next Congressional session. In my case, my freshman class was already halfway through their freshman session by the time I got elected. In Congress almost everything is based on seniority, and I was number four hundred thirty-five out of four hundred thirty-five members of the House of Representatives. That's because I was elected for one year only. I was truly at the bottom of the barrel. All of my colleagues in the freshman class had received workshops on everything from how to run a Congressional office, how to be a legislator, how to get committee assignments, and what was ethical and unethical behavior (even who you had lunch with has ethical implications). I was a freshmen class of one, and all I received was a pat on the back and a quick crash course on parliamentary procedure. But like with many of my previous positions, learning on the job and figuring things out along the way wasn't anything I couldn't handle.

The very first decision I made as a newly elected member of Congress was actually a decision my entire family made together: should Mary and the girls stay in Tennessee or should the whole family move to Washington? If they stayed in Nashville, then I would be a father and husband on the weekends only, and be separated from them during the week while I was in D.C. To me, this wasn't a very tough decision, and I am surprised how many of today's members of Congress come to a completely different conclusion than I did back then. I knew that I wanted my family to be with me and have the Washington experience; I wanted to be there for them, too. The girls needed to have their dad involved in their lives full-time and be there to attend their sporting events and music recitals. The family needed to be by my side as I navigated the tricky waters in our nation's capital. I had the good fortune of representing a district that was relatively easy to get to from D.C. and fairly geographically compact.

Because of that, I could go back to Nashville practically every weekend or when Congress was not in session, as well as for Thanksgiving and Christmas. That way I could remain connected with my constituents. So, for the Clement family the decision was that we would all move together to Washington. Luckily, we found a wonderful home just outside of Washington in Alexandria, Virginia, but we always kept our home in Nashville. It pains me that today there are too many members who shun Washington and can't wait to get out of town as soon as voting is done for the week. They, obviously, don't move their families to D.C., because that would mean they've gone Washington. Instead, they live with other members of Congress as roommates or, worse yet, sleep on cots in their Congressional offices.

I realize that with today's Congressional schedule being shortened makes it much more difficult to get meaningful legislation passed. The fifteen years our family lived in the

Washington area made me a more effective legislator. I got to know other members of Congress on a very personal level because they lived near us, and we would get together on the weekends for BBQs or to watch a football game on TV. You get to know each other and establish trust, so that when you're back at the Capitol you can work together, even across the political divide. There's a cost in institutional knowledge that comes with this weekly escape from Washington, and because these members miss out on establishing important working relationships they are less effective legislators. Not once during any of my campaigns was I accused of Potomac fever or of having gone Washington. Actually, quite the opposite was true: polling year-after-year showed that my constituents felt that they knew me personally, and that I was connected with them and their concerns.

In addition to having my family with me as my support system, I brought to Washington some other trusted aides and advisors from my campaign, including Carolyn Waugh to be my executive assistant. Her loyalty and friendship over the years has been a source of strength to our entire family. As our children say, "Carolyn was always there in the good times and the times of disappointment." I hired David Flanders who was an exceptional legislative director who had Washington experience. Mary and I knew from the first day that we wanted someone with a warm caring and charismatic personality to welcome constituents when they visited the Washington office. We immediately placed a call to Beth Pritchard Geer, who had previously worked at Cumberland University during my tenure, to see if she would move to Washington to work in the front office. She said yes and a few years later went to work for Al Gore where she remains Chief of Staff. This, to me, made for a very smooth transition. I added to that team experienced Congressional staffers who could help us with the business of legislating. Very soon after being sworn in, I had the opportunity to get to know many of my new colleagues during a retreat of the Democratic Caucus at the Greenbrier Hotel, located in White Sulphur Springs, West Virginia. This was the place where secret, underground bunkers had been located for congressional leadership and others to go if a terrorist attack occurred on U.S. soil. I always wondered, though, why they didn't include the families of the members of Congress in those bunkers. I guess they had their reasons.

The retreat's purpose was to discuss policy and determine the legislative objectives for the second session of the 100th Congress. But it was also meant to bring members of Congress together and enable them to get to know one another better. Therefore, in addition to bringing along family, members came together for some informal events during the evening. One such event was headlined by comedian Bill Cosby who was hired to entertain the group in 1988. As luck would have it, he randomly picked our little Elizabeth to join him on stage. He asked her, "Why are you here, young lady," and she replied, "My Daddy just got elected." The ballroom erupted in laughter, and I immediately felt welcome and included. Later that night, House Speaker Jim Wright sought me out and said: "Clement, your daughter got more publicity and exposure than you'll ever get in ten years!" I knew Speaker Wright from my days at Cumberland when he came to speak to our students and at our college fundraising dinner. I always admired him because he had such great interpersonal skills. He not only knew your name, but your spouse's name, too, and even remembered where you were from. He had so much warmth and Southern charm. And, because we got to know each other a little bit at Cumberland, when I arrived in Congress, he was kind enough to open the doors widely for me and helped me as a mentor. I was pleased to know that he also followed my campaign and took an interest in the outcome. To my surprise, he appointed me to the very powerful Democrat steering and policy committee as a freshman member. I was most appreciative of being placed on the fast track, thanks to Jim Wright.

By the way, that was a special committee, unlike all others; it's a group that decides what Democrat member serves on what Standing Committee. I couldn't believe that while I was the new kid on the block, I would have so much influence on other members' careers. In addition to that special committee, my major standing committee was the transportation and infrastructure committee which helped me with my interest in the airport noise reduction issue, and was an important part of my campaign messaging. My minor committee was veteran's affairs which was wonderful since I was a veteran and still a member of the Tennessee Army National Guard; this assignment helped me be an effective voice for veterans in Tennessee and across the country.

The fact remains, though, that the U.S. Congress is like any other large organization. You have people you instantly like, and others you don't want to spend too much time with. There are the big picture thinkers and also others who are the get-the-job-done types. There are some senior members who are not very approachable because of their status and importance, and junior members who are focused on their career paths and will do almost anything to get ahead. And as with any other entity, Congress is a place that thrives on personal relationships. You can't be a loner and expect to be successful in Congress; it just won't happen. Mary and I are the type of people who love meeting people, getting involved in organizations and causes and being involved in our community. For us, Congress was just like being back in Nashville; we made a home for ourselves and the girls, made friends in the neighborhood and found ways to get to know our new colleagues better. Mary immediately joined the Congressional Club, which is an organization composed of spouses of members of Congress. She became chair of the First

Lady's luncheon and was elected president of the Congressional Club several years later. She made so many new friends that way, and I can't tell you how many times a member of Congress would come up to me in the Capitol and say, "My wife met your wife at the Congressional Club, so I wanted to introduce myself." Senator Trent Lott, for example, when he was still in the House of Representatives, became a good friend of mine because his wife, Trish, and Mary became the best of friends. Mary is a quintessential bipartisan who creates meaningful relationships with women in both parties, regardless of affiliation.

One thing I often hear about the current Congress that makes me incredibly sad is that fewer and fewer of the new members seek out the counsel and mentorship of the more senior members. Too many freshmen arrive in Washington and distance themselves from the members who have been there for a long time. They believe that they are part of the establishment. They'd rather blow the place up than work together. This is so shortsighted because to know and respect an institution requires an understanding and appreciation of its history. Valuing the experience and expertise of those who have come before you is essential in my opinion. I was a better legislator because the more senior members of Congress took me under their wings when I first arrived. Take for example, Congressman Lee Hamilton of Indiana.

He was the democratic caucus's voice on international issues, as well as the good conscience of the House of Representatives. Having his advice and counsel were invaluable to me. Bill Natcher of Kentucky, who had entered Congress almost thirty-five years before I arrived, also was one of my mentors. Very early on he took me aside and said, "Bob, don't be a slave to this place, it can just eat you up. If you have to miss a vote so you can get home and see your little girl's music recital, then don't hesitate." Not too long after he gave me that piece of advice, I missed a procedural vote so I could deal with a minor family emergency. The next day Natcher saw me in the hallway, winked at me and said, "Bob, I see you missed a vote yesterday. You're a good man!" When Bill Natcher passed away in 1994 while still serving in Congress, he had never missed a single vote in his entire forty-one year career. All in all he cast more than eighteen thousand consecutive votes. And I do have to wonder, how many freshmen like me did he take aside with his advice in order to keep his record intact? He shouldn't have worried, though, because there is no one who was going to break his historic voting record. I am so glad President Clinton awarded him the Presidential citizen's medal just a few weeks before he passed away.

I had mentors and friends from all political and ideological walks of life, both democrats and republicans and I have learned from both of them. It hurts me to see how Congress' poll numbers have gone down dramatically. Some of the members that I served with such as Congressman Jamie Whitten led by example; theatrics and drama were not necessary to get legislation passed. Congressman Whitten was one of the top Democrats in the House as chairman of the Appropriations Committee. He was one of those members who wielded incredible power and importance, but did not take himself half as seriously as others. I'll never forget chairman Whitten on the floor of the House of Representatives, turning off his hearing aid and refusing to yield his time because he wanted to finish his appropriations report. When we were together during his fiftieth anniversary celebration in the House of Representatives, I asked him whether he had any plans of returning to Mississippi when he retired. He replied, serious as a heart attack and said, "Bob, I would, but I don't know anyone there." I just chuckled, because he had been such an effective member of Congress, and brought a lot of federal funds to Mississippi and the country including the Tennessee Tom Bigbee Waterway and also the Natchez Trace

Parkway; I worked with him to obtain federal funding for these very important projects.

Congressman Natcher told me this interesting story shortly after I got there about Cliff Davis, a Tennessee Congressman who served from 1940 to 1965 and was from Memphis. He apparently had a bad habit of putting his feet on the back of the seats in the House Chamber, and he was frequently chastised for doing this because it was considered rude and not becoming of a member of Congress. But no one could break him of this nasty habit. Natcher was impeccably dressed and looked like a Philadelphia lawyer. He told me how he was able to break his unsightly habit. In 1954, there were four Puerto Ricans who were sitting in the House Gallery, and they came to the House Chamber with their guns in tow. They came to support Puerto Rican independence from U.S. rule. They started firing those guns after unfurling a Puerto Rican flag, and began shooting at the 240 Representatives of the Eighty-Third Congress, accidentally hitting Congressman Davis in the foot. From that day on he never perched his foot on any seat in the House Chamber again! That was surely a painful lesson.

Another lesson I learned very early on in my congressional career was that running a congressional office is very similar to managing a small business. You have a budget to adhere and if you exceed the budget it comes out of your own pocket (which, incidentally, is not a bad way to keep members fiscally responsible). You hire and fire professional staff, and ultimately you are the one responsible for the bottom line. The House of Representatives is like four hundred thirty-five small businesses running concurrently. Some of them operate at a very high level, while others barely function at all. It is the member who sets the tone, and an office's success depends on how they approach that role in the process. For example, anyone working for me knew that they would be in big trouble if I heard of a constituent's call going unanswered or responses being slow.

I gave my staff a lot of independence to grow in their position and build their confidence. I looked for different personalities and experiences for my D.C. staff compared to my district staff, because the type of work was so very different. My D.C. staff was the crew that helped me with the business of legislating. They were the policy people who guided me on an issue and worked with me to navigate the process of making laws. My district staff needed to be people with a lot of patience because their main function was to interact with my constituents. They were compassionate and caring people, because the main thrust of their day was spent with constituents who came to us needing help with social security or dealing with the local VA, among others.

At the end of a successful election campaign you inevitably have a number of campaign volunteers who hope to join you in Washington or the district office. But the reality was that only a small percentage of my campaign volunteers could be brought on board full time. I tried as much as I could to help them in other ways by opening doors or serving as a reference.

A member's experience in Congress is defined most times by the committees on which he or she serves. Members can still introduce or support legislation that has nothing to do with their individual standing committee assignments. The other benefits of serving on a committee are getting to know your fellow members. But there are some challenges of being a member as well. I will never forget when Speaker Jim Wright retired after my first year, and his replacement and I were not exactly on the same page.

The new speaker was Tom Foley a Democrat from the state of Washington. When my term on the Steering and Policy Committee expired, Speaker Foley did not reappoint me. That may have had something to do with the fact that I had encouraged Congressman Lee Hamilton of Indiana and then Congressman Jack Murtha of Pennsylvania to run for Speaker after the departure of Speaker Wright; neither one of them ever ran. As a member I was also serving on the Transportation Committee, which at that time was chaired by Glenn Anderson of California. He had been a great member for many years, but by the time I served on the committee he had lost some of his focus and energy. His age had simply caught up with him. There were at least three different occasions when he asked me where I was from and I responded, "Nashville." And then he would say, "Now that's where they had those racial problems?" I calmly responded, "Yes Mr. Chairman, in the 1950s."

There is no doubt that some members have out-served their usefulness, or succumbed to the ravages of age much like chairman Anderson who was clearly senile and in fragile health. In 1993, we asked him to step down because as chairman of the transportation and infrastructure committee, he was becoming inept and lax in his decision making ability. We were on the verge of passing the transportation bill and we needed real leadership. This was a critical time in rebuilding America. Sadly, chairman Anderson wouldn't step aside, so we decided to take the issue before the democratic caucus and cast a secret vote to oust him as chair. Tim Valentine, my good friend, a congressman from North Carolina, who served with me on that committee, said something I'll never forget: "Remember, Bob, when you draw the sword make sure you use it or he will chop off our heads." I think some members do a disservice to their constituency and country by serving too long. That secret vote resulted in Robert Roe of New Jersey becoming chair in 1991. This was a huge risk, and had we failed, chairman Anderson would have had our heads and this could have had a negative effect on all of our Congressional careers.

Another slice of life as a member of Congress is whether to become active in congressional or party leadership. Those members who aspire to a leadership position often get there by assisting the speaker or the minority leader with running the caucus, setting policy, or counting and confirming votes. I decided against pursuing a leadership post for a number of reasons. First of all, I really enjoyed the camaraderie and issue-specific work of being on a committee. I felt that the substantive experience garnered via committee work was invaluable. For example, having an in-depth understanding of transportation, education and budget issues would prepare me better for statewide office back in Tennessee. Most importantly, I didn't want to end up in a situation where because of my responsibility in party leadership I had to take a position that was possibly contrary to the interests of my district and state. I put all of my energy into my committee assignments and representing the people of Tennessee.

In 1994 a republican landslide swept the democrats out of power, the first time in a generation. It was hard enough going from the majority to the minority. I also knew that it would affect me being appointed to the Appropriations Committee. This was because some democrat members would lose their seat on the Appropriation Committee now that the republicans were in the majority and the democrat/republican ratio changed.

At the time, I didn't get hurt like some more senior democratic members who lost their chairmanships. I was looked upon by my colleagues as a moderate democrat who could work with both parties to get legislation moving and passed. I tried my best to position myself as a consensus and bridge builder, as well as a peacemaker rather than a verbal political bomb thrower. This proved to be a very wise strategy.

With this republican takeover another new speaker was elected. This time a Republican became Speaker of the House for the first time in a generation. His name was Newt Gingrich.

With Speaker Newt Gingrich and his new leadership team, a very different tone and process took hold of the Congress. I, personally, trace today's hyper-partisanship directly back to the Gingrich speakership. His number one priority wasn't governing, but rather to put things in place to keep his majority and make things as difficult as possible for us democrats. He was extremely worried about the 1996 election and whether he could retain the House, so worried, in fact, that they were actively pursuing democrats to switch parties, including me. The other action the Gingrich team put in place was this whole notion of what can be accomplished in the first one hundred days. I don't think before 1994, anyone looked at a newly-elected Congress and said, "Let's see how many laws we can pass in the first one hundred days." But all of a sudden for us that became the litmus test.

Those first one hundred days were incredibly busy, hectic and difficult. Certainly an institution that doesn't change remains static and can become ineffective. To completely trash decades of rules and procedures just to prove you're different from previous management is irresponsible. For example, one of the most impactful rule changes was how committee chairmen and committee members were selected. While the old system, based almost entirely on seniority had its obvious shortcomings, the change initiated by Gingrich made matters much worse. The power to appoint chairmen and appoint members to important committees now became the prerogative of the speaker. Of course, those most loyal to the speaker were the ones chosen as committee chairs and served on the most powerful committees. In addition to loyalty, you could earn your committee assignment by raising funds for the party or other members. In essence, committee assignments were now for sale.

Another policy change was to cut the legislative work week to three days in Washington (Tuesday through Thursday) and Friday through Monday back in the district. Ostensibly, this procedural change was initiated so that members could spend more time with their constituents. In reality, the point was to give members more time to fundraise and campaign back home. An unintended consequence of this change, or maybe it was fully intended, was that the time spent with other members was cut short. The business of legislating is one based on trust, and now the opportunity to build relationships and trust had been cut down to three jam-packed days-a-week. Also, rules were changed so that earmarks were much easier to place into bills. Earmarks are pots of taxpayer dollars that are earmarked by the Congress for a specific project, for example building a bridge. By loosening the process through which earmarks could be inserted, the number more than doubled during the Gingrich years. And, of course, most earmarks went to republicans, so that members could go back to their districts and campaign on how much money and how many jobs they had brought back to their district. This, in essence, was a taxpayer subsidized reelection campaign for republicans.

What happened in those first one hundred days has had far-reaching effects we still have to deal with today. We've lost a lot of what I call institutional knowledge, and that is a tragedy. Many members, particularly senior democrats, preferred to retire than try in vain to accomplish anything under these new rules. We, sadly, had a great many outstanding members of Congress walk away from the job and the institution they loved. The real shame is that some of the ideas republicans were bringing to the table had merit and deserved a full debate. Maybe, given half a chance, democrats would have joined their republican colleagues in deliberating and shaping legislation that both sides could agree on in a bipartisan manner. Take, for example, Newt

Gingrich's Contract with America (or Contract ON America, as President Clinton liked to call it). The entire document, a ten-point legislative agenda republicans were committed to passing in the first hundred days, was phrased in a way that clearly meant to alienate democrats. It completely put the blame on the Democrat Congress that had just been replaced. The very first sentence reads: "In this year of official evasion and posturing, we offer instead a detailed agenda for national renewal, a written commitment with no fine print." Not really language that inspires bipartisanship and a desire to work together! But when you dig a little deeper, the contract certainly had some ideas I and many of my democrat colleagues could agree if given the opportunity.

For example, it ended Congress' little known but truly brazen practice of exempting itself from the very laws it passed to govern the rest of the nation. While all other federal buildings were smoke-free, in the U.S. Capitol you could puff away on cigars, cigarettes and pipes without breaking any law. Also, the contract envisioned a balanced-budget amendment to the constitution. While I did not necessarily agree with amending our constitution, not to mention that amending the constitution is a tremendously difficult and cumbersome undertaking involving both state and federal government, I did agree with fiscal restraint and responsibility. That could have been fertile ground to bring democrats and republicans together in a bipartisan manner to debate and shape legislation. Both sides of the aisle supported the idea but needed to work out their differences when it came to implementation.

Overall, however, the Contract with America was a republican call to arms, filled with measures that would play well with the republican base, and was meant to show republican voters that the Gingrich team meant business. There were a number of tax reforms which clearly helped big business and the top one percent. For example, a fifty percent reduction in the capital gains tax.

But it also included reforms that I could support such as welfare reform. To me, this new tone carried with it arrogance both toward democrat members as well as democrat voters, which I had not experienced in Washington before. Politics, certainly, is a tough business and some would even call it a blood sport. Speaker Gingrich and the new republican majority approached their dealings with the other side of the aisle by abandoning the notion of governing and replacing it with staying in power as the main purpose of the party.

The epitome of the politics of personal destruction and hyper-partisanship came in 1998 with the impeachment of President Bill Clinton. I spent more than half of my congressional career during the Clinton/Gore administration. I had first met Bill Clinton in the early 1980s when he was governor of Arkansas. I was on the Steering Committee to plan the Tennessee Jackson Day Dinner, which is the annual fundraising gala for the democrat party where we had 2,500 top democrats from across Tennessee in attendance. Our keynote speaker was Senator Jay Rockefeller from West Virginia. Bill Clinton was just about to announce his candidacy for President of the United States and was certainly being noticed around the country as a rising star in national politics. I was asked by democrat party officials to contact Governor Clinton to attend the gala and make brief remarks. I told him that we already had a keynote speaker, but we would be delighted to have him speak for five minutes. The night of the gala, Senator Rockefeller became unexpectedly ill and was not able to deliver his keynote speech.

Since Bill Clinton was our back up speaker anyway, he happily agreed to take the Senator's place. At the dinner, rather than Governor Clinton speaking for only five minutes as we had planned, he spoke for an hour, wrapping up Tennessee for the upcoming democrat presidential primary election with his moving oratory. It was amazing to me that Bill Clinton spoke without a single notecard or any other prepared remarks; we were spellbound for the entirety of his speech. In fact it reminded me of President Harry Truman's comments, "If you want me to speak for five minutes it will take me five days to prepare. If you want me to speak for an hour I am ready now." That was my first real introduction to Bill Clinton. I immediately signed on to his upcoming campaign based on his impressive performance.

Over the years, Bill Clinton and I have stayed in touch, and I was very supportive of his runs for the White House in 1992 and 1996. I worked with him on a number of issues and I have the highest regard for him as an extremely skilled politician and executive.

It is a shame that his enemies continue to keep alive his personal failures in an attempt to overshadow his productive eight years as president. There were twenty-four hour news reports as the story continued to be investigated. But it sure sold newspapers and kept the media's ratings high.

The other Clinton nemesis was congressional republicans. When the story first broke in early 1998 the country was in tremendous shape. Unemployment was low, the stock market was healthy and robust and we were dealing with a budget surplus – something unheard of in modern times. Bill Clinton had been reelected to a second term in 1996, and many of the votes cast for him came from Americans disgusted with the Republican-led Congress. The subsequent shut down of the government over a budget impasse was caused mostly by the republican leadership. Republicans needed something to hang their hats on for the 1998 midterms, or there was a real danger that Congress, especially the House, could swing back to the democrats. Bill Clinton himself once told me, "Bob, if the economy in 1998 had been a wreck— high unemployment and inflation, no one would be as concerned with my personal problems." The manufactured constitutional crisis that resulted in the impeachment of the President was nothing but a political strategy to keep Congress in Republican hands in 1998. This set the stage for a Republican White House win in 2000.

The debate in the House was whether to impeach the President or not. This was entirely unnecessary and unfounded. President Clinton's personal failure did not rise to the level of an impeachable offense. But republicans insisted on pushing the process forward no matter what the consequences for the nation. I went to the republican leadership and tried to convince them to allow for a compromise: have the President admit that he had misled the American people (as he stated in a publicized address to the nation on August 17, 1998) and have him apologize for his actions. I was soundly rejected because the republicans were out for blood. Even the fact that a number of the House republicans were being exposed themselves as a result of their own infidelities; this fell on deaf ears.

The process was a highly partisan one, and I knew of no democrats who wanted to vote to impeach the President. Conversely, I did know quite a number of republicans who did not want to impeach the President, too, but felt compelled to do so because of the pressure by the republican leadership. All other business in the House literally came to a complete standstill; we absolutely got no work done on behalf of the nation! This, actually, upset quite a few of my democrat colleagues. They felt that because of Bill Clinton's personal shortcomings many important legislative measures were delayed or derailed. When many of us went back to our districts to town hall meetings, it seemed that most questions focused on the impeachment proceedings. But during my town hall meetings, I also received a clear message from my constituents: they did not want the Congress to go as far as it had and they had hoped that cooler heads would prevail in Washington. Congress changed dramatically in the fifteen years I had been a member. Most of the change was not for the good. The Senate, on the other hand, was not yet as affected by the hyper-partisanship that had eroded the ability of the House of Representative to govern responsibly. I kept a watchful eye on Senator Fred Thompson of Tennessee who was up for reelection in 2002; there was much speculation that he may not run again. This set the stage for another political adventure that would change the course of my career.

Clement's Contemplations

"*A billion dollars might not make you happy, but it will buy a Presidential election.*"

"*Never put your feet on the back of a chair; they may not be there for too long.*"

"*If you can't remember your name, or who your constituents are, quit your day job.*"

"*Cherish your moments with friends and family; they may be gone too soon.*"

"*Congress is like grade school; recess is bliss, legislating is homework on steroids.*"

"*The only things that can be done in 100 days are things that won't last.*"

Chapter 7

The World Before and After September 11

"This place is a target and you're not safe!"
—U.S. Capitol Police Officer

As a member of Congress, and in my case, also a retired colonel of the Tennessee Army National Guard, the greatest emotional burden anyone could have is casting a vote to send young men and women to war. You can't make that decision lightly. I've had to reluctantly cast that vote more than once, a vote that dramatically impacts the lives of our nation's heroes serving in the armed forces during the War on Terror.

One example is Marine Corporal Christian Brown who hails from Munford, Tennessee, only about three hours or so away from the place where I grew up. I met Christian during of one of my visits to Walter Reed National Military Medical Center in Bethesda, Maryland. Today he sits in a motorized wheelchair, yet his spirit is unbroken. This young man is a real hero. He was awarded a Silver Star for trying to save the life of his buddy as he was being shot and returning enemy fire while on patrol in Afghanistan. Getting to know Christian has brought me face-to-face with the difficult choices I made when I was a member of Congress.

Christian suffered many horrendous physical injuries the day that he stepped on an IED in Afghanistan during another tour of duty. The blast blew off both of his legs, part of his finger and left him with the emotional and physical scars of the War on Terror. We relate so well to each other because we speak the same language – our unmistakable Tennessee drawl. In fact, when we are together I can't help but be reminded of our Southern roots and the values we learned from proud, God-fearing parents. Christian and I also share a deep love for this country, as well as the pride that comes with having served our nation in uniform. I remember thinking when we were together how well he bears the burdens of losing so much, and I wonder if I could have handled it with such strength and dignity?

I can't imagine how my life would have turned out, certainly very differently, if I had boarded that military plane to Vietnam on January 4th, 1970. Despite any losses that I have experienced in my life, they are pale by comparison to Christian's. I can sense his resolve to live a purposeful life beyond the terrible pain and suffering he has endured, and I am inspired every time we are together.

I can't explain how good it feels to be a part of Christian's life in some small way. I've had the privilege of meeting him and a number of other severely wounded warriors over the years. I always looked forward to seeing our wounded soldiers and marines—even for just a couple of hours. We usually get together in the Warrior Café, the restaurant that is housed in Building 62 where the wounded warriors live during their rehabilitation. It's a place I wish every American could visit. Why? Because on any given day you can see our nation's finest—many of whom are missing arms and legs and who have sustained horrific wounds, going to and from rehab with so much strength and courage. There are no disabilities only capabilities here. And when I visit the hospital, it feels like any other hospital in the United States.

Nurses and doctors are hurrying from one patient to another, patients are prepped for surgery and families keep vigils around the clock anxiously awaiting a doctor's report. But Walter Reed is no ordinary hospital and their patients are certainly not average either. There is not a day that goes by that I don't think about these young heroes—many in their late teens and early twenties, and how they should be going out on dates, or playing a pick-up basketball game instead of spending their lives surrounded by tubes and monitors.

When I voted in 2001 to authorize military action concerning Afghanistan, Marine Corporal Christian Brown was just a kid. But when I, and the other 419 Members of the House of Representatives voted for the Authorization for the Use of Military Force on September 14, 2001, he was probably doing what most adolescents do. He was learning how to drive a car, going fishing or worrying about asking a young lady out on a date. But on that day, all I could think about was how our country would never be the same again.

Our nation had just been attacked, and a unified Congress gave President George W. Bush the authority to use military force against terrorism, which we all assumed would result in boots on the ground in Afghanistan. I knew I was sending young Americans into harm's way, possibly to their death, and it was easily one of the most excruciating and difficult decisions of my life. I knew we had to deal with the Taliban and the terrorists who were hell-bent on our destruction. I believe that war should be the last resort and not the first option. We had weakened Saddam already in the first Iraq war that I supported when George H. W. Bush was President. In that effort we had shown more restraint, and built more of a coalition; it was less costly in terms of money and precious lives lost.

September 11, 2001, was a bright sunny Tuesday in the nation's capital. While my family was back in Tennessee, I had stayed in DC. Members of Congress spend a lot of time running from one meeting to the next—or rushing off to cast a vote on the House floor, however, on the morning of September 11, I was fortunate to have a rare open schedule. Members never want to be late for committee hearings, and we always are making sure we get back to our offices so our staff can prepare us for the next round of meetings. When our constituents are visiting us in our Washington offices, we especially want to be available to meet with them so it was a really rare treat to have a morning that didn't include so many meetings, events or conference calls. September 11 was that kind of a morning.

Like most members of Congress, I maintained two separate residences, one in Nashville and also a second home in Alexandria, Virginia, a quiet suburb of Washington. A cozy neighborhood where you knew your neighbors, enrolled your children in public or private schools, and became truly a part of a unique extended family. It was like many neighborhoods across our great nation.

This innocence of America that was evident on the morning of September 11 became a very different place by the time the sun set on that horrible September day.

I must have been on my second cup of coffee when I heard the newscaster's voices change from their typically cheery demeanors to something much more ominous. I couldn't believe my eyes. I was stunned to see the first plane slam into the North Tower of the World Trade Center in New York City. Like most Americans, I thought it was just a horrible accident. I called my staff from home, and asked them if they knew what was going on. Then I saw the second plane hit the South Tower. I couldn't for the life of me believe this was happening.

As a member of Congress I felt my place was to be at the Capitol building. Period! I didn't have any information other than what I had seen at home on television. Unlike today, I did not have a blackberry device that would let congressional leaders communicate with members in case of an emergency. And to make matters worse, the phone service was shut down completely due to the volume of incoming and outgoing calls. (That's one of the many lessons we learned from 9/11. Today, members of Congress as well as their senior staff have devices that are equipped to receive messages and instructions in case of emergencies.) With a growing sense of panic and disbelief, it was sinking in that this kind of terrorism was taking place right in our own backyards.

I jumped into my car and headed from Alexandria to the Capitol without even thinking about how fast I was driving. I was pretty much running on gut instinct and pure adrenaline. As I was frantically racing to the Capitol, the news coverage on the radio was uncharacteristically chaotic and disjointed. I could hear the confusion in the reporter's voices. Frankly, I was alarmed. As I made my way along the beltway there were multiple news reports indicating there were other planes attacking targets around the country. In all of that chaos, things were being reported as facts that quickly turned out to be just misinformation or rumors. Sadly, something we have *not* learned from 9/11 is getting those facts straight, especially with traditional and social media's addiction to reporting first and checking facts later. But I'll save that for another discussion.

My drive was an emotionally harrowing experience. And it got even worse when I passed by the Pentagon and saw the flames raging from the building and clouds of thick black smoke rising from the burning concrete. Usually the traffic at that time of the morning would be much more congested, but on the morning of 9/11, I got to the Capitol much quicker than usual, even though the roads were by no means deserted and empty. If I hadn't known that terrorists were flying planes into buildings to kill us, it might have been a pretty average fall morning. But this was clearly a day like no other.

When I pulled up to the guardhouse to get into the garage, the Capitol policeman on duty couldn't believe his eyes. "Congressman," he said, "Get the heck out of here, this place is a target and you're not safe!" Of course, as we would all learn later, he was absolutely right. United Airlines Flight 93, which was brought down by its heroic passengers near Shanksville, Pennsylvania, was headed right for us; its target was the U.S. Capitol. Had that plane hit us, it could have wiped out our entire legislative branch. (Surely, some Americans today believe that we should throw the bums out. But the reality is that without a legislative branch, and the balance of power between us, the U.S. Supreme Court and the President, that is at the heart of our U.S. Constitution, our country as we know it today would not exist.)

Ignoring the Capitol policeman's warning, I drove my car into our parking garage next to the U.S. Capitol. Incidentally, it does disturb me that there are so many absolutely false claims on the Internet and elsewhere about how many benefits and freebies members of Congress supposedly get. I'm often amazed how otherwise rational people would be completely convinced that members of Congress are all driven around by chauffeurs in fancy limos, or have people waiting on them hand and foot. The only real benefit I did have was a free parking space in the garage underneath the Rayburn House Office Building where my congressional office was located. This proved to be a God-send on that horrible day.

As I parked my car, I was again eerily struck by how normal everything felt. The garage was not filled as usual with cars owned by members of Congress and their staff. By the time I arrived, the Capitol was virtually deserted because everyone was ordered to leave the building any way they could—by foot or by car. Apparently, those who had parked in the garage downstairs had evacuated the building on foot. They were told they could come back when things calmed down to retrieve their cars. The other thing that hit me like a ton of bricks was the endless buzzing and ringing of unanswered telephones. There was no one there at all to answer them.

Coming to the Capitol was not some sort of super patriotic act on my part at all. I knew that it was actually a really bad idea to have driven to a place that was clearly a terrorist target. Though I disregarded the first responder's instructions in the process, I still felt very strongly that my place was in the Capitol. My guess was, that had I been on Capitol Hill that morning when the first plane hit, I would have probably evacuated with all the rest of the members and congressional staff. Since I wasn't there when the crisis first unfolded, I decided to do what I thought was best.

The Rayburn House Office Building is just across the street from the U.S. Capitol. It is a striking stone and marble structure that was built in the 1960s, and named after the legendary Sam Rayburn, a Texas Democrat who served as Speaker of the House for almost twenty years. It is one of those buildings where you can actually hear the echoing sound from your shoes as you walk along the stone corridors – or an embarrassing squeaky sound if you are wearing rubber-soled shoes and just came in from the rain. Incidentally, there is also one spot on the floor of the National Statuary Hall in the Capitol where, according to the architect, "Produces an acoustical effect, whereby, in some spots, a speaker many yards away may be heard more clearly than one closer at hand."

However, when you are in the Rayburn Building, in its normal busy state, you wouldn't hear much of anything because of all the noise people are making by opening and shutting doors and having loud conversations going on all the time. (Congressional offices tend to be very cramped spaces, and believe it or not, we often hold meetings in the hallways because there's not enough room inside our offices to accommodate large groups.)

But September 11 was no ordinary day. Rayburn was so barren and deserted that the only other sound I heard, other than the ringing phones, was the clacking of my own shoes as I raced toward my office.

My office was completely deserted, my entire staff had evacuated and I was mighty relieved to know they were at least safe. I didn't want them here for sure, but I felt in my heart that this is where I needed to be. I wasn't trying to do anything heroic at all. I felt I needed to be in the place where I could personally help make some sense out of what was unfolding on TV screens across the nation. Even though I was a senior member of congress, a senior member of important committees that were directly affected by what was happening – most importantly the Foreign Affairs and Transportation Committee – I knew as much, or as little, as anyone else. Nevertheless, since I was one of our nation's leaders, I was very concerned about what direction the country was headed. But at that surreal moment, all I could do was just answer the phones. I wanted to let people know we, the Congress, were still here, even though I'm pretty sure I was one of a few members of Congress on Capitol Hill at the time. Looking back, I was very proud to know that the Fifth Congressional District of Tennessee was being represented in Washington, D.C. during a time of crisis. I was there for my constituents during what was one of the most terrifying days in the life of the United States.

So there I sat, in my small congressional office answering the phones and talking to my constituents and to the media, urging them to stay calm. I have to admit that even while trying to reassure them, I was afraid of what was happening too. This was a seminal moment for all of us. But as I continued to talk to everyone who called well into the late afternoon, I kept telling the callers that the federal government will figure out what was going on and that our first responders were there on the scene.

After what felt like endless days, but probably was only about seven hours, the phone calls stopped coming in, and I decided to drive back home. I gathered some of my important files to take with me, because I wasn't sure when we would be allowed back into the building.

As I left D.C. heading home to Alexandria, Virginia, I was literally only one of a few cars on the road. As I looked over my shoulder, I was horrified to see the smoldering Pentagon, which had just been hit hours earlier by another plane in a gruesome act of terror. I saw the billowing black smoke rising from the building, and, sadly, later learned that one hundred twenty-five-people were dead. I stared at the Pentagon until the image was too small to see from my rear view mirror. Unlike how I drove to my office in the morning, the ride back home was painful. It was raw and emotional too, and it brought back memories of other tragedies in my life that I had gotten through with strength and sheer will power.

When I got back to my house there was a message on the answering machine from the congressional leadership– both sides of the aisle– that members of Congress would be meeting that evening on the steps in front of the Capitol as a show of unity and resolution. After I returned home late in the day, and since I lived a distance away, I didn't get to return to the Capitol for the meeting on the Capitol steps. Later that night, I turned on the television and saw some of my colleagues assembled side-by-side, no democrats or republicans, just patriotic Americans standing their ground. I was so proud of all of them, and I couldn't help choking up when they spontaneously began singing *God Bless America*.

The other thing our congressional leadership announced that night was that we would be back at the Capitol the next morning and that the business of governing and protecting the people of the United States would not come to a halt because of these

heinous terrorist attacks. I was so honored to be a member of
Congress on what was clearly one of the worst days in American
history.

So much had changed for our country in just twenty-four
hours. On September 10, 2001, we were a nation at peace, a
nation that worried about jobs and the rising cost of living and
things many American citizens could relate. Then, on September
11, 2001, we were attacked and now we were a nation at war,
something no one could have ever imagined. And September
12, 2001, was the first day all Americans, including the President
and the Congress, had to pick themselves up and show that great
American resolve and can-do attitude.

We did remarkably well as members of Congress, I must
say. I'm sure we made our share of mistakes along the way.
After all, it was a crisis situation and we had to literally deal
with one emergency after another. But overall, I gave us high
marks for the way we worked together and kept America moving
forward. There was a real sense of cooperation and partnership
between Congress, the White House and among republicans
and democrats. We all appreciated that civility, respect and
trust, something that is woefully missing from our political
leaders today. After all, our great country was built on faith and
confidence and if that is gone, what's left? So as a bipartisan
group, we decided without anyone needing a major briefing or
position paper to work together and get the job done!

I would like to think that even during these very fractious
times that if our nation experienced an extreme emergency,
members of Congress would put aside their politics and come
together for the good of the country. I would hope so, but I'm not
one hundred percent convinced of that to be perfectly honest.

I also believe that our leadership at the time, President George
W. Bush, Dennis Hastert, Nancy Pelosi, Steny Hoyer, Trent Lott
and Tom Daschle, handled this incredible time of crisis in a

very professional and I must say, remarkable way. I know that I was not alone among my democrat colleagues who also felt that if President Bush or his cabinet asked us for support, this was no time to criticize and argue, but rather to rally and unite. In hindsight, it is tempting to judge that we might have been too easy on the Bush administration, maybe too accommodating as well. But if you think about it, how could anyone do otherwise? In such a grave time of national crisis, we couldn't possibly show any weakness to the world by being divided along party lines. Our country had a huge psychological wound that needed to be healed. By showing the world that we as a nation remained strong, we were able to move from chaos back to stability. Whatever President Bush wanted, we gave it to him gladly. In the years that followed I would often ask myself and others, "Why did it take a major crisis or meltdown in order to get members to work together?" We should always be finding ways to work in concert with one another.

Of course, our number one concern at the time was preventing another terrorist attack. As a member of the House Transportation Committee, this became especially important to me. It probably wasn't until about twenty-four hours after the attack that a terrible and unimaginable reality dawned on me. About a month before September 11, I, along with Republican Congressman John Mica from Florida, a member of the congressional Transportation Committee with me, had been in New York City for a luncheon meeting with New York and New Jersey Port Authority officials. For a number of years, we were aware of these terrorist groups and the possibility that they could use planes as weapons to kill innocent Americans. No one knew at the time that it would happen so soon. Though we were briefed on the many scenarios and capabilities of terrorists, the fact was that our government couldn't imagine how terrorists could actually hijack planes and use them as weapons potentially causing such major destruction. Little serious attention was given to those possibilities.

For convenience sake, the luncheon was held in the restaurant called Windows on the World, located on the top of their office building which just happened to be the North Tower of the World Trade Center. We had what I thought was a very productive and informative meeting, and I left there knowing that the Port Authority representatives were informed on the issues we discussed such as transportation, infrastructure and homeland security. Tragically, I learned that all but one of the people who were at that meeting with us died at the World Trade Center on 9/11.

Only a few weeks after the terrorist attacks, I traveled back to New York City with a large bipartisan congressional delegation. As we stood on a platform atop the still smoldering rubble of what was once the majestic twin towers, I couldn't help but think about all those men and women who were at our lunch just a couple of weeks before. There's not a single member of Congress who believed these attacks weren't personal. This was the first time we were faced with such a tragic and vicious attack on our homeland since Pearl Harbor. We were also told, in closed-door meetings by the intelligence community and the military, that another attack was very likely unless we acted decisively and immediately. Our task was to reenergize the American psyche and create an environment where America could pick itself up, go back to work and move forward. That's how we approached the mission that lay before us; we were not going to let the terrorists win.

Many of us knew about Al Qaeda and Osama Bin Laden. Now, all of a sudden, Al Qaeda was lurking around every corner, or so it seemed. The first action the House of Representatives took was to give every single member of Congress a blackberry so that we could receive emergency information and communicate better with our staff and constituents. The second thing that was decided was to put a gas mask underneath each chair in the House Chamber. That took some getting used to, because usually underneath the chairs was the Congressional Record from the previous day. They were there just in case a member wanted to look up the direction of a certain debate, or what was said about a piece of legislation. All they had to do was reach underneath their chair. Now, instead of grabbing a copy of the Congressional Record, there was a gas mask, a constant reminder of our vulnerability and how business as usual had changed forever.

While the Capitol is known as the people's house, after 9/11 access for visitors was severely limited. No one could go in or out without strict security, and to me, that was a symbol of our lost innocence. We were still the people's house, but it was more difficult for the people to get through security in the U.S. Capitol where typically Americans watch their representatives conduct their business from the galleries. It also became much more difficult for constituents or visiting schoolchildren to walk the halls of Congress and get a real feel for how we represented their interests in Washington. From a security point of view I understood there wasn't much of a choice, but it really did upset me. Growing up in the Tennessee governor's residence, Dad refused to put a fence around the twelve-acre property because he wanted Tennesseans to feel like they could come in anytime, made me realize that this was now a new America. Our country also lost its trust.

And when I thought things couldn't get any worse, we were faced with yet another act of terrorism, this time home-grown. Soon after 9/11, several letters containing the deadly airborne pathogen, Anthrax, were mailed to a number of media outlets as well as the Capitol Hill offices of Senators Daschle and Leahy. Now, in addition to curtailing the way our constituents could visit with us, we had to completely revamp the way they could communicate with us, too. The delivery of regular mail was shut down for a while, only to resume after a treatment facility was put together that checked every single piece of mail addressed to a member of Congress. The mail now takes much longer to reach a congressional office, and it goes through a process that leaves the paper all yellow and brittle. The distance placed between us, through no fault of our own, has contributed tremendously to our ever-growing disconnect between members of Congress and the people they represent.

The first 100 days or so after the attack we were moving with lightning speed and spent money like we were drunken sailors. The attitude and belief back then was that there were conspirators around every tree, and that created a sense of urgency for us to spend unlimited amounts of money on security. It also became clear to us very quickly that 9/11 had been master-minded in Afghanistan. Most of the attackers were trained there, though we learned later that a few received pilot lessons in the U.S.. I still question whether all of the terrorists were given the entire master plan, and maybe only those who were in the cockpits on the morning of 9/11 knew they were on a suicide mission to fly the planes into predetermined targets. I often wonder what was going on during those final few minutes of each flight. Sadly, no one will ever really know for sure except for those heroes who took down Flight 93 headed to the U.S. Capitol.

When President George W. Bush asked us for the authority to use military force against the terrorists, he received it with near unanimous consent from both chambers and both parties on October 16, 2002. This was the vote that essentially declared War on Afghanistan, and while we knew the incredible impact it would have, we all felt that it was necessary to protect the American people.

Shortly after 9/11, and the vote authorizing military force to fight terrorism, I traveled as part of a small congressional delegation just outside the city of Rome, Italy. One of my colleagues, Curt Weldon a republican from Pennsylvania, made contact with Afghanistan's exiled king, Mohammed Zahir Shah, also known as King Mohammad VII. After the attack, and after it became clear that the Taliban had given Al Qaeda safe harbor in Afghanistan, the king assembled a meeting just outside of Rome, at his residence. His goal was to bring together members of Congress and leaders of the Northern Alliance. We all boarded the plane, which believe me was not the most comforting feeling so soon after the attacks, and headed to Italy for our meetings. As we sat down with these tribal leaders, some of them were wearing clothing that to me looked like they had just stepped out of the sixteenth century. But the meeting and conversation that followed were something that I will never forget. Here's why: imagine entering someone's home that was surrounded by a huge stone wall and then when you step inside the courtyard, you see a number of soldiers brandishing high-powered weaponry. This furthered my belief that this situation was, in fact, grave and urgent. Along with the soldiers, every major news network was there—including journalists like Larry King and George Stephanopoulos to interview members of Congress who made the trip to Rome that day to meet with the exiled King of Afghanistan and the Northern Alliance. The members of Congress were very interested in hearing their thoughts and recommendations on how they were planning to defeat the Taliban.

I remember after seeing such a heavy presence of media and soldiers, I left thinking that I had just attended the most important meeting in the world on that day.

We met with the exiled king first, then he excused himself from the meeting. He was very gracious and kind, but was obviously very feeble because of his advanced age and poor health. After he left, we promptly got down to business with the members of the Northern Alliance.

The Northern Alliance leaders had a clear strategy for how they could defeat the Taliban with the help of the United States. They weren't asking for boots on the ground, but rather wanted the United States to provide air support. As we all stood around a long wooden table, the Northern Alliance members took out detailed maps for us to review. They showed us the areas where they felt they had control and other areas where they had vulnerabilities. We came away feeling very optimistic and impressed. When we returned to Washington we made the case for supporting the Northern Alliance to help them defeat the Taliban, which they did at the time. We shared our findings in a report which we gave to the President, Congress, the Pentagon, the State Department, and others in the government who needed to be informed. Our problem in Afghanistan from the beginning was trying to force the Afghan people to accept a nationalized government which they have always opposed. I believe that is where we failed.

A good friend of mine, Congressman Charlie Wilson of Texas, once told me, "Bob, we are going to lose in Afghanistan. Those that were fighting for us to get the soviets out of Afghanistan are now fighting to drive us out of Afghanistan. The Afghans are tribal and they will never accept, nor support, a centralized government."

Charlie was right.

In the first full year after 9/11, anything with the words national security in it was given a blank check. While I did have my doubts that Al Qaeda was as strong as we were told, I certainly didn't want to stand in the way of anything that would keep Americans safe and strong. Before 9/11, I believe we, the Congress, acted in a fiscally responsible manner. There was a budget surplus during the Clinton Administration, and our biggest challenge was how to spend wisely and reduce the national debt. We had surpluses as far as the eye could see, according to Office of Management and Budget (OMB) and the Congressional Budget Office (CBO). As a member of the Budget Committee we could foresee a time when there was no national debt. What we had to do as members was to demonstrate discipline and set priorities. It is hard to believe how much unraveling took place in such a short period of time starting with 9/11. That is really a tough pill to swallow now, for sure. But after 9/11, we adopted a fear-based approach to our fiscal management: do what was necessary for our national security and figure out how to pay for it later. We accepted the theory that to keep us safe we had to spend, spend, spend and worry about paying the bills later. That thinking has made the trillions of dollars of an ever increasing national debt acceptable. To this day, we still haven't returned to approaching our finances in a responsible and sound manner.

What started as fiscal policy in response to a national security threat has become not just acceptable but ingrained in our spending habits. I sure couldn't run my household finances that way. It is simply a disgrace that we have accepted the notion of paying for today's bill with an I-owe-you that our kids and grandkids will have to deal with for years to come.

All that free-flowing spending started after 9/11 when we were fearful that all expenditures, no matter how large, seemed absolutely necessary. Take the creation of the Department of Homeland Security as an example. We put everything but the kitchen sink into that Department. Why? Because we were told by the administration that our security depended on one umbrella organization under which all agencies with a similar purpose would be placed. There was much debate on this issue, and one of my concerns was that agencies that had been stand-alone entities would be losing their identities and focus if they no longer had autonomy. A huge part of the debate focused on

FEMA, the Federal Emergency Management Agency. Agencies such as FEMA, that had been once autonomous, would now be losing their independence by being rolled into the newly created Department of Homeland Security. Of all the departments in the federal government this became the largest by far.

Listening to the debate, I was going back and forth on how I should vote, leaning toward opposing it, but at the end of the day I voted in favor of creating the new Department of Homeland Security. We just didn't know what or who might hit us next. What, ultimately, convinced me was the inclusion of the Transportation Security Administration (TSA), which I thought was important to tighten our security. Some people may not appreciate the long lines at the airport, but please don't blame me for that vote. I truly believe the TSA has played a hugely important role in preventing another attack on American soil where terrorists would use airplanes as weapons, or airline passengers as negotiation tools. It pains me that around the world today, many countries that have not put in place such controls have seen planes once again become weaponized.

When the Secret Service, in the name of national security, shut down Washington National Airport, which is about three miles south of downtown Washington in one direction, and five miles north of my home in Alexandria in the other, I voiced my opposition as a member of the Transportation Committee. I felt very strongly that the National Airport needed to be open for business and that our nation's capital can't be serviced by an airport forty miles into Virginia (Dulles Airport) or forty miles into Maryland (Baltimore-Washington Airport). After keeping the airport closed for several weeks, the Secret Service finally relented, and we reached a compromise that reopened the airport, but also addressed some of the security concerns that had shut it down in the first place. I'm sure there are some who will claim that I took such a strong stand against closing it was because it was so convenient for me to fly to and from Tennessee. What bothered me, really, was that we spent an absolute fortune on that airport and we were going to close it down. Honestly, I believed the airport was necessary and that we could provide safety for people, protect historic landmarks and continue to support commerce and tourism without going to such extremes.

Incidentally, I had a tussle over the airport on another occasion, back in the late 1990s. For decades the airport serving our nation's capital was known as Washington National Airport. Then, in 1997, my republican colleagues began naming everything and anything they could lay their hands on after President Ronald Reagan. We had just voted on and passed it into law in 1995. The bill named a brand new downtown building after the former President. What eventually became the Ronald Reagan Building and International Trade Center was a $768 million construction project on prime D.C. real estate. It became the second-largest federal government building in the Washington metropolitan area, the largest being the Pentagon. I thought giving President Reagan that much recognition was very much deserved.

During the debate of the Public Buildings Committee and its Transportation Sub-Committee, I commented that the airport already had a name. "The airport is named after our first president, George Washington. You would not be naming it, but rather, renaming it," I said. After I spoke, Congressman Peter DeFazio, a Democrat from Oregon, spoke in committee right after me. He said: "If you republicans want to name something else after President Reagan, why, don't you name the national debt after him? He tripled that." The debate became even livelier between democrats and republicans. Some democrats on the committee, like me, felt that President Jimmy Carter had been overlooked because nothing had ever been named after him. While it did create much more tension between the two parties, we knew the republicans had us outnumbered!

Then at the height of the debate, the democrat leadership on the Transportation Committee got a call from Leader Dick Gephardt's office, asking us not to object anymore to changing the airport's name. To this day, I have never known exactly why the decision was made, but, perhaps it was part of another compromise regarding another bill that would later come before the House. Finally, the vote was cast and a so-called compromise took place. Then, and forevermore, the official legal name is the Ronald Reagan Washington National Airport. In all of my dealings with President Reagan, I had come to know him as a very decent man and an inspirational leader. Honoring him was not the worst idea that my republican colleagues ever had! I will even say that over the years, it has helped the Republican Party rebuild its image by Ronald Reagan being looked upon as the father of modern day republicanism.

As we continued to deal with the fallout from 9/11, the name Saddam Hussein more and more entered into the national conversation. By the end of 2002, a large percentage of the population, and Congress too, had become convinced that Iraq had played a role in the 9/11 attacks, and that Saddam Hussein posed the gravest threat to our national security. The debate in the United Nations Security Council was fierce, as was the debate in the halls of the Capitol. But the evidence upon which I based my vote was false and misleading. Saddam Hussein had nothing to do with what happened on 9/11, and Iraq had no chemical, biological and nuclear capabilities. The debate that culminated in a heated and emotional vote on the second day of October 2003, led to the passage of the Iraq War Resolution. I am sorry to say I was one of the 296 total votes in favor (only eighty-two other democrats voted for it). I remember when my good friend and fellow Tennessee Representative, Jimmy Duncan, and I had some soul-searching conversations leading up to the vote. I have the greatest respect for him for being one of only six republicans – out of 223 – to vote no. And it is telling that even though we were friends, and did have conversations, he never confided in me about which way he was going to vote. I guess he was concerned about the political pressure he would face if he did come out publicly before such an important and courageous decision.

But, I really regret that I voted yes.

I have thought about that vote many, many times since 2002. The evidence and comments that were presented to us led us to the conclusion that Saddam Hussein played a role in 9/11, which was not true. I also believed at the time that the Bush administration would act much more slowly and in a more measured way, and not rush off to war immediately. As a veteran myself, I wanted our commander-in-chief to use all due diligence before committing our troops to a theater of war. In my mind, giving the President this authority was a sign of unity and strength that would compel the Iraqis to negotiate their way out of the situation they found themselves. In hindsight, I guess I had hoped for a chain of events like we saw in Libya just a year later: faced with the might of both the British and the American armed forces staring him down, Colonel Muammar Gaddafi renounced his efforts to create and deploy weapons of mass destruction. We worked with the international community to decommission his weaponry. Col. Gaddafi's nuclear materials program was transported from Libya to the United States. To show good faith Libya was ending its militaristic actions against the West. Of all things, his nuclear materials are stored in my home state, in the city of Oak Ridge, Tennessee.

Incidentally, four years after leaving Congress, I was affiliated with the Livingston Group as a registered lobbyist, and we worked with the Libyan Ambassador, Eli Ojali, and former Congressman Bill Zelliff of New Hampshire to regularly take the ambassador to Capitol Hill, and on one occasion we also brought Col. Gaddafi's son, Safe, along with us. Bob Livingston and Lori Fitz-Pegado, who are partners in the Livingston Group, were leading the team on this important mission. We were not only instrumental in normalizing relations with Libya, which brought about trade and commerce between the two countries, but we were also able to encourage the Libyans to make final payment to the victim's families of Pan Am 103. This was the plane that was shot down over Scotland killing hundreds of passengers. We were most pleased that Col. Gaddafi did not make a lot of outrageous comments during the period of time that we were trying to get the legislation voted upon and approved. And it did pass without one dissenting vote in the U.S. House and Senate, and was sent on to President George. W. Bush for his signature. That was a good day, and many members were pleased that it was passed, since at the time, there was a great deal of tension between the U.S. and countries abroad, particularly between the West and the East. We were also very pleased to make a new friend and ally. Since that time it has become very complicated again in Libya and that part of the world as it is in so many other countries.

Giving President Bush the authority to go to war against Iraq I thought would show the world and Saddam Hussein that we meant business. That could have exerted some real pressure and might have forced the Iraqis to negotiate in good faith and accept a deal that would remove Hussein from power in a strategic manner. I really didn't expect our administration to go to war so quickly, bombing Iraq before any real progress was made involving the international community to force Hussein into submission. I felt that President George W. Bush was trigger-happy and did not build a coalition-force first. This was a totally different kind of war and very different from the way his father, President George H. W. Bush, had confronted Hussein ten years earlier after Iraq invaded Kuwait. During the first Gulf War, we acted with patience and implemented a focused strategy that involved a clear end-game. The President had also built a huge international coalition ready and willing to help us. In addition, other nations, to the largest extent the Arab/Muslim nations, paid for ninety percent of the Gulf War. Our allies supported and financed the war because they wanted Hussein out of Kuwait, and the deal President Bush struck was that we would not march our troops into Baghdad. I think that left the impression with many Americans that we had unfinished business in Iraq. But it also set the stage for getting in the mess that we're still dealing with today.

There was a reason the Saudis insisted we shouldn't go after Hussein directly. They understood that Saddam Hussein, as difficult, terrible and barbaric as he was, was a known quantity whose actions often were predictable. He also was a survivor who could always be counted on to put things in place ensuring he and his clan would stay in power. It doesn't take an expert in Islamic Studies to understand that thousands of years of religious strife involving the Sunnis and the Shias couldn't simply be wiped away because we presented to Iraq our way of democratic and representative government. The Saudis insisted the first Gulf War end with Hussein still in power. This is because what scared them much more than a Hussein-run Iraq was an Iraq open to religious extremists, assuming power and planting the seeds of chaos and uprising right smack in the middle of the region. Sadly, we still see this happening today in Iraq, complicating things even more by the presence of the super-terrorist group, ISIS that stands for the Islamic State of Iraq and Syria, a group so evil that even Al Qaeda rebuked them. Led by the cleric, Abu Bakr al-Baghdadi, their goal is to form an independent state with territory in Iraq, Syria and Lebanon. Now, America's involvement continues, with more military action to prevent ISIS from propagating their genocidal and terroristic behavior.

President Clinton and I had talked about this very scenario a number of years before 9/11. Clinton said: "Bob, we can take Saddam Hussein out, but who runs the country?" But the fact is, that during the Clinton Administration Saddam was on the move from palace to palace every night to escape a possible U.S. bombing attack. What was keeping him alive was the fact that none of us could come up with an acceptable answer to the following question, "Who comes after Saddam Hussein?"

Where the Bush Administration went astray after occupying the country was that they fired everyone who was in the government and, unfortunately, there was no one left behind with any real experience to run it. The Sunnis and former members of the Bath Party were the ones who had the knowledge and experience. Can you imagine if the Chinese were to occupy America and the first action that they took was to fire everyone who worked for the federal, state and local government? Would we then expect law and order to prevail and necessary services to be provided? If that were to happen, there would be total chaos, confusion and corruption would be alive and well. Just like what happened in Iraq.

When we tried to run Iraq after forcing their leaders out of power we put in place a complete set of new and inexperienced Iraqis who had never been in charge of anything. We also put a bunch of our own inexperienced people in place in the short-term under a provisional authority. Ultimately, they were never accepted by the Iraqi people as anything other than U.S. puppets. We, naively, expected them to step right in and run the country, and were surprised when Iraq began to fall apart before our very eyes. The cost of this failure in death and destruction and trillions of dollars wasted is simply breathtaking. The $2 trillion borrowed and spent is now saddling this generation and future generations with a huge debt. What do we have to show for our efforts? Imagine if we could have had that money available to help people during the economic crash of 2007-2008. Or what our roads, bridges, public and mass transportation, not to mention healthcare and education systems would be like had we invested even half of that money into our infrastructure and economy? During the Iraqi War we never asked Americans to sacrifice, other than our brave military members and their families. No war tax was imposed like in previous times of war. This time we just spent and borrowed to pay for the cost of freedom. We could have rebuilt America and really made a difference for generations to come. What about if we had asked a simple question of the American people before going to war? "We are going to have to raise your taxes in order to pay for this war. Are you willing to vote for and support a war tax?" I expect the answer would have been no.

I do regret that I was one of those 296 yes votes. And if I could have had a crystal ball and known all the things I know now, I definitely would have voted no. But hindsight is always 20/20. In addition to voting yes as a way to put pressure on Iraq and Saddam Hussein, I voted that way because I felt we needed to support our President who was still dealing with an incredible and extraordinary crisis. I believed strongly that we needed to continue showing unity and put partisanship aside for the sake of the country. But that eroded quickly as the misinformation, misleading facts and outright lies became obvious to the American people. On February 5, 2003, when General Colin Powell spoke before the UN Security Council, claiming that Iraq had chemicals of mass destruction, we later learned that much of that pre-war Iraq intelligence was erroneous. He realized soon thereafter that those claims were indeed unfounded. And there were others within the federal government too, who also had their doubts about the veracity of those claims including the CIA, former ambassador Joe Wilson, who had been hired to investigate the yellow-cake uranium claim, and UN weapons inspectors, among others. As a result, that sense of unity and civility from the immediate post 9/11 days was fraying. In my opinion, this may have been the debate and the vote that started turning us back to politics and business as usual.

Our nation has had a number of defining moments that influenced a generation and set us on a certain path. September 11, 2001, is without a doubt such a moment. It really changed how we felt about ourselves – no longer as safe as we thought – and how we felt about other people, cultures and religions—not as trusting and tolerant. That day was a day that inflicted great harm, pain and lasting damage. Of course, almost 3,000 innocent men and women whom we lost on 9/11 were the first and most immediate casualties. Add to that the thousands of warfighters killed or wounded over a decade of combat. Count up the dollars needed to rebuild downtown Manhattan and the Pentagon. Put those dollars into the debit column, along with trillions spent on fighting in Afghanistan and Iraq and then rebuilding those two countries. Lastly, take our system of government and give the executive branch more power and sway than it was ever meant to have. That's the price of September 11. That's just the beginning, because all these things have a ripple effect that will continue playing a role in our thinking and decision-making process for a very, very long time.

Being a member of Congress is a job that comes with great responsibility. In my mind, my colleagues and I lived up to that responsibility on 9/11 and the days and months after to the very best of our abilities. We did what we thought was right and necessary to move our country out of an unimaginable crisis. Dealing with crises is never easy. It is not easy for a President, members of Congress or the military. I like to think that we helped mitigate the crisis from becoming something even more destructive. But we certainly made mistakes along the way. One of the responsibilities of being a public servant is that you are transparent in your debate and analysis. It is important to give future generations the opportunity to learn from your past decisions. What could we have done differently, particularly on the Iraq War Resolution? Maybe we could have questioned the intelligence we were presented more forcefully? Maybe we could have listened more closely to the good counsel and opinion of more of our colleagues and the American people?

I ask myself those questions every time I meet a brave wounded warrior like Marine Corporal Christian Brown.

Clement's Contemplations

"Debate with purpose: vote with courage"

"Members of Congress have just one boss, the people"

"Imagine the unthinkable: planes are not just for flying"

"When tragedy strikes, accept it, then move forward"

"You can name everything after a President, especially airports"

"Never visit a king in exile without bringing a gift"

"Innocence may be lost, but always found"

"Terror is a state of mind, not a state of affairs"

"In a national emergency unify, rally and work the phones"

Chapter 8

COUNTRY MUSIC AND ME: TALES FROM MUSIC CITY U.S.A

"Bob, I'm not Goin' Down!"—Dolly Parton

There is one place in America where both democrats and republicans can agree is among the best places to visit and live in the country. That's Nashville, Tennessee, my hometown and affectionately known around the world as Music City U.S.A. Nashville gets my vote every time.

I guess you could say that country music is in my DNA. As a young boy growing up with a father who was governor and someone who enjoyed gospel and country music, we were privileged to host visitors like Roy Acuff, Eddy Arnold, Minnie Pearl, Dinah Shore and Tennessee Ernie Ford; their songs became part of who am I today. Whether I was on the campaign trail with Dad, going back stage at the Grand Ole Opry or during my many campaigns for public office, country music played an integral part. It infused the room with the music and lyrics that resonated with the hard working, God-fearing people I was proud to know and serve.

Nashville, Tennessee, is a place that exudes excitement. It has a certain rhythm of life that comes from its rich traditions and musical heritage. Nashville is also the home of the Grand Ole

Opry, the oldest live radio show in the country and a place where country music greats still come to perform and see and be seen. It is the glue that connects the people of Nashville together, and is integral to the life of its residents, visitors, song-writers and performers. To this day, when I meet new people and tell them I am from Nashville, you wouldn't believe the response I get. They often say, "You are so lucky. I heard you can even see country music stars hanging out in the Starbucks there?" Of course, growing up and living in Nashville most of my life, I can tell you that we are the most friendly people I know. Even superstars like Tim McGraw, Faith Hill, Taylor Swift, Reese Witherspoon, Alan Jackson, Nicole Kidman, and Keith Urban, feel like they can be themselves and go about their business shopping, eating at restaurants and even attending church without creating a major international incident.

From square dancing and playing the fiddle in the late 1700s, to one of Tennessee's first real superstars and politicians—David "Davy" Crockett, who represented Tennessee in the U.S. House of Representatives, known far and wide for his lively fiddle playing. Tennessee had always had the distinction of being the kind of state where singers, fiddle players, and songwriters come to perform and be among other creative people.

Matter of fact, I remember when I was about twelve-years-old, I heard a story about the famous songwriter, Stuart Hamblen, and one of the greatest actors of our time, John Wayne.

Stuart Hamblen told us this story when he stayed overnight at the governor's residence, which of course captivated me. Hamblen wrote these popular songs including, *This Ole House* and, *It is No Secret What God Can Do.* Apparently, he was having a heartfelt conversation one night with John Wayne, and here's how the conversation went from my recollection: "John, you know I've had some problems lately, but I've turned my life around and it's no secret what God can do," Stuart confided in him. John

Wayne replied, "Well, Stuart, why don't you write a song about that?" "About what," Stuart said quite surprised. "About what you said, Stuart," said John. "What did I say, John?" "You know, it's no secret what God can do." Apparently, as the story goes, shortly thereafter, and in just fifty-five minutes, he wrote the iconic song, which to this day melts my heart; *It is No Secret What God Can Do.*

In the late 1800s, Nashville was *the* place where songwriting got its start and became the hub of music publishing in America.

It has been said that Nashville's moniker as Music City U.S.A. came from one of the first musical groups to ever perform for an international audience. They were called the *Fisk Jubilee Singers* from Fisk University, and in the 1800s they had the opportunity to perform for the Queen of England, who after their performance said that the group must have hailed from music city. The group's funds from their concerts helped pay some of the expenses for the slaves who were freed following the Civil War and wanted to get a college education. Then, in 1897, a group of Confederate soldiers were looking for a suitable place to hold their annual reunion, and they found a tabernacle in Nashville spacious enough to hold the large gathering. That eventually became known as the Ryman Auditorium and was also referred to as the Carnegie Hall of the South because it featured many well-known artists and orchestras at the time like John Phillip Sousa, among many others. Then, in 1925, a radio station known as WSM started an innovative broadcast where they would showcase talented country music artists who performed at the Ryman; that eventually became what we know today as the Grand Ole Opry. In fact, the original Ryman Auditorium, which is now the downtown home of the Grand Ole Opry, is still a favorite place for music-lovers to come and be part of Nashville's dynamic downtown.

But when anyone mentions anything about Nashville, invariably the conversation turns to the Grand Ole Opry. It is not only America's oldest live radio broadcast, but literally an icon of the Nashville music scene, a place where for more than ninety years, some of the greatest county music legends and contemporary artists have performed live every week. It has launched the careers of country music superstars like Dolly Parton, Johnny Cash, Loretta Lynn, Alan Jackson, Vince Gill, Garth Brooks, Lee Greenwood, Taylor Swift, Shania Twain, and literally hundreds of others who are now household names.

I remember going there as a kid with my family, and what a great experience it was being backstage and chatting with the likes of Roy Acuff, who was among country music's greatest artists. Matter of fact, Roy was called the king of country music, and lucky for me and my family he just happened to love politics, too. Roy was always very friendly and generous. He and Dad would talk regularly about what was going on in the country. I always thought that Roy would have made a great governor, but he ran as a republican in 1948 in a primarily democratic state and as a result he lost the election. He was actually our next door neighbor when we lived in Hendersonville, Tennessee. I would hear him practicing with his band almost every weekend. He held his band rehearsals on his boat, and I was sure glad he did. I facetiously told all of my friends that if they wanted to hear Roy Acuff sing the song, *Great Speckled Bird*, they would have to get to my house bright and early in the morning.

Needless to say, at fifteen-years-old that really made an impression and put me in good stead with my group of boyhood friends. Even though Roy was called the king of country music, he never really liked that title. He was more comfortable being with his fans and was known as among the most available country music artists ever. Matter of fact, Roy lived in the house that was built for him right on the grounds of Opryland by my good friend, Bud Wendell, who was the CEO of Gaylord Entertainment at the time. Bud said he did that because after Roy's wife, Mildred, had passed; Roy lived by himself and was fearful that vandals would break into his home. He lived in a big old Southern house across the river from Opryland. At the time there was a rash of crimes where homes were being broken into and people living inside were assaulted. Bud told Roy that it would be Gaylord Entertainment's honor to build a house for him on the Opryland compound and that he could stay there the rest of his life. Roy was a wonderful man and really loved his fans; he was accessible to them throughout his entire career.

To say that the Grand Ole Opry is a legend in country music, in my opinion, is an understatement. It is known all over the world and its influence cannot be underestimated. When I was there as a child, it was a life-changing experience. Why? Because there is no other place on the face of the earth where you can hear a different artist playing their sets live every thirty minutes. It brings together literally thousands of people from faraway places like China and Russia to those closer to home from Seattle, Washington to Miami, Florida.

I think some people who are not from Nashville cannot understand how country music is so much a part of our collective heritage and history. When the Grand Ole Opry was first founded, it was before the advent of television, so the only way they could be exposed to music like this was on the radio. It holds a very special place in the hearts and minds of Nashville residents, whose direct memories and the stories told by their parents are part of the rich music history of this great city.

One of my good friends, Jerry Strobel, worked behind-the-scenes in promotions at the Opry for thirty years, and he was there from the very beginning when it was just WSM Radio. I remember him telling me so many great stories about not only the history of the Opry, but the artists who made it a household name here in Nashville and around the world. Like the time President Richard M. Nixon came to the Grand Ole Opry for the building's dedication on March 16, 1974, which I also attended. It was during the Watergate crisis, and Nixon was in the thick of it, for sure. Apparently, he decided to play *Happy Birthday*, to his wife, Pat, on the piano right on the new Opry stage. The crowd went wild. Jerry was standing with the press corps who was traveling with the President that night, and many of them said that if Nixon showed that kind of caring and humor, he might have survived Watergate and not been forced to resign from office. Matter of fact, every modern President has visited Nashville and the Opry beginning with Nixon, Ford, Carter, Reagan, Clinton, Bush 41, and Bush 43. I was always most honored to be with some of them personally when they visited Tennessee. I flew on Air Force One with President Clinton when he came to Memphis, and also President George H. W. Bush when we both attended the CMA Awards. Needless to say, every President who visits Nashville can't help but fall in love with country music and Nashville, Tennessee!

Jerry also told me another great story about the legendary artist, Grandpa Jones, who he said was the funniest person he ever knew on-stage and off. I knew Grandpa well, too, and I sure agree with him on that. He was funny without even trying. One night, Jerry was watching Grandpa perform backstage, and during his last song he seemed to forget some of the words. When the song was over he collapsed, and Jerry and many other people rushed to his aid. He apparently had a stroke, and while they were waiting for the ambulance to arrive, Jerry asked Grandpa how he was feeling. Grandpa scanned the room with his eyes, and he clearly saw the many people standing around him very worried about his health. He told Jerry, "I don't feel that bad, Jerry. I'm 84 years old and I can still draw a crowd!"

I truly think that country music and Nashville have had a special place in the hearts of not only Americans but people from all over the world. One of my dear friends, Gene Ward, my general counsel when I was chairman of the Tennessee Public Service Commission is a brilliant man. Despite Gene's success as a lawyer, he never forgot his East Tennessee roots. He purchased an old fire truck which he used to drive along the Nashville and White Pine, Tennessee, streets as part of the annual Christmas Parade, giving children the chance to tour the truck and meet the Dalmatian that would always be seated inside. Gene also happens to be married to a country music legend, and host of the Grand Ole Opry, and Grammy winner, Jeannie Seely. She is originally from Pennsylvania, but to me she is country music personified and as Nashville as it gets.

She and I have talked about what it means to be an artist living and working in Nashville, and like so many other people, she says there is no other place like Nashville on the face of the earth. After leaving Pennsylvania to pursue her musical career, she went to LA, and there she met Dottie West who encouraged her to move to Music City U.S.A, and Ernest Tubb, who she credits for moving her career to the next level. Lucky for all of us she did. But what I love about Jeannie is her feistiness and determination. She's been singing with the Opry for forty-eight years now, and in the late 1980s, during a snowstorm, the Opry asked her to host one of the thirty minute shows. Why this is remarkable is that before that time, no woman had ever done that. She was literally the first! And, she lobbied very hard to make sure women would continue in her footsteps. She also led the mission to have women artists dressed in short skirts rather than the traditional ruffles and red checked country attire. She has said, "I told the Opry that I didn't want an all-male or an all-female Opry show, just a great entertainment show." Today, she continues to host at the Opry, performs concerts and is one of country music's most visible trailblazers.

I can also recall a funny example of the influence of country music internationally when I was a member of Congress. I always thought of myself as a goodwill ambassador when it came to promoting my beloved Nashville and the entire state of Tennessee.

One day I hosted a Soviet diplomat, and brought him to the Grand Ole Opry to give him a taste of American culture and the Nashville country music scene in particular. He thought that he was truly in outer space. I am convinced that all of the bright costumes, lighting, fiddle-playing and country dancing were a life-changing experience for him. I can only imagine what he was secretly thinking that night.

I was very nervous about the next place I was taking the Soviet diplomat to visit which was my independent, non-denominational church, named Christ Church on Old Hickory Boulevard. That's where Mary and I worshipped. I was very skeptical that this diplomat from a communist country would appreciate or enjoy this type of spiritual experience, complete with the most rousing music and dynamic preaching ever. Near the middle of the church service, he turned to me and whispered in my ear, "Congressman, this is most contagious." Like the rest of us, he was very moved by the music and sermon by my brother in law, Rev. L.H. Hardwick, Jr. even though the Russian diplomat was a member of the Communist Party and anti-God. That being said, I could understand how this experience was an earthshaking one for him.

When I was a young boy growing up in Nashville, almost no one knew that the city would someday become an international tourist destination and be known around the world as Music City U.S.A. Bud Wendell, however, always had faith that Nashville would be recognized for its diverse music culture and particularly as the birthplace of country music. He knows that all too well, because he spent most of his adult life running Gaylord Entertainment Company, the group that owned the Grand Ole Opry, Opryland and the Opryland Hotel, as well as other properties. I used to tease him and ask him occasionally, "How can a guy from Ohio be so in tune with the country music scene in Nashville?" Matter of fact, Bud started his career selling burial insurance. As far as I'm concerned, that is diametrically opposed to the skill-set that would be needed to run such a creative and artistic enterprise as Gaylord Entertainment. But my friend, Bud, is always full of surprises.

He proudly points out that he is one of the few people in the nation to work for the same company for his entire career. When he was selling burial insurance for American General they eventually sold part of the business to Ed Gaylord, who then bought the rights to the television show, *Hee-Haw*, and eventually WSM radio, the Grand Ole Opry and Opryland. Bud had the vision to realize that if country music in Nashville were to become popular across the country, he needed to promote it on television and through other means such as a museum.

Under his direction, the Country Music Hall of Fame and Museum was born. What started out as a small non-profit operated by the Country Music Foundation is now the home to world-class exhibitions, preserving the rich traditions of country music and educating visitors from around the world. But it wasn't always that way. In 1987, it was accredited by the American Alliance of Museums, and that was the first step in making it a world-class venue. Back then the museum had very little exhibition space and the many country music artists who donated their guitars and other memorabilia were disappointed that many of their items could not be displayed simply because there was no room.

When I traveled overseas as a member of the Foreign Affairs Committee, in every country I visited people came up to me after knowing that I represented Nashville and said, "Oh, country music."

It was fitting, therefore, when Bud and my cousin, Steve Turner, who is now chairman of the board of the Country Music Hall of Fame, called me to let me know that the Tennessee Valley Authority was considering a substantial gift to the museum to help move it to the next level. They knew I had served on the TVA board years before and thought I could help them secure the funding.

Steve had been told that there was a problem and that they might not be able to help as previously thought. I placed a call to the decision-makers at TVA and pleaded my case; tourism in Nashville was growing exponentially because the city was becoming the hot place to be because of country music and Nashville's energy and vitality. I also made the case that the museum is not only special to the people of Nashville, but also the region, the nation and the entire world. To our delight, we were all thrilled when TVA looked into the need and decided to proceed with the gift that dramatically enabled the museum to become the iconic tourist destination it is today. The seeds that were planted by this investment, and the continued progress made by the museum over the years, has helped to bring more than one million visitors to Nashville each year.

Bud told me recently that under Steve Turner's leadership, the more than $100 million they have raised since has enabled: a 350,000 square-foot expansion; the addition of a 776-seat theatre; the Taylor Swift Education Center; multi-purpose event spaces; and thousands of items and artifacts including Nashville's oldest surviving recording studio. And while Bud retired from chairing the museum board I am most pleased that Steve Turner is still chairman. He and the board have taken the County Music Hall of Fame to even greater heights. The Tennessee Valley Authority continues to play a beneficial role in the communities throughout the seven states it serves. As I look back, it still amazes me how much can be accomplished when people decide to work together rather than always being concerned about who gets the credit.

All of these strides have put Nashville on the world's radar screen. It used to be that people would want to travel to visit famous American cities like New York, Chicago, Washington, D.C., or Los Angeles. Nashville usually wasn't on the top-ten lists of desirable destinations. Today all of that has changed and changed for the better. Not only are we known for the Grand Ole Opry, but we are also the songwriting capital of the world. Literally, songwriters from around the world come to Nashville to record their songs and get to know each other and share their love of the genre. I've been to the historic Bluebird Café many times, the place where new and established songwriters can perform songs that others made famous. It's an intimate setting and a great place to hear what's up and coming in the Nashville music scene. By the way, it is owned by the Nashville Songwriters Association, which is headed up by my former congressional press secretary, Bart Herbison.

The famous bar and restaurant, Tootsies Orchid Lounge, is another venue that both Nashville residents and visitors love. And the downtown is booming thanks to many Nashville patrons. In addition, we've added many wonderful eateries and young people are moving into the city in droves. It is no exaggeration to say that we live in an international city where artists and songwriters feel at home here as anywhere in this entire United States.

I must say even I have had my own, brief brush with musical fame. Well, not literally, of course. Many years ago I wrote a song in tribute to the late Dr. Martin Luther King, Jr. just hours after his tragic assassination. His death had a tremendous impact on me as a young graduate student at Memphis State University. It was a patriotic ballad celebrating Dr. King's life and accomplishments.

I wrote the lyrics with my friend, Tony Barrasso, of Italian descent and a life-long Memphis resident. He played my song on his Cordovox-a combination of an organ and an accordion-to the melody of the *Battle Hymn of the Republic*. We were quite a team. I was so excited. I gave the song to Dad in hopes that he would use his contacts to help me get the song published, but darned if he didn't lose my song and that was my only copy. I have never written another one since. That was my contribution to Nashville's songwriting history!

But it's not just country music that sets Nashville apart from any other city in the country. We are also the place where other genres of music are performed including soul, Christian, rock, bluegrass, classical, jazz and pop, to mention a few. Many artists love to come to Nashville to write their songs as well, and in my opinion, it is because of our openness and friendliness. Artists like Sheryl Crowe, John Rich, Justin Timberlake, and Robert Plant, not to mention the Black-Eyed Peas and so many others who find the city a creative outlet and an inspiring place to get ideas, perform new songs and encourage the creative process. We also have what we call the Music Mile, which connects so many of our musical venues together. In essence, the buildings and venues that provide a gateway to the Nashville music scene, to me are symbolic of the bonds that are formed between the artists, songwriters, and performers and the local community.

I truly believe that there is no other place in the country—with perhaps the exception of Los Angeles, or New York City—where the famous feel comfortable just being themselves. When I've seen Tim McGraw and Faith Hill sitting in church on Sunday mornings, there was no entourage protecting them from their fans, just two people taking in a preacher's sermon.

Nicole Kidman often goes to our local Starbucks for a cup of coffee. She is just like all of the others there who are happy to get a jolt from their morning brew. And we Nashvillians let them be because we know that they are just like us; there's no need to make a fuss. The same goes for the not so well recognized artists, but artists in their own right whose music and lyrics are recognized all over the world. I'm talking about Nashville's prolific songwriters.

I bet if I ask any American what their favorite song is they would most likely mention a tune that originated right here in Nashville, or at least had some ties to Music City U.S.A.

For me, there are so many gospel and country music songs that have made me feel happy, sad, motivated and sometimes inspired. What makes those songs even more personal for me is the fact that I have met or known the songwriters and artists personally. But of course, if you live or have grown up in Nashville, mostly everyone has had some interactions with the people who make these songs come alive.

Elvis' songs—*How Great Thou Art*, and *In the Ghetto* have always had a special place in my heart and soul, and as we all know, Elvis' roots were in Gospel Music, too. His working class roots and faith touched a nerve with me and every other working-class person in America. He is a great example of someone who came from modest means, and he worked hard to achieve his dream.

Of course Johnny Cash, and his wife June Carter Cash, and their entire family were not only family friends but people we deeply cherished.

Matter of fact, when I was in Congress, I asked Johnny and June Carter to come to Washington, D.C. and perform for one of my first political fundraising events. This was a special treat for me because not only would I be able to visit with my good friend, but hear some of his songs that I have loved all of my life. To this day, many of my friends in Congress who were at that political fundraiser still say it was the best fundraising event they have ever been to in their lives!

In particular, *Folsom Prison* was among my favorites because it also echoed the theme of people who were down on their luck and living a life that most of us could not imagine. On the lighter side, *A Boy Named Sue* always made me laugh, and only Johnny could make a tune like that a top-ten hit. So, when Johnny came to L'Enfant Plaza in downtown D.C. to perform at my fundraiser, needless to say I was most pleased and excited. I was just a young congressman at the time, and I think all of my guests who attended were taken with Johnny's friendliness and accessibility. He brought his entire family with him and stayed long after the performance to make sure he signed autographs and take plenty of photos with the guests who were there. You just can't take the Southern hospitality away even in Washington, D.C.

I am reminded of another concert when I was a lieutenant in the Tennessee Army National Guard. State Adjutant General Carl Wallace decided we would host a country music concert to entertain the Tennessee troops during their two-week annual training at Camp Shelby in Hattiesburg, Mississippi. The late Little Jimmy Dickens who was beloved and a good friend of the family would headline the show. The general arranged a National Guard plane to fly Little Jimmy and his band to the concert which turned out to be a great success.

But, when it was time for Little Jimmy to fly back to Nashville he didn't want to leave. He told me in no uncertain terms, "Bob, I'm not going home; I'm having such a good time here." He was enjoying visiting with the troops, and he wanted to continue listening to their personal stories as they visited later at the reception. That was quintessential Little Jimmy. He's always been a big hero of mine and an inspiration to millions of people around the world.

Another memorable moment in my life was the time when I nominated country music great—Eddy Arnold—for the most coveted award in the nation that recognizes people who have made a difference in the arts. To my delight, he won and Eddy was presented with the prestigious National Medal of Arts and Humanities Award at the White House by President and Mrs. Clinton on December 21, 2000. Mary and I were thrilled to share this great honor with him. Congress established the award in 1984 to honor promoters of the arts in the United States. Maya Angelou and Barbara Streisand were some of the early recipients. This was a special moment for me because Eddy and his wife, Sally, were great friends of ours.

Over the years I have attended many events where I was asked to say a few words, and sometimes, these events were in honor of some of Nashville's greatest artists like Loretta Lynn, Johnny Cash and Dolly Parton, to name just a few. Matter of fact, Dolly Parton has done tremendous work to promote Tennessee through her Dollywood theme park located in Sevier County, in East Tennessee. It did have some competition from Opryland, which was the popular theme park built right next to the Grand Ole Opry.

It used to be that when a visitor came to Nashville, they could walk out of the Grand Ole Opry Hotel and be right at the entrance to the theme park. This was great for tourism and many people, including me, were disappointed when it shut down. I've always felt that tourists didn't mind paying higher hotel and restaurant bills if they had access to other attractions. I was grateful for the help I received from Opryland, especially because of their generosity in providing summer jobs for the many students who contacted me when I was in Congress.

When the decision was made to close the theme park, the Nashville community, nevertheless, was proud and blessed to still have the Opryland Hotel, Grand Ole Opry, and the Ryman

Auditorium. After Bud's tenure, Colin Reed became chairman and CEO of Ryman Hospitality Properties. The continued growth that the company enjoys is due to Colin's leadership, along with his outstanding team. Back to Dolly Parton, someone I admire, having grown up poor in the mountains of East Tennessee, and coming up the hard way didn't deter her from the dreams she envisioned as a child. What they did have was a lot of love, closeness, and faith, and that helped her rise above her poverty and become one of the most successful business women in the country. As a songwriter her lyrics and music have truly touched people's heartstrings and mine for sure. As a business woman she was fair but tough as nails; her success speaks for itself. An example of her resolve was on display one time when we both were together for the dedication of a highway named in her honor, the Dolly Parton Parkway in East Tennessee.

My good friend, Mayor Gary Wade, who grew up in Sevierville, Tennessee, and later became the chief justice of the Tennessee Supreme Court, organized the event and was also a friend of Dolly's from his high school days, though his brother knew her better because they both played in the same band in high school. His brother Ken and I were ATO Fraternity brothers when we were students at the University of Tennessee. At the time I was on the Tennessee Valley Authority Board and Gary asked if I would say a few remarks at the ceremony. Matter of fact, Gary tells a funny story about Dolly that has stayed with him to this day. Her manager asked him if he wanted to say a few lines in her short-lived and not so well-written Thanksgiving variety show special back in 1987; Gary was happy to oblige.

They brought Dolly's trailer to the courthouse which was next to Gary's office, and there she told him that he would be playing her boyfriend. Rather than have him memorize his lines Dolly said, "Gary, these lines aren't that funny anyway so why don't we just do a quick conversation and wing it." So wing it they did. Dolly looked right into the camera and said: "Gary, I have so many fond memories of us riding together in your pick-up truck." Then she pointed to her newly svelte figure and said, "Now what do you think about this?" Gary, without missing a beat replied, "Dolly, I liked you more when there was more to love!" The headline the next day in the *Knoxville News Sentinel* in big bold print read, "Former Mayor Gary Wade said to Dolly Parton, 'I Liked you More When There was more to Love.'" Gary and I laugh about that to this day.

By the way, Gary took the non-paying job of mayor of Sevierville to get a better understanding between city and state governments and also to understand human nature better. He and I have agreed on many theories about human nature and politics. On one occasion we observed that in political campaigns one-third of people will support you, another one-third will oppose you, and the final one-third are people that you try to persuade to help or support you. Both of us in our careers have focused on that final group to win elections.

Gary and I both spoke at the dedication of the Dolly Parton Parkway. We all sat together as speakers and when it was my turn to speak I stood up and moved to the podium and said these words: "Dolly, be kind to those people as you climb the ladder of success because you will meet those same people on the way back down." When I sat down, she leaned over to me and in a very cute way said, "Bob, I'm not going down." We had a good laugh. I am not at all surprised at Dolly's success and she has continued to rise. She has influenced many generations of people through her music, films and philanthropy. In recent years she founded the Imagination Library whereby parents who enroll their newborns in the program receive a book called, *The Little Engine that Could.* This program encourages reading aloud to children and it has proven to increase early childhood literacy. I have always been so impressed with Dolly's accessibility and drive, and she has said that she traces that back to her inclusive family background.

"Anytime I get a big head, one of my family calls me down and reminds me where I come from. I stay grounded with the help of my family and husband, Carl Dean. All of them stay out of the limelight and live fairly normal lives," Dolly told me recently.

Matter of fact, Dolly shared her thoughts with me about that day. "I was honored by the naming of the Dolly Parton Parkway and the statue of the courthouse in Sevierville. Having your own people pay tribute is the highest of all honors. If they are willing to honor me, I should be willing to give back for my success."

One thing about Nashville that most people don't realize is that we are what I call a big small town. We're known all around the world as Music City U.S.A and a prime tourist destination, but the fact is, we pride ourselves on keeping our Southern roots and hospitality. I've tried throughout my career to not only help other people, but care about them, where they came from and where they want to go. I couldn't have done all of the things I have without strong mentors in my life. I always knew that if I were in a position of power I would try to do the same for others.

One example is Bart Herbison who worked for the governor of Tennessee, Ned McWherter, back in 1988. Bart recently told me that I was one of his mentors; I was flattered that he would consider me in that role. I never looked at myself as a mentor, but hope that the young people that I have worked with over the years can take away some of my better qualities instead of my weaknesses. I hired Bart to work for me as my press secretary when I was a member of Congress after his stint with the governor. As a former reporter he was perfect for the position. Bart is a lot of fun, and he is such a positive person which made it easier when schedules get hectic and travel demands dominate one's time. We became friends and are still very close to this day. When I was in Congress, I had a wonderful opportunity to attend an event that I knew would be a thrill of a lifetime for Bart. Bart like me was a country music fan, and he especially loved Elvis Presley. I wanted to surprise him and so I called and told him to meet me at Stevens Aviation in Nashville. He told me in no uncertain terms that I needed to stay in D.C. for a vote. I didn't tell Bart that I already voted, but said he needed to meet me ASAP because we were going to Memphis. He asked me if I were serious and I said, "Bart, I'm as serious as a heart attack!" To his surprise, we flew to Memphis, Tennessee, with Marvin Runyon, postmaster general of the United States. We were there for a ceremony dedicating the unveiling of the first U.S. Postal Stamp of Elvis Presley at Graceland. The room was filled with many notable people including city, county and state officials and many others. This event was truly a big deal. When Bart and I finally settled in we couldn't believe our eyes when we saw none other than Elvis' widow, Priscilla Presley. I asked her if she would sign our commemorative books that were given to every guest, and she very graciously agreed to do so. The Elvis stamp was issued on his birthday, January 8, 1993. Lisa Marie, the only child of Elvis was also in attendance. I am told that the Elvis stamp holds the record of being the best-selling commemorative postage stamp of all time. What an honor and thrill for me to be able to attend such a special event since the music of Elvis is embedded in my mind since childhood.

Today, Bart is the executive director of the Nashville Songwriters Association, and I am most proud of what he has accomplished in that role for the past eighteen years or so. When Bart took the job, the association was in serious financial trouble. Today their organization has 165 chapters around the country. Bart has always said, and I agree, that country music has always made people feel something. It makes us cry, think or act." But I am most proud of Bart for his mentorship of so many young singer/songwriters, and his willingness to listen to a song, or travel anywhere in the country to promote, protect, or defend the rights of these creative and talented Americans.

One of these Americans is Taylor Swift. Bart first met Taylor when she was fourteen years old. Her father, Scott Swift, brought her by to join the Nashville Songwriters Association International (NSAI). She played a few songs for Bart who noticed she was one of the most talented young songwriters he had ever met. On another visit to NSAI at age fifteen, already signed as the youngest songwriter with Sony ATV Music Publishing, Taylor played Bart songs that would soon become very well known and sell millions of copies, including "Tim McGraw," "Our Song," and "Picture to Burn." By 2015, Bart and NASI had presented Taylor their prestigious "Songwriter Artist of the Year" award.

Even though she has many Grammys to her name and is wealthy and famous around the world, she never lost her sense of balance and self. As Bart noted, "Taylor has been a big part of not just country music but the pop world, too. She has conducted herself with dignity, and she has very deftly dealt with issues head-on and with honesty and grace; politicians can certainly learn a lot from her in this regard."

Being a native son of Music City U.S.A. has been the greatest blessing any man could have. Even though I've traveled around the world as a member of Congress, and in my role as a volunteer civic education advocate and business executive, there is no place like my hometown of Nashville. I've always fought for the underdog and helped people rebuild their lives. Country music tells their everyday stories about the trials and tribulations of life. Country music is clearly the champion of the common man.

It is where I first heard Roy Acuff's band rehearsing on his boat next door to our house, Elvis' rousing gospel music at the governor's residence, and Johnny Cash strumming his guitar when he sang at one of my political events. I've laughed and cried in the audience at the Grand Ole Opry, and hung out backstage with the likes of Little Jimmy Dickens, Minnie Pearl, Loretta Lynn and Grandpa Jones. Sometimes when I am by myself, I can hear the words and music of my favorite country songs, and it is no exaggeration to say those lyrics have helped me in times of trouble and inspired me in the good times, as well. Like every American, and people from all around the world, country music is an art form that brings us all together, and has a special way of mirroring our emotions, and telling stories that resonate with our hearts and minds. I tip my hat to the artists and songwriters who have inspired me, and especially to Elvis who filled my young mind with curiosity and awareness. His words from *In the Ghetto* will live in my heart forever: "As the snow flies on a cold and gray Chicago mornin', a poor little baby child is born in the ghetto. And his mama cries, cause if there's one thing that she don't need it's another hungry mouth to feed, in the ghetto."

Clement's Contemplations

"If you're going to write a country music song and you're a politician, don't quit your day job."

"When taking a Russian Diplomat to the Opry make sure he wears a spacesuit."

"Country music is the soul of the people and the heart of the world."

"Even when they're down for the count, country music stars can still draw a crowd."

"Names don't mean a thing. Little Jimmy Dickens was as big as a man can get."

"Songwriters are artists whose words paint a picture of our shared hopes and dreams."

"Always ask a country music star to headline your political fundraiser. You will raise a heck of a lot of money and you're popularity will be legendary."

Chapter 9

THE REWARDS AND CHALLENGES
OF LAWMAKING

"Clement, you're nothing but a liberal; you said it,
now back it up!" Anonymous voter

I loved being a politician. No matter what people think about the profession today, to me it is and always will be a noble pursuit with its genesis in service. Politics has given me the opportunity to lead a purposeful life, to bring about positive change and to truly help people deal with their problems. While many Americans may be frustrated with their elected officials, and while politics is undeniably messy at times, it is still one of the hallmarks of our democracy and it's a career that can change lives for the better.

Despite the negative perception of politicians in general, I can say with great confidence that most people who enter public service are sincere. That being said, politicians are no better or worse than the society that elects them. They are a reflection of society. The American people are generally perceptive enough to know the difference between an elected official seeking to feed his or her ego, versus the one who truly wishes to serve the public. For me, having the opportunity to serve the people of Tennessee, from being elected to the Tennessee Public Service Commission, being a director of the Tennessee Valley Authority, president of Cumberland University, serving in the military and finally as a member of the U.S. House of Representatives, has fulfilled me. That was because the rewards have always outweighed any of the challenges or setbacks. Very few careers can have such a profound impact on improving the quality of life for all Americans. This is one of the most important messages I hope to leave with future generations: that politics and public service are still and always will be noble callings.

I am concerned that in today's destructive political climate, America's future leaders are turning their backs on politics. They do not realize how impactful and gratifying a life in public service can be. It's a job where no day is like the next, where you can help a constituent solve a problem, or protect the country from terrorists. Politics helps people in so many ways. I can honestly say that after spending my entire career in elected or appointed office, or as a volunteer in public service, I am humbled by having the opportunity to serve my fellow man and make a difference in their lives.

Today, the word politician has evolved into something less than honorable and decent, and unfortunately now it carries a negative stigma, which really pains me. The word politics actually comes from the Greek language and means "of, for and relating to citizens." My Aunt Anna Belle Clement O'Brien, who was among the most influential women in my life and served as a Tennessee State Senator, had a wonderful description of what politics means. She used to say, "Politics is a beautiful word to me. Politics builds roads and bridges. Politics educates our children and helps handicapped children walk. Politics builds schools. Politics is compromise!" I've never heard anyone quite express it that way, and I most likely never will again, but I've always tried to live by her words throughout my entire political career. Like many members of my family, Aunt Anna Belle had a winning personality, and she was for sure a people person of the highest degree.

Perhaps the greatest reward in politics is the opportunity to help people. There were many times that I was a constituent's last hope and resource, and I'm touched that even today, years after I left office, people still call and ask for my help. Others call to just thank me. Whenever I do get these calls I always consider it an honor and privilege and feel very humbled. I was extremely fortunate to serve in Congress with four Presidents including Ronald Reagan; George H. W. Bush; Bill Clinton; and George W. Bush during times when major legislative changes truly made the lives of Americans better. Sadly, today, regardless of Congress' achievements, they continue to get no respect as the late comedian Rodney Dangerfield used to say. Trying to convince the American public that members of Congress are mostly individuals who love this country and truly want to serve is an almost impossible feat. It is discouraging at times when people make comments such as, "All politicians are crooks," "They are only interested in themselves," or "They've all sold out." No other profession seems to get so little credit for doing a good job. Believe it or not, once upon a time we were rated above a used car salesmen, but now members of Congress are at the bottom of the barrel in terms of professions worth pursuing. Regardless, as a member of Congress, I had a lot of inner satisfaction that my efforts brought about positive change.

For example, during President Reagan's administration, we witnessed the fall of the Soviet Union and the end of the Cold War. During George H. W. Bush's presidency, we passed the Americans with Disabilities Act, which for the first time forbade discrimination against people with disabilities when it came to employment or transportation. We passed the Clean Air Act to cut down on smog and pollution. Congress also ratified a number of nuclear arms reduction treaties with Russia, which, eventually, helped us win the Cold War. During Bill Clinton's years in the White House, Congress helped people with legislation such as the Family and Medical Leave Act and our Student Loan Reform. We created a surplus, negotiated a balanced budget agreement and governed in a fiscally responsible manner. We created the Head Start Program to hold our school administrators and teachers more accountable. We passed Megan's Law, so that communities and parents had greater resources to keep their children safe from dangerous sexual predators, as well as passing the Brady Bill. Congress also put new standards in place to make our drinking water safe and to increase the standards for our food quality. We passed welfare reform and increased the minimum wage. We also helped American families by passing the Child Tax Credit and created a children's health insurance program or CHIP.

During President George W. Bush's administration, the main focus, of course, was 9/11, and we worked on the many pieces of legislation that needed to be passed to keep the homeland safe. In addition, we improved America's standard of learning, created a number of free trade agreements, modernized Medicare and Medicaid, and protected America's children by passing the Adam Walsh Child Protection and Safety Act. In addition, and this to me was especially rewarding, we put in place a number of benefits and safeguards for our veterans and military members. This is what I believe is the power of politics!

One of the bills I am most proud of is the Intermodal Surface Transportation Efficiency Act of 1991, of which I was an original co-sponsor. If you like riding your bicycle on bike trails, or having paths designated to take walks on public lands it is because of the way we drafted the bill. The legislation (ISTEA -pronounced Ice-Tea) is a great example of why politics and public service can positively affect the lives of Americans. We worked in a bipartisan manner to help rebuild America and keep our roads and bridges safe. By coming together as elected representatives rather than as democrats and republicans we created jobs and strengthened our infrastructure. For me personally, the bill was extremely gratifying, because we were able to include language to create greenways all over the country. To me, this was a quality of life issue, and every time I take a stroll on one of the greenways we created, I have to admit I feel like I made a difference. Believe it or not, the legislation came with some controversy because the road contractors fought us tooth and nail; no pun intended. They were worried about millions of federal dollars that should have gone into concrete instead going into nature trails. We argued successfully that in addition to this being a quality of life issue, the greenways were family-friendly and an environmentally sound policy. In addition to the road contractors, who wanted every federal penny to go toward building roadways, there also was some sizeable opposition from NIMBYs or not in my backyard! I was accused of all sorts of things, including wasteful government spending and creating unsafe zones with increased crime rates. But I strongly believe this legislation was worth sticking my neck out. Now in Nashville, due to public and private funds, we have more than 200 miles of nature-friendly pathways for residents and visitors to enjoy on a daily basis, and thousands of more miles across the entire United States.

A similarly rewarding political experience was witnessing President Clinton sign the International Religious Freedom Act of 1998 into law. The bill was passed to promote religious freedom as a foreign policy of the United States, thereby avoiding future conflicts with religion being the primary catalyst. I became a leader in drafting and negotiating this bill out of a very strong personal conviction that we were not holding other nations, even allies of ours, in any way accountable for the religious discrimination they were imposing on their people. What persuaded me to become involved in this issue was a meeting with then-President Hosni

Mubarak of Egypt. While the Pentagon was pumping millions of taxpayer dollars into Egypt in the form of military support and weaponry, Egypt was persecuting its Christian citizens. This issue became so important to me, that I had a full-time volunteer who worked on nothing else. It is truly wonderful to think that because of the good work of my staff, colleagues and organized coalitions, there are now some people around the world with greater freedom to practice their religious faith, regardless of whether that faith is Christian, Muslim, Jewish, Hindu, Buddhist or something else. My involvement with this cause, and my opportunity to speak with President Mubarak at the Blair House next to the White House about my concerns were made possible because I served on the International Relations Committee. Because of that committee I had the good fortune to learn about other cultures, countries and governments. In all of my legislative work, this exposure to other points of views and other experiences has always served me well.

The challenge, but also the reward, of passing legislation is that you are one of 435 voices in the House of Representatives. Other members of Congress had a tremendous influence on my life, both professionally and personally. Some of my best friends are former colleagues, and among them are probably as many republicans as there are democrats. I had the honor of serving with so many great and impactful legislators. Being around them and hearing their thoughts and ideas truly served as an inspiration to me. I came to Congress via a special election, so I didn't have a great number of other freshmen members to rely upon the way members do after a normal election is held.

But instead of feeling ostracized as either a democrat or a rookie, I felt welcomed by members from both sides of the aisle. When I left Congress in 2003, the political divide was much more palpable, but in recent years the divide has grown into the fissure that now defines Congress.

During my time in office, democrats and republicans could sit down together over lunch, before and after committee hearings and between votes. We could exchange ideas and thoughts freely without having to worry that being seen with someone from the other party would brand us as a traitor. I'm sure that there are still a number of democrats and republicans who get along well and are good friends, but that number certainly has dwindled over the years and is getting smaller with each election cycle. These friendships are so incredibly important, and without the level of trust that is founded upon personal relationships, how can members of Congress negotiate in good faith over very difficult and emotional issues? This gets me back to my earlier point: politics is based on being able to connect with people.

When I look at our politics today, I often wonder, "Who are our elected officials listening?" I don't think it's their constituents, because the perception is that today's politicians only seem to care about that small percentage of voters who turn up for their primaries. They're also not really hearing what their voters are saying as much as they pay attention to some super PAC or millionaire who doesn't even live in their district let alone their state. I even have my doubts that they listen to the expert witnesses who come before their committees to share facts and information. That's because many members of Congress can't even agree anymore on what constitutes a fact or a piece of information, so that committee hearings are more about grandstanding rather than education and fact-finding. I'm sorry to say that because of the vitriol in Congress, elected officials won't even listen to their colleagues from the other side of the aisle because having the wrong party label means your opinion automatically is wrong.

In our current political environment we've, unfortunately, developed a system where tunnel vision gets you elected and where politicians want to interact only with a mere ten percent of their constituents. Why? Because that's the ten percent who finance political campaigns and come out to vote on primary day. And more than that, we also have a system, thanks to gerrymandering and redistricting, where the people no longer choose their politicians, but rather the politicians get to choose their constituents. You want a district where your party is sure to get elected every two years? No problem, let's draw a line right here where the math tells us you will get elected no matter what. While all of these issues have negatively affected our politics today, I know first-hand how politics and politicians coming together can do great things. I am hopeful that someday politics in general will return again to a profession worthy of trust and respect.

Politics is one way to serve the public and public service is an honorable calling. But the current state of our political debate discourages the very notion that by entering politics you can do well for your community. I am extremely concerned that we are losing the next generation of America's leaders, not because they are not bright enough, but because they are unwilling to consider politics as their vocation. The young Americans I get to meet when I speak at colleges or high schools across the country are just as informed and engaged as previous generations. The difference is that they don't view Washington as the means for achieving great things, but rather as the obstacle toward achieving great things. One of my regrets from my congressional career is that I didn't accomplish creating a system of mandatory public service for young people. The law would have required them to serve his or her country for a specific period of time, either in the military, or in the Peace Corps, or some sort of domestic service. Giving the next generation some buy-in and getting them involved in service-oriented activities at a young age would also give them a sense of understanding of how our democracy works, what is involved and to what standard they should hold their elected officials.

Everyone should own a piece of the rock, so to speak, and feel accountable as citizens. In addition, for those who may be lacking focus or discipline, this would be a way to help them early on, rather than letting them slip through the cracks. I think this current generation has to deal with so many challenges and distractions and this is leaving them feeling alone and isolated. The whole notion of becoming involved in a larger group or for a larger purpose is lost on many of them. I believe that generally young people today are not joiners or so-called belongers. They don't join civic organizations or religious groups the way we used to when I was growing up. And this discomfort with being part of a larger cause translates directly into their attitudes toward politics. It breaks my heart when I hear young people say, "I hate politics," because to me it sounds like they are saying, "Democracy is dead." But given how politics tends to be in this volatile, partisan age, who could really blame them? No wonder so many young people are materialistic and individualistic, because everything that is thrown at them is geared in that direction. For example, we now communicate by typing out 140 characters on our phones and never have to look up from the screen to have a chat with someone. Combine that with what we are witnessing these days as part of our politics as usual, and you have to wonder where our next Abraham Lincoln or Jack Kennedy is going to come from.

I really think that our responsibility for engaging the next generation is to lead by example. Leading by example is one of the problems facing young people today. They watch our current political leaders behave like bullies and recalcitrant teens, not great leaders. They witness members of Congress who believe that dialogue and finding common ground are signs of weakness. Is that really how the American public should view our political leaders? I'm sorry to say that is what is playing out on Capitol Hill these days, and in a great number of our state capitals, on television, the internet and even more and more at the local government level.

For Congress specifically, I fear we are no longer as unified as previous generations and the rift is only getting worse. Through retirements and election losses, mainly during primaries rather than general elections, we have lost decades of institutional knowledge. We are not replacing retiring legislators with new members of Congress who operate with respect for Congress as an institution and know the process of legislating. The moderates from both sides of the aisle have been exchanged for extremists and hyper-partisan members. Members of Congress don't really know each other anymore, often they don't like each other and they certainly don't want to work together! A lot of the consensus-makers are long gone from Congress, including me. I always felt very comfortable working with other members of Congress on legislation because I never thought of them as political enemies, but rather as fellow representatives. When you listen to people, when you give them the courtesy of engaging in a respectful dialogue, they repay that courtesy in-kind. We are political beings and we certainly have strong views and opinions. And that is the way it is supposed to be. But listening and having a dialogue means you attack the issue, not the person and certainly not someone's honesty or integrity. Today's politicians have an almost impossible time finding common ground and solutions because there is no trust, no dialogue, no listening skills and for sure, no give and take. What we are truly lacking is political courage.

Politics also gets a bad rap from the many political ads that flood the airwaves especially during an election cycle. I can't blame anyone for wanting to change the channel when a political ad comes on TV – mostly the messages depict a candidate running *against* Congress rather than running *for* Congress. It seems that every candidate, and that includes incumbents, is running for Congress so that they can *fix* Congress. They want to go to Washington, but promise to spend as little time as possible in Washington. When I was there we worked from Monday through Friday. Now they fly in on Tuesday and fly out on Thursday. You don't know me and I don't know you. And, since we don't trust each other, why should we work together and try to find solutions? That's the result of the shortened congressional work week.

Can you imagine this scenario if you were interviewing for any other job? "I want to work here, but I really disrespect everything you do and stand for, and my main goal is to spend as little time at headquarters as possible." We have inherited from our Founding Fathers this tremendous gift of true participation and representation in our government. But, we have allowed the process and system to hijack this gift, to the point where it has deteriorated so much that I'm afraid they wouldn't recognize their own creation.

It seems to me that there are three main reasons causing the deterioration of our current political process: the money, the media and the primaries. All three were issues I, too, had to live with during my time in politics, but they have become tremendously amplified in recent years. This larger role they play in the lives of our current generation of politicians has led to a system that is near broken unless we make some changes soon. I don't hold our current members of Congress totally responsible though, because for the most part members chose to be public servants who come to politics for the exact same reason that led me to Capitol Hill: a desire to make our communities and country better, to help solve problems and to lead our nation into a healthy future. But what I do hold them responsible for is perpetuating a system that they know has become abused and is hurting our democracy. There are ways to fix what ails us, but it takes leadership and guts to make that happen.

There has always been a need for money in our politics. It takes money to run a successful campaign. You have to pay campaign staff, print flyers and other materials, buy advertising time on television and radio and keep campaign offices open. Depending on how competitive a campaign is, the more money you'll have to spend. Also, depending on where your district is, you may have very expensive TV markets where thirty-seconds of advertising time becomes very costly. Of course, a statewide campaign for office is much more expensive than a race for a single congressional U.S. House seat. Political campaigns have become outrageously expensive. We have truly gotten to the absurd stage of candidates trying to buy an election, rather than earning one. Candidates are spending more of their time raising money than meeting people, organizing, making speeches and sharing their message. I have come to the conclusion that we must have limits on campaign spending. If it means public financing of congressional campaigns to get around recent U.S. Supreme Court decisions, we may have no other choice. U.S. citizens are voting less and getting involved in politics less. Our citizens are shying away from running for political office because it is too costly, too risky, and too dangerous. This is not healthy for democracy and our way of life.

Over the years, campaigns have become more and more expensive. By the time I ran for the U.S. Senate in 2002, I spent ninety percent of my time fundraising, the main activity for any political candidate; this is outrageous! In addition, raising more dollars has an impact on the number of staffers, offices, media visibility, and so forth that you have to maintain in order to win. Political campaigns have literally become an industry in and of themselves, with consultants, experts, analysts and pollsters that every campaign has to employ. The days of running for Congress from your kitchen table with the help of family and friends are long over.

What changed exponentially are the sources of funding, and the fundraising requirements that are put upon each member of Congress by their party and leadership. And, unfortunately, the U.S. Supreme Court, with two recent decisions, has made it almost impossible now to reverse course. In 2010, *Citizens United vs. The Federal Election Commission*, the Supreme Court held essentially that corporations, unions, trade associations and any other group have the same freedom of speech rights as an individual. They, therefore, cannot be limited in the way they donate money to political causes and political issues.

This decision has opened the floodgates when it comes to campaign contributions and has created PACs that no longer are held responsible for how much they spend and how vile their campaign advertising. The other 2014 Supreme Court decision, *McCutcheon vs. The Federal Election Commission*, took this notion one destructive step further and struck down all limits on federal campaign donations. Now the notion of a single vote per citizen is completely moot because the richest Americans can outspend everyone else without limitation. In addition to the malignant effect these two decisions had on campaign financing, they also had a tremendous effect on who will run for political office. More and more of them will either come from great personal wealth, or have connections to great amounts of money.

Money for congressional campaigns used to come primarily from someone's district or state, because that was one way their constituents could ensure that the voice they supported could make it all the way to Washington. Today, few congressional campaigns can survive on the accumulated ten dollar checks their constituents might send in the mail. Instead, candidates turn to PACs, those political action committees that bundle vast amounts of money to support candidates based often on a single issue. If a PAC is opposed to gun control, they will spend money all over the country in support of candidates who will stand up to gun control activists. And candidates who might be complete lunatics on every other single issue affecting our nation will pocket a huge check because they have an opinion on one single issue that might never come up for a vote anyway. Other PACs dole out the cash of a single millionaire or a group of extremely wealthy individuals who will pick candidates across the nation to form a large enough voting block in Congress, either for or against a certain policy. The anti-tax crowd is a perfect example of that. A candidate for office has to make one simple pledge – never to raise taxes under any circumstances – and he or she will receive financial support no matter how extreme or dangerous their positions. I am astonished by candidates making this reckless pledge.

In addition to where the money now comes from, there also has been a change for what is expected of members of Congress. Leadership positions and committee assignments are no longer determined based on experience and expertise, but rather on how much money they brought in as a fundraiser. And there even is an unspoken quota system, where members of Congress are held accountable within the party for raising a certain amount of money every quarter. These are elected representatives, sent to Washington to represent the people and to govern, and they are being held accountable and publicly shamed in front of their peers into raising large amounts of money for the party. This is ridiculous!

I don't think there is something inherently wrong with political fundraising, by the way. I have spent untold hours doing so. I believe if someone wants to support you and views you as his or her voice in Washington, then they should be able to help you. That help can come by volunteering for your campaign or writing a check, as long as we instill rules for full disclosure and limitations on campaign spending. But, clearly, the system is being abused. I would say there are some simple fixes that could help change this, such as the requirement that a percentage of monies raised comes from within either the district or the state. Also, we need to limit the amount of money a candidate can contribute to his own campaign, because we are giving an unfair advantage to the super rich. You cannot limit and control the flow of money from outside groups without also limiting the amount of money coming from the candidate; otherwise only well-to-do candidates would have a realistic chance of winning a campaign.

What it boils down to is that all of this money freely flowing into our political campaigns is distorting and hijacking our political process. And there's another thing I would surely address about our political system, and that is manners and decorum or a lack thereof.

I always attended the State of the Union Address on the floor of the U.S. House of Representatives, because I believed it was my responsibility as the elected representative of the 5th District of Tennessee. I came to hear the President speak as he laid out his plans and initiatives for the country. I did this for every President during my time in Congress, no matter which party the president belonged. I find it not only distasteful, but also highly disrespectful for members of Congress to be sitting in the House Chamber and tweeting their every comment and thought during the State of the Union Address. Or what was even worse, talking to other members, chewing gum, falling asleep or yelling at the top of their lungs. As parents, we would be outraged if our children tweeted during their history classes, but we cheer a member of Congress who tweets during the President's message about the health and future of our country. That is nonsensical!

I certainly believe strongly that the office of the President of the United States should be held in the highest regard and respected, especially by elected officials such as members of Congress. They may disagree with the President's initiatives but that does not give them license to demonize the office holder and sink to such lows as name-calling personal insults. We have let our politicians get away with launching the most outrageous personal attacks and this makes our country weaker and undermines our position in the world.

But regardless of all the problems with our politicians today, being a member of Congress was among the best experiences of my life.

One of the greatest thrills of my very young congressional career was meeting President Ronald Reagan even though we were from different parties. I won my first congressional election at the height of Iran-Contra, when the Reagan administration was explaining to Congress how the proceeds of illegal arms sales to Iran (via Israel) were used to fund the anti-communist rebels in Nicaragua. I had won my seat through a special election because the incumbent, Congressman Bill Boner, was elected mayor of Nashville. I was the new kid on the block, and I guess the White House thought I'd be a willing supporter and was in awe of the President of the United States. So about a week after I took the oath of office in January, 1988, the phone rang in my office and it was the White House inviting me to meet with President Reagan. Just to show how inexperienced I was, I took a cab all by myself to the White House, and I walked into the Oval Office with not a single staffer accompanying me. And there was President Reagan and General Colin Powell who at that time was National Security Advisor. There were another ten or so senior staffers, and there I was sitting across from them all by my lonesome. President Reagan was cordial and nice, and at the end of a very long and very pleasant conversation about Iran-Contra he asked me whether he could count on my support. I explained to him that while I did want to work with him and support him on a number of issues, this was one vote where I simply could not join his side. I also explained that as an army veteran, I had concerns about the way our military was being used in support of the Contras, and that we were getting entangled in a war of attrition and containment. I voted, no. The Contras quit fighting because they were not being paid to fight. Shortly thereafter, the people of Nicaragua voted the communist-inspired Sandinista's out of power. The rest is history.

We shook hands and left it at that. On a number of other occasions we did work together. Somewhere along the way President Reagan discovered that my wife, Mary, had worked for a republican member of Congress in her early-to-mid-twenties. When we attended the White House Christmas Gala that the President and First Lady hosted for members of Congress, President Reagan leaned over and whispered in Mary's ear, "Mary, talk to Bob about switching from democrat to republican." In late 1994, the republicans actually did court me pretty heavily about switching parties; I stood my ground.

My point is that even though politically President Reagan and I certainly came from different sides of the aisle, we never let our political differences deteriorate the respect we had for each other, and the recognition that for the good of the country we could find plenty of things on which to work together. In the spirit of you win some, you lose some, we could part cordially on the issues where we just couldn't find a compromise, yet keep our relationship intact so that future opportunities to find common ground would be preserved. I really don't think that our current members of Congress and the White House have left themselves open for that kind of give and take.

One reason for that is because of the media becoming so polarized, as I said before. Our elected officials communicate in sound bites, and the only way you get some exposure is by saying something derogatory about your opposition. Not the best way to keep your friends.

We are blessed to have the First Amendment in our constitution, though our resolve to protect the freedom of speech has been tested often during our nation's history. Just imagine the pressure the journalists and editors of the *Washington Post* were under during the Watergate investigation. But we are fortunate that our courts and our society have always been protective of our right to state our opinions freely. And that is the way it should be. However, have we really sunk so low as a society that only those shouting loudly with a message we agree with one hundred percent are worth listening? Can't we be more discerning where and from whom we get our information? Today, in order to fill massive amounts of air-time, every network employs pundits whose job it is to interpret, not always report the news. In my opinion, I would like to see more engaged and informed citizens who can make decisions themselves based on unbiased reporting. While it takes a bit more time to make our own interpretations, I believe it is healthier for our form of government.

We for sure cannot prohibit media outlets from filling the airways with political commentary, sometimes barely veiled as journalism and independent reporting. In my opinion, we need to bring back the moderate voice in journalism with a balanced point-of-view reflecting the majority of the American people. This is evidenced by the losses of moderate democrats and republicans across the country, especially in their primaries. I have no problem with the left or the right being represented, but I think more balance is needed. Members of Congress need to participate if they want to be seen as current, plugged in and influential. They tweet their every thought, and their followers dutifully gobble it up. And they have no problem acting out on the U.S. House floor, even when the President of the United States comes to visit!

Members of Congress also need to take responsibility here. It is too simple to claim they are just the victims of the system when they are also contributors and beneficiaries. We have far too many members who think political discourse comes in thirty-second sound bites and that a debate should be conducted through the media rather than in personal meetings, during committee hearings or in the House Chamber. The answer is simple: stop feeding the beast! There is no need to send out a tweet every thirty-seconds accusing the president of this, the speaker of that, and opponents of everything in-between. When doing interviews, how about actually engaging in a discussion on the issues that affect all of us, instead of wasting air time on the exact same three talking points that some pollster determined might play well during the next primary?

If someone were a republican, they shouldn't be afraid of MSNBC, and if they were a democrat they might give Fox News a try. Hearing the other side's points of view, truly analyzing their arguments and responding in a partisan yet level headed manner, is actually what the Founding Fathers envisioned when they created Congress in the same document that also gave us the First Amendment. This country and our system of government are founded on compromise and debate. The location of our nation's capital was the result of a compromise. The fact that we have a Senate as well as a House of Representatives was the result of the Great Compromise. The responsibilities given to state governments through the federal government was the result of a compromise. The powers the executive branch has, and how they are monitored by the legislative branch was the result of a compromise. I am often amazed how the same political crowd that opposes dialogue and common ground most of the time will misquote our Founding Fathers to hammer home their point.

There are many brave men and women in history who risked it all and paid the ultimate price for their political beliefs. Our Founding Fathers would surely have been tried for treason and executed had we lost the Revolutionary War. You need to be awfully thick skinned to get into politics, that's for sure.

I remember one particular incident when as a member of Congress I got a real earful. It was a Sunday morning and I was home in Nashville for the weekend. My family and I were at church and the morning service had just ended. As we said our goodbyes to neighbors and friends I excused myself to use the restroom. There I was, as vulnerable as a man can get, when this agitated fellow walked into the restroom and headed straight for me! I had just enough time to finish my business and pull up my zipper when he said to me: "You're nothing but a liberal," to which I replied, "You said it, now back it up!" I don't know what was more shocking, the fact that this exchange was taking place in my church, or that it was taking place in the men's room! It took me about a second to regain my composure and I very calmly said: "Yes, I certainly am a democrat, and there are probably a number of issues where I am more liberal than others, but which position of mine exactly has upset you so much?" In other words, I asked him to get beyond the political label and actually explain to me where our points of view were so dramatically different that he needed to accost me at church and in the bathroom no less. Turns out he couldn't name a single issue or position of mine where he had heard me specifically taking an extreme position. He probably had started his morning reading some newspaper or seeing something on television where he thought those damn democrats in Congress were running the country into the ground. Then, when he saw his democrat congressman in church, he seized the opportunity to share his point of view. There was nothing wrong with that at all, though next time I would prefer a different venue. To the gentleman's credit, when he saw me the following Sunday he came up to me – not in the men's room this time – and apologized. My point is that he was thinking in labels, was painting me with one huge political brush, and he probably could have found lots of issues where we were in near agreement if only he had moved beyond calling me what he thought was a derogatory and insulting name – liberal!

This anecdote, unfortunately, describes where we are now when it comes to our elections. Our elections are label driven. Most voters cast their vote not for a candidate necessarily, but for the d or r label. Traditionally, voters turn out in the greatest number for a Presidential election rather than the congressional midterms. They have formed an opinion about which candidate for President will receive their vote and then, because often they really don't know much about any other candidate on the ballot, they blindly vote the party label. Since most congressional districts are drawn to favor one party over the other, the general election, particularly during a non-Presidential midterm cycle, is of little consequence since the winner is predetermined in the party primary election.

If a district is solidly republican, then the winner of the republican primary will win the general election and vice-versa for democrats. The primary election rather than the general election, therefore, is where the voter actually has somewhat of a say. Yet, only about five-to-ten, at most fifteen percent of eligible voters bother to participate in the primary election. And that gets us right back to the influence of labels rather than substance. In our current political system, primaries are fought over whose party label is more stellar. Inside the beltway we often refer to RINOs and DINOs – republicans in name only and democrats in name only. The theory is that if you are not completely in line with conservative or liberal thinking on every single issue, you are not truly a republican or democrat. What's the point of debating an issue if you are just electing mouthpieces who will simply mirror whatever Rush or Rachel tells them? On the republican side, the RINOs —employed a purity test that conservative republicans have even applied to their own members who are suspected of harboring a moderate thought. This debate involves mainstream republicans versus TEA Party candidates.

On the democratic side, the same is true for liberals, blue dog democrats, and new democrats. Candidates from these subgroups now have to advocate to just a small percentage of their party rather than all voters of their party. In other words, success depends on how many voters from these subgroups a candidate can rally to come out on primary day. Money is poured into convincing the subgroups that you are one hundred percent in line with their thinking on one hundred percent of the issues. An individualistic approach is shunned, and group think prevails. That is today's primary system, and that is why we have more and more elected officials unwilling to stray even one inch from the fringe group's party line.

When I talk to current members of Congress, they tell me that they used to focus on the general election and that was what they worried about. How will I stack up against a challenger from the other party? How can I highlight my differences and the differences of my party versus the other candidate's party? Where might my record get attacked by the other party? What votes have I cast that the other party's candidate could use against me? These days the primary is what they are most worried about. Now they question, was I conservative or liberal enough to avoid having someone from my own party run against me in the primary? Did I do enough to convince the ultra-conservatives or the ultra-liberals in my party to vote for me in the primary? Are there super PACs out there across the nation that might fund a primary opponent against me based on one single vote out of the hundreds I've cast since the last election?

That's not to say that general elections can't get pretty rough also. I remember during one of my campaigns a man coming up to me who kept focusing on the fact that I was vertically challenged. He said, "I can't vote for you because you are too short," and knowing the real reason for his putting me down was that he was a strong republican. I said that's interesting because I admired Howard Baker and the two of us are approximately the same height and it certainly never kept him from becoming the Senate Majority Leader, White House Chief of Staff and later the U S Ambassador to Japan. On another occasion I was called, Little Bob, to which I immediately replied, "I accept that characterization as long as you understand that I represent all the little people of Tennessee!" I also put little Bob on the side of my campaign truck and he never used that derogatory comment on me again. Not having learned the lesson, on another occasion one of my opponents called me a wimp, and I immediately responded, "I believe what you are saying is that I'm going to 'Win In Most Precincts.'"

Anyone reading my story, probably has a general interest in politics, but I wonder how many have actually voted in more than one primary? My guess is, not that many. With election day traditionally being held during the week, casting a vote means either missing some work, going very early in the morning or taking care of voting after work around dinnertime. That's why, historically, the United States has a much lower voter turnout than most other democracies – all of which schedule their election day on a weekend. It requires some effort to cast a vote in this country. In Tennessee, to encourage a higher voter turnout, we implemented early voting, which I supported. I thought this would help democrats, but it turns out republicans have done a better job of organizing and getting out the vote through early voting.

And the very lowest voter turnout occurs for party primary elections to determine each party's candidate going into the general election. In Tennessee, these primaries tend to happen in late summer. Since gerrymandering has already pretty much determined which party will win the general election, the only time American voters have a real choice about their representative in Congress is during the primary.

Who, then, participates in the process and actually bothers to show up during a congressional midterm primary? Usually, it is those people who feel so strongly about an issue or a candidate that they can be counted on to show up. So what is a candidate for office going to do to get elected? Make sure that their voters are energized, agitated, and ready to fight it out and then make sure they show up on primary day. That's where you get the extremists who advocate to a hyper-partisan crowd in order to win the party's seat going into the general election. Of course, this doesn't happen for every seat and for every election, but it has happened more and more during the past few cycles so that we now have some members of Congress who truly are on the extreme fringe of their party.

A number of states have taken a look at this and have come up with some reforms that deserve time and study to see whether they can make a difference. For example, in Iowa, districts are drawn by a non-partisan commission rather than by a state legislature controlled by one party or the other. The districts become more competitive and there is less of a certainty that a democrat or a republican is a safe bet. Another example is California where there is an open primary, meaning all candidates for office, regardless of party label, run against each other and then the top two candidates move on to the general election. Also, there have been a number of respected experts on elections who advocate moving our election day to a weekend rather than a week day. That certainly would increase voter turnout and get more people engaged in the political process.

I became well known in Congress as someone who wanted to reach across the aisle, even though I am a democrat. But to be an effective member of Congress you need to work together, as I've said. For example, my good friend, John Kasich, Governor of Ohio, a former member of Congress, and a 2016 Presidential candidate and I worked together on many budget issues and we had a terrific relationship. He was chairman of the Budget Committee when I was one of its members. In fact, he visited Nashville recently and told a group of reporters at his press conference, "Bob and I had our differences but we reached across the aisle on many budget issues that benefitted the country and believe it or not, we actually worked to balance the budget." John Kasich is a great example of a leader who always puts his country first and did not participate in petty partisan politics. He was a master at reaching across the aisle because of his vast experience as a congressman and governor.

Serving as a member of Congress was the most challenging and the most rewarding experience of my professional life. I would be lying if I said I wouldn't change a thing, but every day, whether I was legislating or campaigning, it was always interesting and exciting. I am privileged to have served in the House of Representatives for fifteen years. But the U.S. House I served in, and the campaigns I was involved have changed so much in the past few years. I've tried to address some of the main causes of this change and how they have contributed to our current, dysfunctional political gridlock. I've also tried to suggest some solutions, or at least some general ideas worth thinking and talking about.

How can we get more people to run for political office and get voters involved more in the process?

The only real solution is by re-engaging America's voters. We have a history of more than 200 years of representative government. Like few other places on this planet and in mankind's history, we are blessed to live in a country that empowers citizens and offers us choices and participation. However, the system only works if we safeguard it and if we live up to the responsibilities that come with citizenship. At the very minimum, Americans need to educate themselves about the issues and the candidates running for office, then make the concerted effort to vote. That is the absolute lowest standard that each of us has to meet, participate in our representative process by actually showing up for primaries and general elections! There are other democracies that have a voting requirement and a citizen may be fined for not showing up on election day. In Australia, for example, people are subject to a fine of about twenty-five dollars for not having their names crossed off at a local polling station on election day; Chile does the same.

All Americans should know how important primaries are versus the general election and have their voices heard through their vote. And, if candidates for office had a real expectation that fifty percent of eligible voters will turn out for a primary, they would be forced to run mainstream campaigns that go well beyond convincing just the extreme wings of their parties to vote for them. Simply showing up in great numbers for a primary election will have an immediate impact on the types of candidates who run and get elected. If citizens are hoping for mainstream, compromise-seeking candidates, then they should never hand over that power of choice to the hyper-partisans of both parties.

The other very easy thing we all can do right now is turn off the network pundits. Walk away from all the mouthpieces that make a very good living getting one side of the political spectrum riled up against the other. Let's hold our journalists to the highest possible standard where news is actually news, not editorial interpretation. These hour-long diatribes are on the air only because they have enough viewers and high enough ratings to be of interest to advertisers. Once the demand subsides, the supply shrinks. There absolutely is a place for partisan advocacy on our airwaves, but not if it is veiled as news and journalism. If we stop tuning in, then members of Congress and other elected officials also will no longer have a reason to populate these shows and use them as their personal soapboxes.

We all should be willing to go beyond simply voting, and reclaim some of the ground we have lost in our democratic process. Putting our energy and efforts toward real change and starting a nationwide conversation about the role money plays in our politics should be a goal. Let's discuss what system we can put in place that eliminates the need for candidates to raise millions of dollars. And while that goal may take a while to reach, one thing we can immediately demand is transparency from every candidate and from every PAC. There is no good reason why a candidate for office or a PAC should be allowed to keep the names and dollar amounts of their supporters' secret. Every dollar should be accounted for and should be publicized. Americans should know who pays for their representative's campaign and how much it is they are contributing.

The long and short of it is that the voter ultimately has the power. That is how our system is set up, and that is the tremendous gift we received from the Founding Fathers. We all really have the power to demand better and set a higher standard our candidates and elected representatives should meet. We have the power to hold the media accountable for what they report and how they report it, and to select who we send to Washington. They give the people power by being a true representative for all their constituents, not just a small percentage.

The greatest reward of being a lawmaker is giving that resounding voice to the people who put us there. The challenge is keeping it alive and well.

Clement's Contemplations

"Don't vote for the designer label; it's who is wearing it that counts."

"It is irresponsible to make blanket pledges, such as never to raise taxes."

"Ronald Reagan was one of the nicest and most difficult men to have to say no to."

"Institutional knowledge averts costly mistakes."

"When you use the Church restroom, lock the door!"

"Paying it forward pays off."

"Vote with your heart, not with your wallet."

"Money is the Achilles Heel of Politics."

"If you want a friend in Congress, get a pit bull."

"You can survive Ebola but Potomac Fever will kill you."

Chapter 10

THE SECRETS OF GREAT LEADERS

"I will leave you a rich name; but not a rich
pocketbook"—Governor Frank G. Clement

My life has been one of great privilege. Not the privileged
existence of a billionaire's son or the heir to the British throne.
No, I am referring to the privilege that comes with being in the
presence of some of the nation's and the world's most renowned
and influential leaders. Whether presidents, kings or convicts,
each in their own way has taught me valuable lessons about
integrity and leadership. Even at the tender age of nine-years-
old when Dad began taking me to all of his campaign stops
I was beginning to see how people reacted to someone with
charisma and tremendous oratory skills. As the years went by
and I matured I gained my own experience as an adult. I formed
in my mind important parameters as to what makes a great
leader. While applying these lessons to all seven of my different
careers and over thirty years of public service, I am appreciative
that each person the good Lord brings into my life is there for a
reason, a season or a lifetime.

There have been many studies on what makes a great leader and
I have read a number of them. But one simple Proverb—13:20NIV
to me says it best. "He who walks with the wise grows wise."

In my years of public service I hope that I also have grown wise along the way.

I was fortunate to meet some of the country's most respected leaders including Harry Truman, Dwight Eisenhower and John F. Kennedy, among many others. I vividly remember, even at a young age, why these impressive men made such an impression on me. Harry Truman had a good sense of humor, John F. Kennedy great charisma and Dwight Eisenhower a strong and dynamic presence. Then, as my own career progressed and I made my way from Nashville to Washington, D.C. I got to know many other influential leaders who possessed both position power and personal power. Some of them such as Former House Speaker Jim Wright, Presidents, Jimmy Carter, Ronald Reagan, George H. W. Bush, Bill Clinton, George W. Bush and Barack Obama; each had their own leadership styles and different ways of governing. Each had a career that included great triumphs as well as the type of failures that would have debilitated lesser men. Great leaders face adversity head on and view failure not as a personal crisis, but as an opportunity to learn and grow.

In fact, in an article written for the American Management Association, Robert Hewes, PhD, outlined the top-ten characteristics that make a good leader. Some of them include: being results oriented; having vision and a strategic focus; asking questions; dealing effectively with conflict; making high quality decisions; being a trusted leader; getting work done through others; and being an incredible communicator. Most of these qualities I have observed in the leaders I have met and worked with over the years.

America has become the greatest nation in the history of mankind for a number of reasons. We are blessed with an abundance of natural resources that helped us grow our country; two large oceans that serve as a natural protective border while other countries – particularly in Europe – learned that their borders are just arbitrary lines drawn on a map. But more than that, we have human capital—great leaders like our Founding Fathers who sacrificed so much to create a nation founded on freedom and liberty for everyone. Our military has shed blood for those freedoms. The thousands of stark white crosses and Stars of David at Arlington National Cemetery serve as a reminder that we have been willing to die for the fundamental principles that make our nation great.

Since our Founding Fathers decided to risk it all, their privileged existence as well as their lives, America has been able to develop inspirational leaders who stepped to the forefront when the nation was in peril. Whether it was Jefferson drafting the Declaration of Independence, Lincoln keeping the Union intact, Roosevelt and Truman battling the evils of Fascism, Dr. Martin Luther King, Jr. fighting for civil rights, Golda Meir, the iron lady of Israel, Kennedy staring down Khrushchev over Cuba, or Reagan winning the Cold War, we have witnessed inspirational leadership, vision, integrity and courage. This leadership is akin to a natural resource that we were able to discover, nurture and harness for the good of the country. What do these great leaders have in common? In essence, history thrust them into a time of adversity and extraordinary circumstance, and they met the crisis head on. They faced it and through courage, vision and determination, led our country through the perilous time so that we could emerge a stronger and better nation. They all had common character traits, among them honesty, vision, a sense of humor, decisiveness, preparation and a willingness to listen to others. They were goal-oriented and driven. No matter how great the obstacle they refused to be defeated.

One of my favorite subjects in school has always been history, particularly American history. As soon as I had mastered the skill of reading I devoured history books as my favorite past time. By reading about people who did remarkable things, like Thomas

Jefferson, I could just image him sitting by candlelight in the Assembly Room in Independence Hall in Philadelphia, putting pen to paper – or rather quill to parchment – and drafting the Declaration of Independence. First, what vision he must have had to put into words why the colonies had a right to break away from the crown and create their own destiny as an independent nation. He imagined a country where the citizens, through an experiment called democracy, would determine their leaders and their path. As a student of history I always wondered what it would be like to be able to have a conversation with some of these inspirational leaders.

What would I ask Thomas Jefferson given the opportunity? I certainly would want to learn more about those days and nights he spent drafting the Declaration of Independence, and putting into words the notion that the colonies, part of the greatest empire of its time, greater perhaps than the Roman Empire, had a right to self-govern. That meant giving citizens the power to determine their country's destiny based on the notion that men (and much later women) may participate in government by choosing their representatives and leaders. How had he become so convinced of his vision of a self-governing citizenry that he was willing to risk it all – life, liberty and everything he owned – to make that vision a reality? And then I would want to ask him about his relationship with John Adams and how their conflicting visions of democracy led to a falling out that they almost took to their graves. It turns out that they renewed their friendship later in life, but both died within hours of each other on July Fourth, 1826. While Jefferson believed in a hands-off federal government where individual states' rights trumped the powers of the federal government, Adams framed his presidency within the notion of a strong, centralized federal government dictating overall policy to the states.

Within a few short years of winning its freedom, our nation was thrust into its first crisis because of conflicting visions of its leaders.

Abraham Lincoln's challenge, among others, was the conflict between a centralized government and individual states' rights. That is, of course, the root cause of our Civil War. Slavery was the catalyst for the war, but what caused Southern states to secede was the question of the federal government's power to dictate to individual states whether they may or may not be slave states. Lincoln's leadership was severely tested like few others in our nation's history. Not only did he have a vision and conviction about the importance of our union, he also had a decisiveness and resolve that preserved our United States for future generations. I think of Lincoln as one of our history's leaders who combined all the attributes that I believe are important for leadership: honesty, vision, humor, decisiveness, preparation, a willingness to listen to others and surrounding yourself with talented people who are not yes-men. Given the opportunity, I would ask him about his cabinet, made up almost entirely of political rivals who had opposed and denounced him on his way to the White House. Lincoln was a man of faith, and he certainly turned the other cheek when he made his political opponents his closest advisors. By the time of his assassination, Lincoln's leadership had turned most of his former rivals into trusted allies and close supporters. They had signed on to his vision of a restored union and were engaged in his deliberations when it came to dealing with a defeated South. I wonder how different reconstruction would have been had it been led by Lincoln and not his successor Andrew Johnson. Johnson was a Southerner and former governor of Tennessee, whose loyalty to the union was never in question, but who none-the-less could never win the trust of Lincoln's cabinet.

I would add one more former president to my imaginary conversation with great American leaders and that would be

Dwight Eisenhower. I would ask him about leading the D-Day invasion during World War II. Like Jefferson and Lincoln, Eisenhower was a man of vision. His courage and conviction that he was setting the right course for our nation was tested like few others. Despite many leading voices to the contrary, Eisenhower picked Normandy, France as the best location for the invasion. He knew that countless lives and the eventual success or failure of his war effort rested on his decision. He was denounced by much bigger egos (British Field Marshal Bernard Montgomery certainly comes to mind) as lacking military understanding and dooming the allies to failure, but he stood by his decision and prepared the greatest military invasion in the history of mankind.

I would love to talk with him about those last few weeks of preparation, where the weather, timing and location all seemed to conspire against success. It would be a tremendous lesson to hear how he handled the burden of leadership, the certain knowledge that huge success as well as terrible failure all rested on his shoulders. When he settled on Normandy as the invasion location, how much time did he spend considering the catastrophic effect it would have on the war effort should the Germans succeed in keeping the allies off the beaches? How lonely a night was the evening of June fifth, knowing that the next morning could decide the outcome of World War II? These questions are very near and dear to my heart because unlike the Revolutionary War and the Civil War, World War II happened in my lifetime. I grew up with men whose lives were changed forever by their experiences on the battlefields of Europe and the Pacific.

When I was growing up I had a sense, though probably not an appreciation, of the fact that I had a front-row seat to history in the 1950s and 1960s in the south. I remember how excited I was when I got to meet great leaders, such as Presidents Truman, Eisenhower and Kennedy, as well as the Reverend Dr. Billy Graham. I remember when President Kennedy came to Tennessee to speak at Vanderbilt University in May 1963 to give the school's ninetieth convocation address. My father hosted a luncheon at the governor's residence and I had the honor of offering the opening prayer. In my mind Kennedy was another example of a great leader. President Kennedy was one of those men who simply walked into a room and people paid attention. He and my father had a lot in common. They were from the same generation of new democratic leaders, having been born within three years of each other. They both served their nation during World War II, my dad in the army and Kennedy in the navy. They were charismatic leaders who had a vision for America that accepted the reality of the Cold War and appreciated America's responsibility in the free world. My father had been helpful to the Kennedys during JFK's first primaries in 1960. One reason Kennedy was in Tennessee in May of 1963 was to shore up Dad's support for his reelection campaign. But what was really interesting about that visit was Kennedy's focus on the possibility of being a one-term president. I remember clearly that Kennedy spent a lot of time in private with my father. He asked him about his experience leaving the governor's residence after his second term ended in 1959 when my father was only thirty-nine-years-old. While never admitting so publicly for even one second, privately Kennedy was extremely concerned that he would not be reelected to a second term.

My father's experience really interested Kennedy and he turned the conversation back to 1959 numerous times. Now, in hindsight, those conversations gave me an insight into Kennedy's soul. The great lesson in leadership, and no matter what his innermost thoughts regarding his reelection, Kennedy portrayed a sense of self-confidence to outsiders. He'd never allow his doubts and the possibility of failure to seep through to his supporters and distractors. They would have been shocked to learn that he even for a second, thought about losing his re-election campaign because of racial unrest and labor problems.

As a young man these great American leaders from history inspired me so much. As my own political career unfolded, I came into contact with many other leaders whose commitment and devotion to a cause or their country served as a lesson. I would definitely put Presidents Ronald Reagan and Bill Clinton into that category.

And, of course, great leadership is not confined to America's shores. I met many international leaders who I admire such as Nelson Mandela when he addressed a Joint Session of Congress, Mother Theresa when she came to Washington for the National Prayer Breakfast, and Shimon Peres and Yitzhak Rabin when I visited Israel. All of them were great leaders of their times. They sacrificed for their ideals and vision, showed courage and stood up to adversity. None of them was afraid of controversy. They met history's challenges head on. They were sometimes discouraged, but never defeated.

I believe great leadership is based on a number of attributes. Most importantly, an effective leader needs to have honesty and integrity. It used to be that a handshake was all you needed to know a deal was sealed, and that's the way I believe it ought to be. Also, leaders have a vision and a way to communicate that vision. They bring people along and inspire a loyal following. Often, part of the ability to communicate is having a sense of humor. Abraham Lincoln loved telling stories and jokes, for example, and both Presidents Reagan and Clinton were extremely quick-witted and could put you at ease with an unexpected remark. Great leaders are also decisive people who can weigh the pros and cons, determine a strategy and stick with the chosen path, no matter how great the adversity. That decisiveness includes listening to the advice of others, weighing that advice and listening to smart and talented counselors. A commitment to preparing properly for the mission ahead and an ability to delegate responsibility when necessary is another important element. Many of the leaders I admire combine nearly all of these characteristics.

One of the benefits of studying history is that you can learn from the mistakes of others and have the foresight to not repeat them. But no amount of academic knowledge can completely prepare someone for what they will face in the real world. I've learned quite a bit from on-the-job training. For me there never was any doubt that the positions I held professionally would involve the responsibility of making decisions and implementing my vision.

My exposure to politics as a child allowed me to observe the workings of government and understand what makes a leader. The other paramount lesson in leadership I learned was this: a leader who inspires people is one who is honest and has integrity. I remember my father telling me when I was young: "Bob, if I wanted a million dollars in cash sitting on this table by the end of the night, all it would involve is a couple of phone calls to those who have been trying for years to purchase my favors. But I will leave you something much more valuable: I will leave you a rich name, not a rich pocketbook."

Because of Dad's guidance and the qualities of so many other leaders I observed as a young man, I was able to formulate my own vision and understanding of what leadership really means. For example, it became very important to me that my own leadership skills involved being part of a team and being able to lead that team. To me, therefore, an important aspect of team leadership is the ability to share credit rather than take credit. I was also not risk adverse. I am very much focused on identifying opportunities and when an opportunity presents itself, going after it even if that is the riskier of two options. One thing I try to avoid is looking back and thinking what if? While my willingness to take a risk has certainly contributed to my fair share of mistakes and losses over the years, I believe that's how we grow. One of my favorite sayings from sports is by the hockey great, Wayne Gretzky. He said: "You miss one hundred percent of the shots you don't take." Boy is that true!

Different professional situations call for different qualities and leadership styles. Generally, I've always been able to formulate a vision and a plan, articulate that message and do it with a sense of humor. A sense of humor can take people very far in life and help them through adversity and challenges. Also, being an unselfish leader and having a willingness to share credit with those who work for you have always been hallmarks of my leadership approach.

At Cumberland University, I was the sole person in charge of all day-to-day operational decisions and answered to forty members of the board of trust. They all had very strong and quite varied points of view. Here the leadership challenge was to filter through priorities and negotiate a strategy with the university board. While my overall approach to leading and making decisions was always the same, sometimes different positions called for different leadership skills.

Two examples that reinforce this point are my service in the military and my time in Congress. You cannot find a more structured environment than in the military. Every position is defined down to the minutest detail. Rank comes with authority and responsibility, an order is an order, and the expectation is that it will be carried out exactly as instructed. There is a rigid chain of command with pages upon pages of rules and regulations.

I spent thirty-one years in the military, starting in the Army ROTC at the University of Tennessee, and retiring as a colonel in the Tennessee Army National Guard. With each step up the ladder my areas of responsibility increased and the pool of soldiers (men and women) serving under me grew accordingly. I was assigned to the Adjutant General Corps. During my military career, I served under exceptional commanders who helped me to grow and succeed. But after several years into my military service I reported to a commanding officer who was difficult to work with; that was surely an understatement.

I'm not sure what exactly our problem was, but we didn't see eye-to-eye on even the simplest issues. There were a couple of times when I was ready to call it quits and leave the military altogether because of this one man. I stuck with it and I am sure glad I did. That experience taught me a lot about myself, life and leadership. You can go through the storm but the sun will ultimately shine brightly once again. These were lessons I applied to all my other professional positions. You can learn a lot from success, but even more from being challenged and having to overcome adversity.

As one of the few veterans, I was honored when members of congress sought my opinion concerning military issues, especially during the budgetary process. This was a new leadership challenge for me: being one of 435 votes requires you to be the ultimate team player. There's a fine balance between leading from the front on an issue, and at the same time allowing others with more seniority to call the shots. For me this balance required applying all the lessons I learned over the years, to effectively represent the people of my district.

I resolved to be very critical of myself so that I never would cause embarrassment for my constituents. I also wanted to make sure I spoke up early and clearly on issues that I deemed important for my district and the well-being of our nation. I didn't want to be a bench warmer, but rather wanted to display the political courage necessary to speak out about the important issues of our times. I resolved to be decisive and specific so that my voters always knew where their representative stood.

Congress is the most unique work environment I have ever experienced. On the one hand, I was lucky to work with so many smart and dedicated people. On the other hand, it was a challenge having to listen and compromise.

Most members of Congress are so-called Type-A personalities, people who are most comfortable being in charge and are convinced that they have the right vision and strategy. But once they are no longer a candidate for office but rather an elected representative, they are only one out of 435 people. And, depending on which party has the majority, you are either on the winning team or on the losing team. Either way you need to be a team player. In other words, the House of Representatives is filled with 435 men and women who have a natural affinity for taking the lead and are now asked to be team players. That may explain some of the gridlock we are witnessing currently on Capitol Hill.

I decided to turn this dichotomy into an advantage for my district by seeking out the counsel and expertise of other members on issues that were new to me. I also was willing to offer my experience and advice to other members on issues where I had the requisite knowledge. This served me well in many ways and made me a popular member who got along with many of my colleagues from both sides of the aisle. My congressional experience was, therefore, a very positive one and it was defined by collaboration, partnership and friendship. Instead of thinking, "I'm only one of 435 votes," my approach was, "My vote counts just as much as the most senior person in the room."

In addition, many of my colleagues have said what makes this very tough job so rewarding is that they can make a real difference in the lives of people. You can play a direct role in helping a specific family in your district, or crafting legislation that will positively impact people all over the country. Each day is different. It seems like every thirty minutes you change focus, meet with new people or work on new issues. The current Congress, I'm afraid, does less and less legislating and more and more grandstanding. They are depriving themselves of the very thing that makes the job so important and rewarding. I believe many current members do not have the respect for Congress as an institution that my colleagues and I had because they do not experience the good that can come from working as a team to get things done.

I didn't have a difficult time at all going from being the sole man in charge as president of Cumberland to being one of 435 as a representative. I got the committee assignments I sought, I made good friends on both sides of the aisle, and I felt challenged each and every day. And the leadership skills that had served me well in my previous positions all made a positive impact on my life as a member.

One realization I had during my time in Congress was that good leaders, no matter what position they held, all have certain things in common. For example, even the President of the United States needs to be a team player if he (or she) wants to get things done. In my view, the presidents who were most successful in the toughest job on the planet are those who were coalition builders and reached out to Congress. I'm thinking specifically about Presidents Reagan and Clinton. They were incredibly personable, invited rank-and-file members to spend time with them at the White House or on Air Force One, and recognized that they would not be successful by simply dictating policy from the White Houses' bully pulpit. Bill Clinton, for example, had a heck of a time with congressional republicans, particularly after Newt Gingrich became speaker in 1994. But President Clinton's leadership style was such that instead of shrinking from interacting with Congress, he doubled his efforts and sought out members of Congress from both sides of the aisle even more. He realized that in order to lead and accomplish his mission, he needed the support of as many of us as possible.

During the Bush/Gore campaign and with some extra time on his hands, President Clinton decided a round of golf with a member of Congress might be productive. "Bob," he said, "Meet me at the Army Navy Country Club in Arlington in half an hour." "Mr. President," I replied, "I would be honored to play with you, but I don't have any clubs here at the office." "No problem, Bob. I have an extra set of Callaway Clubs," the President said." So off I went, racing down the highway to get to the Army Navy Country Club next to the Pentagon, because the last thing I wanted to do was keep the leader of the free world waiting.

When I arrived, I was wearing a suit and tie, which would not be the appropriate golf attire. I headed to the pro shop where I spent $240 dollars on golf shorts, shoes, gloves and a cap. When President Clinton's motorcade pulled up, I was ready to play. We had a great time playing golf until we got to a particularly tricky par-four. After my first drive, the ball was situated in a wooded area and no matter which angle I took, I somehow had to play the ball by trying to hit it between two trees. The president was sitting in the golf cart and I said, "Mr. President, you might want to move that golf cart." "Bob, just hit your ball; I'm okay." I hit the ball with a lot of power, but the odds were simply against me. It somehow ricocheted off a tree, flew right back at us, and slammed into our golf cart just about an inch from President Clinton's head. It made a tremendous thud. President Clinton jumped; the Secret Service jumped; and I really jumped.

"Bob," he said to me, "You almost made a lot of new friends today!" I visualized the worst. I could just see the headlines in my mind: *Tennessee Congressman Kills President. Tennessee's Vice President Becomes President.* After the golf game, there was an article written in *Time Magazine* about this incident. Shortly thereafter, when I was back in Nashville, someone came up to me and asked, "You know what would have happened if you had killed the president on the golf course? "I responded, "I don't want to think about it." Then the man said, "You would have re-written the rules of golf, and anyone from that time on that hit a tree, an obstacle, or someone else, would say, 'I pulled a Clement today.'"

George W. Bush, for example, had a very folksy and down to earth style. I may have disagreed with him on some political and policy issues, such as the rush to go to war in Iraq, but he was approachable on other issues where he sought an ally. The same is true for President Reagan who enlisted my support on Iran-Contra aid (Nicaragua). That didn't prevent us from working together on a number of other pieces of legislation. And I believe that President Obama is a talented and gifted communicator. I think that most Americans, even those who differ with him would agree. Unfortunately, the political climate that he inherited has deteriorated to a level, whereby, the hyper-partisanship that has emerged in recent years greatly lessens the trust between the administration and Congress. As a result, President Obama's attempt to form friendships and alliances across party lines in the Congress has been diminished over the years. Unless members can regain a level of trust through fostering relationships with other members with whom they disagree, gridlock will continue. The next generation is watching. At the very least I hope in the future our leaders will wake up and show them that they can work together on the major issues facing our country and the world.

I believe there are a great many leaders upon whom this country has relied in and out of political office such as Bill Gates, Warren Buffett, Colin Powell, Lee Hamilton, James Baker, Madeline Albright, Wesley Clark and former presidents to name just a few. Great leaders are a natural resource in America, just like water or land. We are blessed in that regard. But while in the past we have found ways to nurture and encourage great leaders to rise to the top, I believe our current system actually stifles the growth of future exceptional men and women. Using the natural resource analogy, it is like we have access to water but have decided instead to build a dam. Fewer and fewer people are willing to go into public service and put their name forth because of the incredible scrutiny their personal lives will be subjected. The political commentator, Charlie Cook, said that when he meets a young man or woman thinking about running for office, he tells them to get a pad of paper and on each line write the year from present day going back to the year in which they were born and then, next to each year, jot down the most embarrassing thing they did that year. If they can stomach having everything listed appear on the front page of a newspaper or be talked about for hours on a news channel or online, then they are ready to run for office. Today we want our leaders to be perfect people. That's like asking Franklin D. Roosevelt to rise from his wheelchair. Would we have asked Harry Truman to stop playing poker and enjoying his Scotch, or John F. Kennedy to quit flirting? Would Thomas Jefferson survive the rumors involving his slave Sally Hemings? Even Pope Francis in his Christmas address in 2014 condemned gossip and the politics of personal destruction, a very bold move on his part for sure. But by judging personal shortcomings so harshly and indiscriminately, we are discouraging the next Jefferson or Kennedy from ever stepping forward to lead. We have many highly qualified leaders who have had failings in their personal or professional lives. Our society is judging them so harshly that they can never rise to the highest levels of their capabilities. Since leaving Congress I continue to try to encourage the next generation of leaders. I hope to pass on what I have learned from the mentors in my family and others whom I have met or worked.

The secret of great leadership is really no secret at all, because our country has been so blessed with outstanding men and women ready to meet a challenge head on. They are honest and fundamentally decent people. While each may have different leadership styles, they share many of the same qualities. The challenge for our next generation of leaders is to learn from the lessons of the greatest leaders of the past and embrace the tried and true qualities that have stood the test of time. It is now our responsibility to the next generation to inspire them to study leadership principles. No matter whether they are electricians, teachers, farmers or plumbers we all should look at ourselves as public servants. That's the least we can do.

As Mother Teresa said, "To keep a lamp burning, we have to keep putting oil in it."

Clement's Contemplations

"When playing golf with the leader of the free world make sure to yell, "duck."

"Leadership is a set of qualities that can be learned if you are not afraid to make mistakes."

"Humor is no joke. Take it seriously and share it with friends."

"Put your money where your mouth is, but take it out of politics."

"When you throw stones at glass houses you will shatter someone's dream."

"Study the lives of our Founding Fathers and their fabulous mothers too."

"Being a team player transforms the 'I' into 'We.'"

"Have the vision to see the future and learn from the past."

Chapter 11

WHY CAN'T WE ALL GET ALONG? OUR HYPER-PARTISAN AMERICA

"Nothing is sweeter than the sound of your
own voice"—John Jay Hooker

The one good thing about growing up with prisoners, movie stars and politicians is that you learn to respect and appreciate people's differences. I wish the same could be said of the U.S. Congress.

This great nation of ours has always been one of contrasts, differing philosophies and struggles between classes, races and parties. We have always found ways to overcome our divisions, and often it is our internal struggles that made us stronger. The most poignant example is the Civil War, which pitted brother against brother. But just one generation later, the country united to fight and win the Spanish-American War, which resulted in our expansion into the Caribbean and opened the way for the Panama Canal. My point is that we are a nation that distrusts marching in lockstep to the same tune. Our history and culture are based on differing points of views clashing until a common ground solution emerges. This has been ingrained in our psyche since the Founding Fathers and is reflected in our form of government: all three branches clash with each other, with not one being more powerful or important than the other.

Differing points of view being argued vigorously is an integral part of our political experience. It was so important to the Founding Fathers that they shaped their vision of representative democracy on the core belief that debate eventually leads to consensus and solutions. The parties have always clashed and partisanship not only is nothing new, it is actually a healthy and necessary ingredient to our political process. Yet the current hyper-partisanship seems to me to be more than merely a continuation of our usual political struggles and there are many reasons for this.

A June 2014 study by the highly respected Pew Research Center supports the notion that as a country we express our partisanship much more eagerly than in the past.

When I served in Congress you could find republicans more liberal than the most conservative democrats and vice versa. In today's Congress the most liberal republican is still more conservative than the most conservative democrat. The most conservative democrat is still more liberal than the most liberal republican.

Why are these hyper-partisan members of Congress on Capitol Hill in the first place? That's because we sent them there. Or, more accurately, because we are sitting on the sidelines while hyper-partisan representatives are elected by hyper-partisan voters in a primary system that protects the incumbent. How is the system distorted? Because state legislatures controlled by one party or the other get to draw congressional districts that have as their sole purpose to group as many like-minded voters into each district as possible. We have elevated gerrymandering to a science; I do not mean that as a compliment.

Those determining the often completely arbitrary lines on a redistricting map have a very good idea how each and every one of us is likely to vote. They know what TV shows we watch – particularly where we get our news, which primaries we have voted, who we have given money, what church we attend, what schools we send our kids, whether we have served in the military, and other factors that slowly but surely add up to a pretty accurate picture of our political leanings. Big brother is alive and well, for sure.

For a political candidate, the easiest and most obvious way of picking his or her voters has become the zip code. Generally, the rule of thumb is that urban areas tend to vote for democrats, while well-to-do suburbs and mostly rural areas tend to vote republican. That's why, on election night, you'll see the vast majority of a map of the United States painted red, with large blue blotches where you find cities such as Washington, New York, San Francisco or Chicago. During the past twenty-years or so there has been a shift in America's population, precipitated by an urban flight of middle class and upper middle class families moving from the cities to the suburbs. And when picking a new neighborhood to move into, families consider factors such as schools, churches, local government and taxes, for example.

This sad reality is documented by the American National Election Survey, which asks Americans every two years how they feel about certain institutions and groups in the United States.

For the past ten years or so the survey has seen a sharp decline when people were asked whether they felt positive about someone with a different political persuasion; often the word hate is used. Subconsciously, our society has created enclaves of like-minded political persuasions. We have adopted group think, within our communities to such a degree that we view those who think differently than us in very negative terms. These communities become congressional districts drawn to protect a party's hold over the district, or make it impossible for a candidate from the other party to win the district. By having grouped more and more like-minded voters into specific congressional districts, our political process pressures elected officials to stand firm and defend their values rather than seek compromise and common ground.

However, let's not forget that there are still some current members of Congress, in both the House and the Senate, who are more than willing to cross the aisle in order to get things accomplished. I am so impressed by the group of women senators especially. In the One hundred fourteenth Congress there are twenty women from both parties who continuously set aside party labels in order to work together and bring real progress to the Senate Chamber. One of their secrets is that they meet regularly as a group for informal lunches and dinners. They talk about policy, but also about their lives, their families and their concerns as mothers or grandmothers. This commonality unites them. It has given them a strong foundation of trust upon which they can rely when difficult problems call for pragmatic solutions. Routinely, these women senators can overcome partisan differences in order to compromise. I'm hopeful that we can identify and groom more women to run for office and have successful political careers. I am pleased to say that during my congressional career and beyond I have seen my female colleagues pass significant legislation in areas such as, women's' healthcare, education, children's welfare, fair and equitable pay, and support for military families, among others.

As a father of two daughters, I most certainly hope we can find ways to engage the next generation of female leaders. Many of the most influential and impactful people in my life were women, so to me it is second nature that women make outstanding leaders. The success of the women senators clearly demonstrates the importance for members of Congress to get to know each other better on a personal level. They have invested the necessary time to understand each other as people first and elected officials second. The only way you can regularly engage in difficult negotiations is by compromise and trust. I believe strongly that enabling our elected representatives to create those kinds of bonds would go a long way to overcome today's hyper-partisanship.

One of the benefits of having the time and opportunity to get to know your colleagues on a personal level is that they can forge long-lasting friendships. These relationships go beyond party labels and make it possible to work together across the political divide in order to accomplish important goals. Don't get me wrong, just because we were friends does not mean we all left our partisan point of views at the front door. No, being friends meant that while we had strong political points of view we were still able to communicate those views in a respectful and productive manner.

Here's a story about a challenge I faced when I was in Congress and had to try to find a solution to a national issue in a bipartisan manner.

It had to do with rail passenger service that I strongly supported for the entire country. I was working on local passenger service projects that I wanted to pursue and had tried with no success to persuade CSX, a Class I railroad, to operate rail passenger service on their freight lines. They were not helpful. They had concerns about their freight scheduling and liability if their lines were going to be used for rail passengers in and out of Nashville. Matter of fact, one local mayor had this to say about the project, "We don't need it; no one will use it; and it costs too much." It took another year to get him on board and get the U.S. Department of Transportation to get back in the game. I actively pursued getting the short line railroad, Nashville Eastern, to work with me, and I discussed getting them federal funding. I was able to get the federal funds with matching funds (state and local) to make it a very successful project. But I couldn't have done it alone. I worked with my colleagues from both parties to get federal funding for a local commuter train called, Music City

Star. We were most fortunate to also have the strong support of the Regional Transportation Authority, and MTA, who made the deal possible. Rail passenger service is a must for our country to relieve traffic congestion, help the environment and bring about quality of life for all Americans.

Also, by working with a bipartisan group of members of Congress from the South and West, we were able to rewrite the highway funding formula that was diverting a disproportionate amount of highway funds to the North and East compared to the South and West. This was because of an antiquated highway formula that penalized the South and the West. For the first time in U.S. history the South and the West had more population than the North and the East but the old formula did not reflect that. We sprang into action and made changes to that formula to bring about fairness in all parts of the country. We had many heated debates about the issue but our efforts paid off. This resulted in more than a sixty-two percent increase in federal transportation funding for Tennessee alone, taking us from $360 million dollars per year to $800 million dollars.

As someone who always worked across party lines, Republican Roy Blunt of Missouri and Democrat Ray Thornton of Arkansas and I helped to create the House Education Caucus. To this day, it involves members from both sides of the aisle in a dialogue about public education and the importance of giving our children the very best classrooms, teachers and resources.

In 1993, I worked closely with Congressman Jim Clyburn of South Carolina and a diverse group of members of Congress from both sides of the aisle to help the Congressional Black Caucus pass the bill I introduced, Historically Black Colleges and Universities Historic Buildings Restoration and Preservation Act. This assured that federal dollars were available to colleges and universities in an effort to preserve their historic buildings. We passed the legislation. This meant five million dollars for

Fisk University. Dr. Henry Ponder (president of Fisk) worked diligently to get this legislation passed. That same year, I was part of a bipartisan group of members who worked together to create the National Service Act, which offered college aid to students in exchange for community service in areas such as teaching, health care, environmental cleanup and public safety.

I also co-sponsored the Family and Medical Leave Act. While a tough assignment, and at times a heated and trying debate, the groundbreaking legislation allows workers to have up to twelve weeks of unpaid leave per year. This can be when a new baby is born, or when a loved-one has a serious illness that requires full-time care. It was a tough bill to pass for sure. The republicans thought it was a mandate; the democrats felt the opposite.

To help our nation's veterans receive the benefits they deserve, I assembled a bipartisan team to pass legislation that provided special health care benefits to Desert Storm veterans experiencing illnesses. This may have been caused by exposure to chemical agents such as Agent Orange. Sadly, I am disappointed in how Veterans Affairs has fallen short in their duty to take care of their own. This is a national tragedy!

Not one of the above accomplishments came easily. They all involved coalition building, negotiating, giving up on some ideas and accepting others. In a partisan legislative world, that is the system our forefathers envisioned. Better laws are created because people with differing points of view come together to address an issue.

While we certainly live in a more polarized world, and have surrounded ourselves with mostly like-minded neighbors, are we really more staunchly conservative or liberal than previous generations? Do we seriously despise those who think differently than us than previous generations? Certainly the statistics support that premise. But I am convinced that the root of our hyper-partisanship is that we are moving toward polar opposites—either more liberal or more conservative. We have so disenfranchised the independents and moderates that the hyper-partisan crowd has become the only political voice still being heard. This behavior has certainly given rise to the behavior and actions of the candidates during the 2016 presidential race.

I believe we are not more partisan as a nation than in previous years. It's just that we hear no louder voice other than the hyper-partisan one. They have become such a forceful group that an entire industry, ranging from media outlets to professional political fundraisers, lives extremely well through their rhetoric. Most people are simply less engaged politically because they view Washington or their state capitals with apathy and cynicism. People have lost trust in their government and are wondering what their government can do for them other than raise their taxes. When they think of politicians they think of the person who reaches out to them more often than not to ask for a campaign contribution.

This may have resulted from the McCain-Feingold Campaign Reform Act that sought to stem the undue influence of money in politics and achieved just the opposite. Also, fundraising is now a full-time profession in which the candidate has to engage several hours every day, something as I've said before, really short-changes constituents.

One of the other realities some members of Congress face is the temptation to be one type of candidate depending on their audience's zip code, and then a different candidate the next day when they have moved on to a different part of their district. I believe I stayed true to my character and message. I let the chips fall where they may. As an incumbent, I never lost an election for my U.S. House seat. It seems to me that my constituents knew where I stood on the major issues and were comfortable sending me back to D.C. even if they didn't agree with everything I stood for all of the time. I'm equally sure there were a number of hyper-partisan democrats and republicans who would never vote for me because of one particular position or another. Inevitably as a member of Congress, when casting hundreds of votes throughout the year, someone is bound to become upset with you for one reason or another.

Matter of fact, what people would do is sometimes single shot me. They would agree with me on everything but on one issue, and, therefore, were against me. It was difficult to swallow that some people would not vote for me based on one issue only; I always hoped that they would look at my overall record and find some common ground.

I certainly served with my share of so-called bomb-throwers. Jim Traficant, a democrat from Ohio, one day during debate in the House Chamber shared his opinion of the IRS. He said: "From the womb to the tomb, the internal rectal service is one big enema." Or Bob Dornan, a republican from California, who had this to say about the right to keep and bear arms: "The Second Amendment is not for killing little ducks and leaving Huey and Dewey and Louie without an aunt and uncle. It's for hunting politicians, like in Grozny and in the colonies in 1776, or when they take your independence away." It never bothered me to interact and work with such a polarizing and controversial group of politicians. I find different points of view, even ones I object vehemently, to be worthy of consideration. It surely keeps things lively!

Healthy debate challenges your own positions and forces you to articulate an argument in favor of your analysis and conclusion. In addition, it reminds you that there are many moving parts to our nation, with many different districts, constituencies, experiences and points of view. To me serving with these hyper-partisan members was educational; it made me a better member. However, this only works if it is a two-way street. I think during my time on Capitol Hill there still was enough respect to engage in this type of back-and-forth. Today's extremists have neither any interest nor incentive to listen to anyone who has a different philosophy.

Also, when I served in Congress, many of these hyper-partisan members mellowed considerably as they rose in leadership and were tasked with actually getting things done. Specifically Newt Gingrich, really came into the speakership alienating so many different people, you couldn't have fit them all into The University of Tennessee's Neyland Stadium. It quickly dawned on him, however, that he will have a very unsuccessful and meaningless speakership if he didn't at least occasionally tone down his hyper-partisan rhetoric and extend an olive branch to the other side. Today, I wonder whether a bridge-builder and middle of the road speaker can succeed. Only history will be able to fairly and accurately judge the speakership of John Boehner. I certainly think of him as someone who seeks to find consensus and pragmatic solutions, regardless of his party's approval ratings. It seems to me that during any other time in congressional history he could have made his mark as an exceptionally capable and successful Speaker of the House. Having been handed the most hyper-partisan republican caucus in modern times, we will probably never know his true potential, which is too bad.

On the national level, with hyper-partisans in both parties drowning each other out, there might be an opportunity for a viable and electable third-party candidate to rise and capture a lot of attention. The moderates and independents feel like they do not have a voice and that they are getting lost in the shuffle. There's a real void here that could be filled by an independent or third-party candidate who might be able to unite a large percentage of these disenfranchised voters under his or her umbrella. I hear this all the time from my past constituents and supporters. They feel that they are being left out of the political process, almost as if they are intentionally overlooked. They tell me that their vote means nothing and that there is no one who is speaking on their behalf.

To me, it is pretty clear how we have arrived at this stage of hyper-partisanship. Certainly, money in politics plays a pervasive role that has become out of control and has outrageously elevated the importance of Wall Street at the expense of Main Street. Money has become such a determining factor that both parties now recruit candidates based on their ability to raise money or self-finance a campaign. The most viable candidate, therefore, is the one with the deepest pockets, not the one with the best ideas or the greatest concern for the American people.

Both parties have succumbed to the sway of the all-mighty dollar. In addition, social media and our way of receiving news have brought us to this point. Social media is a two-way street, asking candidates to stay relevant by posting often irresponsible comments, and giving supporters the necessary anonymity to feel comfortable posting inflammatory statements as well.

My Aunt Anna Belle was a career politician in Tennessee, culminating in her election to the Tennessee State Senate (where she was the first woman to ever chair a committee). She would have people ask her for help all the time, and the first question she asked anyone walking through her door was: "Are you registered to vote?" She didn't care who they voted for—of course she hoped for her—but she did care that someone asking their elected representative for help was someone who took his or her civic responsibility seriously enough to actually be a registered voter. She would say, "Are you registered to vote? If you are not, go home and register to vote and then come back to see me, and I will help you." These were words of wisdom, for sure.

Ultimately, communications, understanding, tolerance and forgiveness are principles that have been at the forefront of my life for years, my anecdote for hyper-partisanship. I have tried to embrace them as a politician and throughout my careers in education, business and the military. Once we fix the problems hampering our nation's political system such as redistricting, voter apathy, etc., we need to be better listeners. I've heard all of my life from my friend, a political activist named John Jay Hooker, "Nothing is sweeter than the sound of your own voice." Maybe the time has come for us to all truly listen, and realize compromise is not a dirty word. Only by taking the time to hear others' concerns can we change the paradigm from arguing to communicating.

Clement's Contemplations

"God gave us ears for listening, not blocking out our opponents."

"From the womb to the tomb, the Internal Rectal Service is one big enema."

"There are no Democrats; no Republicans; just those who come to the party without a date."

"How can you distrust someone who lives next door to you and you actually like?"

"If there is such a thing as a wise man in politics he would say, "Be thankful to have a voice in government no matter how tough it is to be heard."

"Forget about getting everything you want: compromise will sustain you for the long haul."

I was addressing the crowd after winning the
1987 primary for the 5th Congressional District
seat while family and friends cheered me on.

Speaker of the U.S. House Jim Wright of Texas, left,
holds a re-enactment of the swearing in ceremony on
Capitol Hill for my 5th Congressional District victory.

My daughters, Elizabeth and Rachel join me on the floor of the House of Representatives during my swearing in ceremony in January, 1988.

My appearance on PBS's Washington Week. Left to Right: Bob, Congressman John Tanner (Union City, TN), moderator, Congressman Jimmy Duncan (Knoxville, TN), and Congressman Zach Wamp (Chattanooga, TN).

Speaker of the House, Newt Gingrich, and
Bob in his office in the Capitol.

Senator Bill Frist, U. S. Surgeon General
David Satcher and me.

*President Reagan and I meeting at the White
House in early 1988 to discuss Iran Contra aid.*

*President Ronald Reagan whispering in Mary's ear
asking her to encourage me to switch parties.*

President George H. W. Bush signs the Noise
Reduction Reimbursement Act of 1989, the bill
that I introduced to help Nashville and other cities
solve the noise problem in and around airports.
General Moore, president of the Nashville Authority,
joined Mary and me for the signing ceremony.

President Clinton and First Lady Hillary Clinton, greet
us at the annual Christmas Gala at the White House.

Bob listening to Minister of Defense for Israel Yitzhak Rabin's presentation regarding Israel and the Middle East.

Bob and Mary showing "The Watch" to Yitzhak Shamir, seventh Prime Minister of Israel during their trip as a Member of Congress. The first Prime Minister of Israel, David Ben-Gurion, gave the watch to my father, Governor Frank G. Clement when he was Governor of Tennessee.

Welcoming Israel's Prime Minister, Benjamin Netanyahu, and his wife, Sara, to the U. S. Capitol prior to his speech before Congress in July, 1996.

Bob and U.S. Senator Tom Harkin of Iowa welcoming President of the Russian Federation, Boris Yeltsin, to the U.S. Capitol in 1992.

Former exiled King of Afghanistan, Zahir Shah, and me at the King's Residence outside of Rome, Italy. We met with Northern Alliance leaders from Afghanistan that asked for U.S. military assistance to defeat the Taliban, shortly after September 11, 2001.

The meeting after September 11, 2001, with the Northern Alliance leaders from Afghanistan outside of Rome, Italy. They include: Congressman Curt Weldon (R-Pa); Cliff Stearns (R-FL); Bud Cramer (D-AL); Dana Rohrabacher R-CA); and Bob Clement (D-TN).

Bob, Charlie Daniels, and Alex Haught, my chief of staff who was later tragically killed in an automobile accident in Nashville in 2000.

Mr. and Mrs. Eddy Arnold with Mary and me at the White House where President and Mrs. Clinton presented Eddy with the prestigious National Medal of Arts and Humanities Award on December 20, 2000.

Little Jimmy Dickens (center) with me, Mary and others back stage at the Grand Ole Opry.

Johnny and June Carter Cash (center) had entertained at a political fundraiser for me in Washington, D.C. It was a spectacular event – promoting country music and Nashville, TN (Music City, USA).

Governor Frank G. Clement, Minnie Pearl
and my mom, Cille Clement.

Mary, Dolly Parton and Bob at the Grand Ole Opry.

Dolly Parton, Mayor Gary Wade, Bob and others dedicating the Dolly Parton Parkway in Sevier County, the home of Dolly Parton.

Earl Scruggs, Mrs. Scruggs and me during their visit to my office at the U.S. Capitol. Bluegrass pickers and singers, Lester Flatt and Earl Scruggs, were the background musicians for the popular "Beverly Hillbillies" television show.

U.S. Postmaster General, Marvin Runyon and Bob discussing Elvis Presley's upcoming dedication stamp ceremony, which was held in Memphis, Tennessee. The Elvis stamp became among the country's most popular stamps in history.

Priscilla Presley signing the book featuring the inaugural Elvis Presley postage stamp. Bart Herbison and I happily looked on.

Vice President Joe Biden attending a political event in Nashville where Mary and I had a chance to visit with him. He supported Amtrak for years as he rode the train each day from Wilmington, Delaware to Washington, D. C.

Speaking at an event in Washington, D. C. to promote expanded rail passenger service as a member of the Transportation and Infrastructure Committee and ranking Democrat on the Railroad Subcommittee.

*Bob attending a high level briefing with U.S. Senate
and Congressional Leaders with President Hosni
Mubarak of Egypt where he had the opportunity
to ask President Mubarak a question.*

*General Colin Powell, Bob and the President of
Fisk University, Henry Ponder. General Powell was
the guest speaker at the university's graduation
ceremony where his wife, Alma, was a student.*

My meeting with Jim Hall, chairman of the National Transportation Safety Board discussing the major transportation safety issues facing the country.

Tom Simpson, president of Railway Supply Institute (RSI) the RSI board, and I meeting with U. S. Transportation Secretary, Ray LaHood, to discuss major transportation issues.

*Speaker of the U. S. House of Representatives,
Tip O'Neill, with Mary and me in 1979.*

*Bob, Dale Wiley, King Abdullah's brother, Dr. Peter Konrad,
and our host, Dr. Osama, during our humanitarian trip
to Saudi Arabia to discuss spinal cord injury research.*

Bob visiting with Marine Cpl. Christian Brown in Bldg. 62 at the Walter Reed National Military Medical Center in Bethesda, MD. Cpl. Brown received the Silver Star for his valor and now is medically retired and living in Munford, TN.

Chapter 12

LIFE AFTER CONGRESS: KEEPING THE SPIRIT OF SERVICE ALIVE

"Service is the rent we pay for being. It is the very
purpose of life, and not something you do in your
spare time."—Marian Wright Edelman

Many Americans believe that members of Congress enter the profession of politics for their own personal gain.

Fortunately, this perception isn't true for most members. They enter politics because they want to serve others, keep America as the exceptional nation it is, and help the American citizens achieve the dreams they have for themselves. At least that was the case when I served. For me, and so many of my fellow members of Congress with whom I have had the privilege to work, we are saddened by the many roadblocks created by partisanship which has caused much of the public's national skepticism. During my public life I have given many speeches and ended with this proposition, "I am only one, but one is one hundred percent greater than none, and that which I can do, I will do, so help me God."

I have thought about this principle many times throughout my life. It has always reminded me to continue to renew my dedication to live a purposeful life of service to others. There were many times in my life when I have felt so small in the world where there were so many needs. There were never enough people or resources to meet them. This principle has helped me on my journey and allowed me to make a difference. Knowing that I was leaving Congress, I still wanted to help restore hope and enthusiasm and try as one individual to give one hundred percent of myself to achieve those goals.

Being a member of Congress for me was a dream come true. After serving the people of the 5th District of Tennessee for fifteen years, the thought of leaving them was bittersweet. Even though I cast many votes that not only helped my constituents, but every American, knowing that I would not be part of the political system as a member of Congress was, nevertheless, painful for me.

Why? Because I had been engaged with thousands of people during my tenure and many of them had become my good friends. I helped them get their social security, veteran's benefits and at times find them jobs, get their passports for travel and many more services that members of Congress do on a daily basis. It was an empty feeling knowing I would have to not only change my own daily routine, but develop new daily patterns devoid of many of the encounters I enjoyed with my constituents over the years.

Throughout my career I have taken one day at a time and tried to not project very far in the future. As a member of Congress this came in particularly handy, since legislating requires great focus. While we need to be knowledgeable about the issues, we also have to understand the political ramifications of what we do on a real-time basis. It was a tricky balance for sure. I can illustrate that with this analogy. Many times I have seen politicians shake a constituent's hand at a reception and at the same time, be looking at the next person in the receiving line and leaving the constituent behind. This has always been one of my biggest pet peeves.

After spending much of my life around politics I have learned to try very hard not to look backwards. Life has a way of taking detours and turns in the road. I truly believe that wherever we are and whatever we do prepares us for the next chapter in our lives.

Fairly soon after I left the U.S. Congress new and interesting people came into my life, yet there were some speed bumps along the way. While my phone started to ring and people were seeking my consulting services, I still knew that position power can be a fast and fleeting thing.

Clearly, as a member of Congress you have position power, meaning you have the authority to make decisions that affect others' lives based upon the position you were elected to and the power it inherently holds.

Most politicians, I do believe, understand that when position power in political office ends there will be change. The same people that came to your office with their own political interests and agendas will naturally move on to the next person taking your position. That is politics 101. It has always been that way and is not going to change. However, as I have said before, there are those who you befriend and help who will always remain in touch. There are others who will abandon. But regardless, a successful transition for anyone in a position of power requires two essential qualities: a sense of purpose and an even greater sense of humor.

There is no question in my mind that if you are a member of Congress and have a fragile ego it can be an emotionally devastating combination. Believe it or not, I have seen some members become immobilized after their defeat. When they were in power everyone was hanging on their every word. Now those same individuals who once worshipped them won't even return their phone call. I learned that lesson myself at a very young age and that served me well throughout my political career.

Not only were some members of Congress shocked when people wouldn't return their phone calls they were even more devastated by their perceptions of themselves as failures. I have seen way too many times when members who lost their elections refused to go home and face their constituents. Many simply stayed in Washington, selling their places back home to avoid the reality of defeat. The loss was personal and painful. During their time in office they were consumed by their power and thrived on knowing that they were important and indispensable. Power overcame them and they just couldn't handle it. I am reminded of a quote of an unknown origin that went something like this: "Cemeteries are filled with people who thought they were indispensable." To me, that mindset just leads to bitterness and self-loathing. Even more troubling, I have watched some former members physically and emotionally retreat and not stay engaged and involved in their communities. I have always been a person who was not just one-dimensional. That's where personal power enters the picture, as well as not taking yourself too seriously. I believe that people can have a purpose other than what they simply do for a living.

However, scandals are a different matter. They present their own sets of unique challenges for members of Congress who for one reason or another find themselves in the thick of it. In the days before mass media proliferation and the Watergate scandal, behaviors that might be ripe for ridicule today might have gone unnoticed and underreported. Still, for those members who clearly broke the law—think about Former Congressman Bill Jefferson of Louisiana who kept $90,000 cash in his refrigerator, or Randy Duke Cunningham of California who pleaded guilty to charges of tax evasion, bribery and mail fraud, their actions were inexcusable. But, their departure from the halls of Congress was necessary.

Others, like Congressman Gary Condit of California, who was falsely accused of murdering his young intern, Chandra Levy, left in a cloud of suspicion; he never fully recovered politically.

That cloud of scandal overshadowed his successes in Congress. I knew Gary very well, since his office was down the hall from mine. We often talked about his love of country music. In fact, when Johnny Cash performed at a fundraising concert for me in D.C., I arranged for Gary, as well as Congressman John Kasich, to meet Johnny and his family backstage. That's one reason why Gary's situation was especially troubling to me.

Back to what I mean by personal power and not taking yourself too seriously. Personal power is something that you are not always born with but you can always attain. It is the belief that you can be comfortable in your own skin regardless of your position power and what others think about you. I had loving parents who instilled that sense of confidence and purpose in my life. But I would be lying if I were to say that confidence wasn't tested at times. Part of having personal power is the belief that no matter what happens to you in your life, you have the power within to change. There is no one on God's earth who is perfect. In politics, like in other fields including business and entertainment, for example, there are many individuals, who because of their position power will endlessly flatter and cajole you. That constant adulation can breathe the life out of your humility and sense of emotional balance.

That's why I always say that humor is sometimes the best cure for what ails you. Even in those moments when I had to deal with political defeat, health issues and personal losses including the deaths of my father, brother, and mother, and two of my chiefs of staff, at some point I tried to find some humor in the wake of those darkest moments. A funny memory, or a joke that made them laugh—those happy times are what I choose to remember. Mary and I, and our children and grandchildren, share many great laughs together and keeping those positive thoughts makes all the difference. I once heard someone say, "Don't let toxic people rent space in your brain. Raise the rent and kick them out."

For people who don't keep humor and balance in their lives, when their position power is suddenly taken away because of losing an election, loss of a job or even as a result of a scandal, they often become the most vulnerable and unhappy. One of the best ways I've dealt with avoiding that downward spiral is by focusing on what motivated me in the first place to want to pursue a career in politics; that is service!

After leaving my congressional career behind I was now ready to begin another chapter. As the poet T.S. Eliot said: "What we call the beginning is often the end. And to make an end is to make a beginning. The end is where we start from."

I consider service a high calling no matter whether one is elected, appointed, or serves as a volunteer. I have always felt a deep void in my life when service wasn't an integral part. Although I have spent most of my career in politics, people surely don't have to be in politics to serve. It is a great feeling to help others. Research suggests that people who give back to others on a regular basis are the most fulfilled. I have always shared with my children the idea that people you help may not be able to help you, but others will help you that you couldn't help. I believe that is one of life's most important realities. I have found it to be true over many years working in politics and public service.

When I walked out of the Capitol for the last time, my heart was heavy. I knew I wasn't going to be there to make a difference in people's lives, and I would surely miss my colleagues. The race for the U.S. Senate was particularly painful because it always hurts to come up short. I felt like I did a great job as congressman but now my time was over. And the worst part was that I needed to vacate my office in just thirty days and begin a new life for myself.

Still, I thought about all of the people I met along the way who had a great influence on my life. Contrary to public opinion today, most of the members of Congress when I served were more concerned with governing than marginalizing their colleagues from the opposite side of the aisle. The popular Netflix series, *House of Cards*, depicts the life of fictional U.S. House majority leader, and President, Frank Underwood, as a scheming leader who murders his adversaries and is a complete narcissist. It is not so far-fetched a portrayal in terms of the acrimony and vitriol that exists in the Congress today, without the murder of a member's political enemies notwithstanding. Nevertheless, the American people, as witnessed by the current congressional and presidential elections, made the choice to throw the bums out. I am convinced that this was largely due to their frustration with the grid-lock and partisanship in the Congress today and seems to take place every eight years or so. People want different things at different times. Sometimes the public wants experience, and other times experience is a negative rather than a positive attribute in some election cycles. They have a different feeling or attitude about whom they want as a leader based upon what the previous leader did or did not do in office.

The public should never forget who in Congress really cares and who are in this business for the right reasons. In my fifteen years in Congress I have known some dedicated leaders who have stood out among the rest and who deserve accolades for their work both inside and outside the Beltway. I will never forget my Tennessee Congressional Delegation that I served with during my eight terms in office. They include people like my fellow Tennesseans and former members of Congress—Al Gore; Jim Sasser; John Tanner; Bart Gordon; Marilyn Lloyd; Ed Jones; Jim Cooper; Don Sundquist; Harold Ford, Sr.; Van Hilleary; Ed Bryant; John Duncan; Harold Ford, Jr.; Jimmy Duncan; Jimmy Quillen; William Jenkins; Zach Wamp; Harlan Matthews; Bill Frist; Fred Thompson; and many other of my dear friends and colleagues around the country. Even though we didn't always agree on all the issues they became my political family and I was quite emotionally attached.

One might think that when you spend a lifetime in politics surely you must be able to name many, many people who have been your role models in terms of public service.

However, as I reflect back over my life one non-political family stands out for keeping that spirit of service alive. Cal Turner, Sr., and his wife and children who have mentored me and my family, and who founded the Dollar General Corporation are at the top of my list. Mr. Turner's wife, Katherine, and her side of the family are related to my family through my grandmother, May Belle Goad Clement who was my father's mother. I knew Mr. Turner, Sr. from the time I was very young. I can still remember my grandparents talking about their family with admiration and warmth as we sat around the dinner table. They were very giving and dedicated people. They spoke highly of their children, Cal, Jr., Laura Jo, Steve and Betty. I always heard them speak fondly about the projects they loved, and I have used them as examples on numerous occasions to highlight outstanding examples of philanthropy.

Many former members of Congress as well as business leaders never left their love of service behind when they left government or the corporate world. They also helped me realize that retirement was not an end but a beginning, and for that I am very grateful.

I must say, the weeks following my departure were both exciting and at the same time frightening. After fifteen years of serving my constituents in Tennessee, I wondered what I could do to continue to help others, support my family, and also keep structure in my life and make me want to get up early every morning.

Having been in business before, it was an easy and natural progression for me to start another venture of my own. That's when I founded Clement and Associates, a public affairs company headquartered in Nashville, with my Vice President Terri Dorsey.

She had worked as a reporter for television news and had an excellent background in research. It was great to be back full time in Tennessee. Being close to family and friends was a blessing for sure. Even though Mary and I traveled frequently to Washington D.C. to visit our grandchildren and to pursue my other business opportunities, we were thankful to be home again.

Mary was a big help to me during this period. Her family had a strong belief that serving others was something that should be an integral part of your life no matter what profession you choose.

Even though Mary didn't grow up in politics, her parents were always very involved in the lives of the people around them. They were the first to show up at a funeral home, make a hospital visit, or take a hot meal to those who were sick or downtrodden. She learned that type of love and service at a very young age.

I have seen way too much selfishness in my life to not try to do something about it. That selfishness is hard to swallow when there are so many people who are isolated, suffering and totally disconnected. To be truly engaged in our society today is difficult at best. People go to their one church, shop at their one grocery store or pharmacy, and continually see the same people each and every day. Technology, while a terrific tool, has also made us more isolated, with many preferring to send a text message rather than truly communicate in person or in a deep and emotional way. We need to break out of our old habits and have more exposure to people from all walks of life, people who may have different interests and needs than our own. We are entirely too isolated. A lot of people who need help are not getting help, and those who could help don't realize the significance of the problems in the inner cities and rural areas.

When I was in Congress I witnessed the needs of so many people all around the world and knew I had to do my part to help. Here in Nashville we have the largest Kurdish population in the country. Their lives back home are fraught with extreme violence and despair. I was very pleased to know that I was able to get a significant aid package to the Kurds that was delivered in northern Iraq which included medical supplies and many other much needed items. One of the area's most prominent local Kurdish leaders, Pakeza Alexander, sent me a note of appreciation. I saved it because it meant so much to me to know that I had helped people in their time of need. She said: "Congressman Clement, you were an integral part of our efforts to help the Kurds in Northern Iraq during the Gulf War. You were at the forefront in Washington, D.C. in the early years, pushing for a no-fly zone which was responsible for saving tens of thousands of Kurdish lives in Northern Iraq. Your unwavering support, when you realized the terrible treatment and abuse of the Kurdish people, was evident when we asked for your help and you came to our rescue right away. You were instrumental in leading the effort to send medical supplies to the refugee camps which was critical to the survival of so many women and children. And you were also able to work very effectively with the State Department to overcome travel restrictions in the area and brought Fred Smith, the CEO and founder of Fed-Ex, on board to fly the much-needed medical supplies halfway around the world. For that I am eternally grateful."

Here at home, poverty and homelessness were two issues that I've always tried to address as a member of Congress. As a volunteer, though, I worked with Habitat for Humanity to sponsor and build a home for a family in need right here in Nashville. I'm proud to say that I broke the world's record for building a Habitat home in the shortest period of time in their history—four hours, thirty-nine minutes, and eight seconds! I couldn't have broken the record without the full support of the Middle Tennessee Homebuilders Association. Millard Fuller, Habitat's founder, came personally to the build, and even President Jimmy Carter was excited about what happened that day; he wished he could have been there.

I was committed to giving of myself even when I left Congress. There were so many projects that I will never forget, especially my trip to Liberia (West Africa), where our humanitarian delegation met with the tyrannical leader, President Charles Taylor to encourage him to resign. A few weeks after we left, because of the encouragement of many countries and organizations, Charles Taylor finally resigned and left the country, moving to Nigeria, where he was arrested and transported to The Hague and was tried as a war criminal. He was convicted. I suspect he will spend the rest of his life behind bars.

I am also an active volunteer for a program through the U.S. Association of Former Members of Congress (FMC) called Congress to Campus. It has been a real eye-opener for sure.

Many of the former members who belong to the association volunteer in bipartisan groups. They travel to colleges and universities talking to students about what civic engagement means and how they can become involved and active citizens. We try to explain to them the benefits of living in a democracy. Through our extensive travel as former members of Congress we discussed the suffering that people living in developing nations experience.

When I visited the United Kingdom, and spoke at two Oxford colleges, the British Library, Wellington College and The University of Northampton, I was shocked that the students were more interested in learning the ins and outs of our democratic form of government than their own. Matter of fact, students in the UK, when asked what they were studying, would always respond, "I'm majoring in politics." It always amazed me that they would say politics rather than political science. It was obvious to me that they were most proud of that. You could see how excited they were about politics, and this was such a hopeful sign to me and my colleagues.

I have seen that same enthusiasm in universities here in the U.S. when I was a Congress to Campus speaker. Some of them include the University of Massachusetts, University of Central Florida, Richard Stockton State College, West Point, Rollins College and Wabaunsee Community College, where many of the students' questions revolved around common themes. Some of their concerns were: how to reduce the national debt; will there be jobs for them in the future; how can the gridlock in Congress be fixed; global climate change; what will happen with healthcare and education; and whether social security will be around when they retire. Despite the lack of civics courses being taught, I am always encouraged during my visits that our country has many young people who are engaged and enthusiastic about the future.

In addition to talking to students, I feel very committed to helping our brave wounded warriors as they transition from the military into civilian life. As a veteran and someone who loves the military, I feel it is the least I could do to honor our brave men and women in uniform.

And, what better place to honor our nation's veterans than in Philadelphia, the birthplace of our country, the city where the Declaration of Independence and the U.S. Constitution were ratified, and our own Congress was created. It was a fitting location to recognize another group of heroes the mothers who care for our brave wounded warriors.

I was in Philadelphia on Veterans Day, 2014, at The Union League of Philadelphia. This organization was founded in 1862 as a patriotic society to support the union and President Abraham Lincoln, and was the model for other Union Leagues created as a result of a nation torn by civil war. The league has hosted many U.S. presidents, heads of state, industrialists, entertainers, and dignitaries from around the world. It has supported the American military in every conflict since the Civil War.

Since I was a child I spent most Veterans Days listening to passionate speeches about patriotism and the sacrifices of our brave men and women who served our country in the military. As a college president and member of Congress, I continued this tradition and made many speeches at American Legion Posts, VFW Posts, military events, and throughout my home State of Tennessee and around the country. But on this Veterans Day, 2014, The Union League of Philadelphia hosted a group of hidden heroes, often suffering in silence as a result of their sons and daughters who were severely injured during the War on Terror.

Ten of these mighty moms and their wounded warrior sons and daughter are profiled in a new book to which I wrote an endorsement. The book is called, *Unbreakable Bonds: The Mighty Moms and Wounded Warriors of Walter Reed* by Dava Guerin and Kevin Ferris. All of the moms and wounded warriors were the highlight of the Union League event. I was fortunate to spend time with them, and watch them reluctantly be recognized from the podium for their own suffering and sacrifice. One mom, Lyn Braden Reed, has been at Walter Reed National Military Medical Center for more than three years taking care of her son, Cpl. Christian Brown, a Silver Star recipient who I mentioned before. I know their journey hasn't been easy. I asked Lyn how much they both have changed after their harrowing experience. It is no surprise that she replied,

"It hasn't been easy for Chris because of all his physical challenges, but his future is falling in place. We are so thankful for all of the wonderful Americans who have supported us." Lyn and Chris know first-hand what the price of freedom really means. As former members of Congress we share the belief that service helps us own a piece of the rock.

The mighty moms know this all too well. They have literally given up their jobs, homes and even marriages to care for their children, many of whom are the most catastrophically wounded and will need support for the rest of their lives. Though they have a heavy weight on their shoulders and unimaginable hardships and burdens to deal, they stand together as solid pillars of strength.

Their stories need to be told and I am thankful *Unbreakable Bonds* was written as a testament to their great strength and resolve. I hope every American will not only thank a veteran for their service, but the caregivers who serve their loved ones on the home front.

I have found that it has been among my greatest opportunities to have been an elected official in Tennessee and in the U.S. Congress. People have often asked me, "Bob, if you weren't in Congress what job would you have wanted to do?" Aside from serving as a university president, I would have loved to be a CEO of a humanitarian organization such as Habitat for Humanity, the U.S.O, the Red Cross, or become a U.S. ambassador—but I must confess they were jobs I never sought. When I tell my friends about those bucket-list jobs, they would sometimes say, "But wouldn't you miss being in the spotlight and having all the power you had as an elected official if you were just doing charity work?" Then it hit me. What I did in politics was to serve others, the same as if I were working for a non-profit. I loved and cared about people, I had a positive view of what I could do for them, didn't judge them, and I was a bridge builder not a divider. What you saw was what you got.

Is there life after Congress? For sure. But that life would not be worth living for me if it didn't include some aspect of service. It is for sure a calling, but it can be learned at any age. As the great South African President and civil rights activist Nelson Mandela said, "We must use time creatively, and forever realize that the time is always ripe to do right."

Clement's Contemplations

"Never use your refrigerator as a bank. The price you pay for convenience is a spoiler."

"When leaving Congress, leave your crown at the door."

"When you take the time to help someone else, you leave your troubles behind."

"Great men and women give a heart, a dollar, and lifetime of faith."

"Service on the home front and on the battlefield is the noblest of pursuits."

"Congress is like a dream: when you awake it doesn't always make sense."

"Living without giving is as empty as a guitar without Johnny Cash."

Chapter 13

Fixing America: My Prescription for Getting the Country Back on Track

"America is a shining city upon a hill whose beacon of light
guides freedom-loving people everywhere"
—President Ronald Reagan

America is the greatest nation in the world. Despite the political and fiscal challenges, we are a country blessed with one of our most precious commodities—freedom. Living in a democracy we often take for granted what we have here in the United States. With a world in chaos, it is even more obvious that America is a better place. While we may have different visions of how our nation should be governed, and polarizing politics, still, we are the land of opportunity. There are challenges to maintaining it, and we need to be vigilant to keep that sense of optimism alive.

Throughout my career, I have had the opportunity to not only observe, but participate in making the laws of the land, and hopefully, I've made a difference.

Many of our country's pressing needs such as education, transportation, energy, foreign affairs, national defense, the environment, and a host of other issues, affect us both in the short and long term. These are issues that are never fully resolved because there is a constant need for upkeep, reform and refinement. In my opinion, here are some of the most important challenges our nation faces, and I believe will continue to face for many years to come.

Education has always been a major focus in my life. As a young man I was told over and over by many different people, all of them meaning well, that as the son of a governor I didn't have to worry about a thing. All the doors would magically open for me. I strived to get a good education knowing full well that in order to be my own man; I needed the insurance policy of a college degree. I also worked toward my doctorate degree; those classes sure paid off when I became president of Cumberland University. Out of all the issues I have been able to work on over the years, education is the one that is closest to my heart. In high school and later in Congress in the 1980s and 1990s, I saw the same struggle play out that the nation still is grappling with today: what is the role of the federal government in our educational system?

I believe strongly that the easiest, best and cheapest way to retain and keep a strong, viable middle-class is to educate our citizenry. The private and public schools, which provide the K-12 experiences, need to be the responsibility of the state, not the federal government. Local leaders know best what the needs of their children are and what will or will not work in any given community. However, I also believe that the federal government has a fiscal responsibility when it comes to education. I have always supported federal aid to the states in support of education. What bothers me is financial aid from the Federal government leading to the Department of Education trying to assert control. Take Common Core, as an example. On paper and in Washington, Common Core sounds like a great idea because it creates formalized standards that every student, no matter where in the country, has to meet. This, also, makes it easier to compare the quality of our education to other countries. However, Common Core has resulted in us falling behind instead of surging ahead. Specifically, because of Common Core we now teach to pass standardized tests, rather than focusing on the main components of basic education: reading, writing and arithmetic.

We are not preparing our children for the changing workplace where they need more advanced skills rather than simply filling in a, b, c or d on a multiple choice test. We are failing both our students as well as our teachers. While Common Core makes comparisons and collects statistical data more easily, it has taken control away from state and local government in how to best educate our kids. No educational leader sets out with the goal of failing our kids, but the requirements and bureaucracy thrust onto educators make their jobs unnecessarily challenging.

When I was in Congress, I founded, with two other members of Congress, the Education Caucus. Roy Blunt of Missouri and Ray Thornton of Arkansas both were college presidents before coming to Congress, just like me. We shared a passion and a concern for public education, and sought to keep members of Congress involved in a productive debate about this vital issue. We addressed classroom concerns such as high drop-out rates, a lack of motivation and appreciation for the importance of a good education, as well as a lack of discipline. And we started talking about solutions. For example, schools are under-utilized. We spend more than any other country on education, yet we are the only one that lets students take three months off in the summer. While I'm not advocating for a year-round school year, I do believe strongly that kids should go to school more, not less. Also, even though we spend so much money on education, we are constantly cutting subjects or classes that some bureaucrat or another deemed unnecessary.

How can an appreciation of the arts, music, or civics be unnecessary if the goal is to create a civilized society of well-rounded citizens? Also, while helping our teachers is imperative, we are failing our families. Too many students lack discipline, support and love because of the changing family dynamics in this country. Two-income homes are the necessary norm. A great number of kids come from a single-parent household. Teachers often have become babysitters rather than educators. As a society, we need to ask ourselves what we can do to support the American family, and where do we want to put our priorities?

Part of this problem ties in with poverty and the growing income gap in this country. Just one mile from the Capitol Building in Nashville you can find the type of homelessness and poverty that should never be possible in the richest country in the world. Some people are having a really tough time making ends meet and keeping their families together. To me the solution to our poverty problem is education, and creating a safety-net that includes better public transportation, after school programs and welfare-to-work programs. We can lift these people into a solid middle-class status where the welfare check no longer is a way of life, but rather a bridge from poverty to opportunity. There needs to be incentives so that people will want to succeed rather than succumbing to the feeling of being trapped. Our Federal Government is the largest employer in the country, but it is the private marketplace—including large and small businesses that create the bulk of jobs for average Americans. However, government can do a lot to help Americans obtain gainful employment. Some of these include creating tax incentives, exposing young people to the workplace through the military, Peace Corps, Job Corps, Domestic Corps and many others. While government isn't the end all and be all in terms of creating jobs, it does have a vital role to play. If not, we will have a melt-down in our society because of the disparity between the rich and poor and the shrinking of the middle class. I have always admired FDR's ability to communicate to the masses and his innovative ideas and projects to get America working again. This wasn't just big government; it was big ideas. He was a master at building confidence and trust. I believe FDR had the right approach at the time and history has proved him to be correct in his strategy.

All of this begins and ends with access to a good education. It can come in many different forms. That is why I have always been a supporter of charter schools, which, in my mind, helps public schools improve. But public schools will only be as good as the principals running them, the teachers conducting the classes and the administrators overseeing them. We need to provide all of the necessary resources to succeed. We need to reform our twentieth century school system to twenty-first century realities. One such reality is that the job market has changed and we are much more of a service-oriented society heavily dependent on technology. Therefore, jobs and job requirements have changed. How we prepare our young people for entering the workforce has to be changed, as well. Another reality is that schools are being asked to fill too many roles rather than just educating our kids. They now have to cope with huge social problems not as prevalent just one generation ago.

Strengthening our educational system surely is of utmost importance, but it is not the only area where we need to focus right now.

I view our failing infrastructure and transportation system as another pressing challenge, which our elected officials have to address immediately. We have entered a period where our roads and bridges no longer are safe, and where our public transportation system is so outdated that it no longer sufficiently serves those who depend on it the most. There is also a role for the Federal Government to supplement what the private sector is doing by creating what I call a Domestic Corps. This idea would put people to work rebuilding our nation's infrastructure. I've always said that if someone can use their hands, they can always make a living.

At the root of this problem is the Highway Trust Fund, which represents the federally appropriated funding necessary for upkeep and improvement of our nation's roads and bridges. The Highway Trust Fund is subsidized through an eighteen percent tax on every gallon of gas purchased. This tax has not been increased since 1993. The challenges are two-fold: first, we are producing cars that consume much less gas per mile than any car that was on the road over twenty years ago when the gas tax was last adjusted for inflation. Fewer gallons sold means less tax collected. And, second, republicans who have taken the, "I will never raise taxes" pledge are steadfast in their opposition to raising the gas tax. In essence, that figure barely was sufficient in 1993. Eighteen cents, over twenty years later, is still the amount earmarked for keeping our roads safe; lives are at stake.

For example, on August 1, 2007, thirteen people were killed when the I-375W Mississippi Bridge outside of Minneapolis collapsed. Federal inspectors for a number of years had classified that bridge as structurally deficient and recommended its replacement. Yet traffic continued to flow back and forth, night and day, 365 days-a-year. The really scary part: the same year the I-375W Mississippi Bridge collapsed, approximately 75,000 other bridges in the United States carried the same structurally deficient classification! This is outrageous! This should be a bipartisan issue where broad consensus and collaboration should yield solutions to keep our citizens safe.

Yet an irresponsible pledge made solely to appease hyper-partisan primary voters is keeping us from doing just that. Meanwhile, federal dollars put toward strengthening our infrastructure and improving our transportation system would yield tremendous revenue due to jobs' creation and increased tourism. Transportation dollars would be incredibly well spent and should be a no-brainer. And since it takes years to implement infrastructure planning, every day Congress lets pass without reaching consensus is making the situation more costly and dire. I can only imagine the improvements we could have achieved with the taxpayer dollars that have been wasted on first destroying and then rebuilding Iraq.

Our failing infrastructure is one side of the coin, but our failure to implement a coherent public transportation strategy is the other. We need to focus on making public transportation more desirable, efficient and available. Transitioning consumers away from their gas-guzzling SUVs and into buses, trains, trams, or at minimum car pool lanes is optimal. This is not just an environmental issue it is a quality of life issue. How much time can a family devote to having dinner together, working on homework, and spending quality time when one or both parents are inching along a congested highway for hours each morning and night? It is getting more and more difficult to get around in our major urban areas. The vast majority of vehicles on the road are cars with one driver and no passengers. We have conditioned our consumers that bigger cars are an achievement and a status symbol, instead of presenting public transportation as a viable and desirable option. And the stranglehold exerted by the oil industry and the automobile industry over our elected officials will continue to prevent us from moving toward a more practical public transportation system. That is, unless we as voters and as consumers demand better.

Clearly, we live in a global world, and education as well as transportation and foreign relations are the keys to remaining competitive. Serving on the House Foreign Affairs Committee made that abundantly clear. Usually congressional service is structured so that members will serve on one major committee and then on one or more minor committees. For me, things fell into place differently, when I served on two major committees, the Foreign Affairs Committee and the Transportation Committee. I also got a special assignment to serve on the Budget Committee. Back then, not only were we able to pass a budget, but also a balanced budget. Those days, unfortunately, are long gone. As a result, I have a deepened appreciation for how each and every issue carries with it a global aspect simply because we are a superpower.

When I served in Congress, the Cold War was coming to an end, and thanks to the reforms by Mikhail Gorbachev and Boris Yeltzen, relations between Russia and the United States thawed considerably. Whether that means we won the Cold War I will leave for others to decide, but it did result in a very long period where the United States was the sole superpower. I think that period is now coming to an end with China joining the United States in the league of superpowers. Being a superpower comes with a heightened responsibility to protect global stability even if it puts the lives of our troops in harm's way.

The first Gulf War is an example of the United States taking the lead to form a coalition of like-minded partners. They recognized the tremendous threat Saddam Hussein posed to world security when he invaded oil-rich and Western-leaning Kuwait in 1990. I supported the first Gulf War because I agreed with President George H. W. Bush that Hussein had to be stopped from expanding into neighboring regions. I also supported the war because President Bush committed to leading a group of partner nations rather than going it alone. That meant that ninety percent of the costs of the first Gulf War were borne by countries other than the United States. Compare that to the second Gulf War, initiated by President George W. Bush. Without any real international support, the United States had to assume the total cost of that war. We paid a tremendous price in blood as well as dollars, not to mention the lives lost in Iraq. We basically put that war on a credit card, and the fiscal instability of the last ten years can be traced back to a very large extent to our irresponsible decision to invade Iraq. As I've said, that war cost the American taxpayers in excess of $2 trillion. I'm not the only one who thinks so, even the President's own brother, Jeb Bush, has made it clear that he disagrees with the way the Iraq War was handled.

The world we dealt with during my time on the Foreign Affairs Committee is very different from the one we live in today. For example, I am very concerned with the rollback of freedom and democracy that Russia is experiencing under Vladimir Putin. He clearly has decided to dismantle many of the accomplishments of President Gorbachev, and he is turning the world back toward a Cold War mindset. Russians always preferred strong and assertive leaders. The current Russian mindset is that they are being treated like a regional power when, in fact, they consider themselves a global superpower. I have been to Russia, as well as to Crimea and to the Ukraine, and I feel deeply for the many families that are now living in fear because of Russia's aggression toward Ukraine. I hope and pray that eventually cooler heads will prevail, because the world is a much safer place when Russia and the United States cooperate and treat each other with respect.

We understood and appreciated that America's leading role in the world made it a target. We were aware of the extremist role some Muslim clerics in the Middle East had adopted. We witnessed the growing threat of terrorism, first with the 1993 bombing of the World Trade Center, and then with the horrors of September 11. The terrorist threat has taken on a new and even more frightening reality with the incredibly barbaric actions of ISIS in the Middle East. I do believe we now have a situation on our hands that is similar to what our fathers and grandfathers faced in World War II; an existential struggle of good versus evil. To be clear: I am referring solely to the extremist, criminal terrorist groups such as ISIS and Al-Qaeda, who have taken Islam hostage, but are just a small fraction of the Muslim world. They have radicalized the teachings of Muhammad. It would be a mistake to hold more than one billion Muslims responsible for the violence perpetrated by a group of terrorists.

What makes ISIS and other organizations such as Al Qaeda in the Arabian Peninsula so dangerous is that they have such an easy way to communicate directly with their target recruits: young people from the Middle East and all over the world who are looking for adventure and do not believe life holds any opportunities for them. They often blame the West, specifically the United States, for their society's ills, such as the stranglehold of poverty and hopelessness. Some of our actions play directly into this narrative, for example the Second Gulf War. We have driven a great number of young Middle Easterners away from the West and Western values. I think that having a great respect for the Muslim culture, history and heritage would go a long way toward restoring our relations with that part of the world. We should not paint all Muslims with one broad brush, or characterize this as a war between religions, when it is actually a war against criminals who have hijacked their own religion for their radical and militant purposes.

One danger that exists now but was not necessarily on our radar screen when I served on the Foreign Affairs Committee is the homegrown terrorist. By this I mean young men or women, who were born and raised here in the United States, became radicalized often via social media and the Internet, and now are able to move freely around the country, ready to strike at any target of their choosing. These are young people whom we have failed as a society. For whatever reason, they see no hope in their present environment. They were never given a sense of discipline or responsibility; they slipped between the cracks.

I believe strongly that we need to do a much better job involving our young men and women in our society and government. This generation has an opportunity to buy into the American dream; they belong and have a role to play. Give them challenge, responsibility and hope. Bring civic education back to our public classrooms so that future generations have an appreciation for our way of life, as well as an understanding of the responsibility that comes with living in our society.

We would lose fewer young men and women to extremist and violent groups, whether they are radical Muslim groups or inner-city gangs, if we instilled a sense of purpose and hope.

Equally important is securing our borders. Our border with Canada is almost 4,000 miles long, and our border with Mexico comes close to 2,000 miles. It is critically important for security reasons to know who is crossing the borders and for what purpose. But right now our borders are more like a porous sieve than a protective defense against those who seek to harm us. The Department of Homeland Security, created by me and my colleagues in the House and the Senate as a response to September 11, is the largest federal agency. Yet on a daily basis people cross into this country illegally, and we have yet to figure out a way to stop them. But we need to know who these people are first. Congress, instead of holding the department hostage by threatening to defund it, should increase the number of border patrols, increase funding for better technology, and increase its support for border-states like California, Arizona, New Mexico and Texas. To me this is a security issue, not an immigration issue. True immigration reform, in my mind, is much more about dealing with the people who are already here. One of my ideas would be to bring those who are in our country illegally out of the shadows, provide them with work permits, and send the criminals back to their country or adjudicate them here. The president and Congress have to come to a unified decision on this issue and do it now.

Throughout our history, immigrants have contributed to our nation's achievements, not taken away from them. This is not an open invitation that comes without any limitations, though. First and foremost, everyone should know English so that they can be an integrated and productive member of our society. Having a common language is very important and unifying. Just ask Russia, which witnessed the Soviet Union falling apart rapidly in part because they lacked a common heritage and a common language.

But part of the problem we face today, as I've often said, is the lack of trust and cooperation between the executive and legislative branches of government. President Obama and Congress are still struggling with an immigration bill that can be passed by both the U.S. Senate and U.S. House of Representatives. President Obama's decision to use executive orders more and more is a direct result from the hyper partisanship that didn't exist as much when I was a member of Congress. I do not recall any other president who has had such a contentious and dysfunctional rapport with the legislative branch. Congress and the executive branch have a problem with trust due to the deterioration of respect and friendships formed across the aisle that foster compromise. As a result, working together effectively is more of a pipe dream than the dysfunctional reality that exists today.

Being President of the United States is undoubtedly the toughest job on earth, and it has only gotten more complicated in our hyper-partisan environment. How can one restore hope and optimism? No matter what words are said, at least half the country believes strongly that they are disingenuous? The next democrat president will inherit the same atmosphere as President Obama, and the next Republican president will get the same cold shoulder from Democrats in Congress.

What is the solution? In my opinion, it is this: an end to voter apathy; an electorate that is involved and demands better from its elected officials; more vigorous voter turnout during presidential and primary elections; getting information from a diverse group of sources, not just the ones that are most closely aligned with a person's political beliefs; an understanding of how government works; and the civic responsibilities that come with being a citizen.

What I witness in today's America truly worries me. We have always been a partisan and political society, but never has it inhibited us as it does today. When this country has had to face a national crisis, we always were able to put our differences aside and rally around the flag and our commander-in-chief. I wonder whether we are currently eroding our ability to come together for the good of the country. I pray we do not have in the future a catastrophic event that will test our resolve to put party over country.

Like most Americans, I am an optimist. I prefer to see opportunity where others see nothing but challenges. Ronald Reagan famously referred to America as the, "Shining city on a hill" that had a promise that was boundless. This well-known quotation was from John Winthrop, and it goes back to Puritan times though it has been repeated many times throughout American history. Are we still that city? Of course we are! Are we still a beacon of light? Absolutely, although right now that light seems to be flickering a little bit.

The American spirit has always been one of can-do, and never one that thought a hurdle was too high. I came of age during the Vietnam War and Watergate, where trust in government was at an all-time low. The war was dividing us like no other experience since the Civil War. Yet we have always overcome.

My vision for the America I would like my grandchildren to inherit includes optimism rather than obstacles. To paraphrase Hubert Humphrey, vice-president under Lyndon Johnson, "Why shouldn't the government play a leading role in ensuring that every American who wants a job can have one?" Why not take the tremendous resources we are expending on welfare and instead put them toward putting people to work? There is great dignity in having a job. There is pride in earning a living and providing for your family. And there is an opportunity here to lift up young people who have become disenfranchised and feel trapped in the unemployment rut.

Re-engaging citizens is a way to make America stronger. Engage Americans in the basic tenets of citizenry, and turn mere spectators into participants, increasing our dismal voter participation. We need to focus on American exceptionalism without glossing over some of our failings like slavery or the treatment of American Indians, as an example.

We can also put our resources and energy toward lifting up the middle class. Shrinking the income gap and eliminating the disproportionate difference between the haves and the have-nots could also make a difference. The tax code has gotten too complicated, as well. It is broken. Why not adopt a modified flat tax where people can still deduct mortgage interest and charitable contributions with all taxpayers participating? Having a fair and workable tax system would go a long way towards improving the lives of every American. We can also strengthen our public education so that future generations have all the tools they need to succeed. We need to address the deeper issues affecting these communities, as well as the increase in poverty throughout the country. It troubles me that more and more people are dropping from the middle class into despair.

Fixing Congress and our representative democracy is an achievable goal. It is the responsibility of every citizen of this country. All Americans should be engaged in the political process and educate themselves about the issues. Getting to know the candidates and showing up to vote for each election, whether it is a primary or general election, is optimal.

I admit to being worried about our country's future, but I truly believe in the American experiment and the American experience. I foresee an America where the power of ideas prevails rather than the power of the pocketbook. I am convinced that as a nation we can overcome any obstacle, and that we will always come together for the greater good. I am living proof that this is a nation of opportunity and that hard work, determination, and a little bit of luck will always see you through. My journey from the governor's residence to the halls of Congress has been the greatest adventure of my life. It was only possible because I was born and raised in the United States of America.

My story of meeting presidents, kings, and convicts is one that could only have been written in this glorious nation of ours, this exceptional beacon on the hill.

Clement's Contemplations

"Bridge the income and education gap, but don't forget to fix the bridges"

"Take the road less traveled, but drive home the fact that they need fixing"

"Vote with your mind, not your pocketbook"

"Education is the real road to prosperity"

"If you are the leader of the free world, stock up on antacids"

"Congress should be held to a higher standard. No short work week, recess, or extra time on the playground"

"Fixing America is easy. It's not that complicated. Cooperate and communicate; that's the ticket"

Chapter 14

Behind-the-Scenes with Presidents, Kings and Convicts

"I've been an eyewitness to history,
made some of my own, and I have embraced every moment"
—Congressman Bob Clement

Sometimes I have to pinch myself when I think back on the wonderful life I've had and the exposure to some of the world's most celebrated people and events. Growing up in a fishbowl for me was an honor. It came with all the benefits of success and privilege, and very few, if any, of the drawbacks. I often have said, jokingly, about my experience growing up in the governor's residence, "I grew up in public housing with prisoners and highway patrolmen as my best friends."

But, growing up in a fishbowl wasn't as awkward as some might think. Back then we didn't have reality television, but our lives were truly open books. Millions of Tennesseans knew our family's every move. However, I never felt like I was restrained in a strait jacket, and matter of fact, my parents let me live a relatively normal life, even though it wasn't normal at all. To me, it was perfectly natural to have visitors at the governor's residence like President Kennedy, Elvis Presley, and Billy Graham, to name a few. But no matter, I never felt like I was better than anyone else. I do think at times that I might have tried too hard to make friends, and I guess one might say that I over did it sometimes.

Way back when, if someone saw me in the hallway at Hillsboro High School I was probably the only person who would stop and speak to my fellow students at least four-or-five-times over the course of the day. By this over-compensation, I wanted them to understand that I was no different than they were; I so badly wanted to fit in. I guess it would come as no surprise that I was voted the friendliest student in my high school year-book, an honor that I treasure.

I believe that when children grow up in families with great wealth, fortune or fame there is the potential for them to feel a sense of self-importance, not gained through accomplishment, but solely on the basis of their parents' success. My parents never fell into the trap of making us feel special because of who we were. Mary and I raised our girls to stand on their own two feet and become confident and conscientious women in their own right. As Dad often said, "I left you a rich name, not a rich pocketbook."

But for me it always felt very comfortable being around movie stars, musicians or politicians. It was a natural feeling for me, and there was never a time when I was uptight, or didn't know what to say or how to act. I was an eyewitness to greatness most of my life. Being around so many accomplished people at a young age taught me to be a good listener, and learn from them as much as I could. All of my life I believed that whether people were on the low or high end of the spectrum, on top of the world or hitting rock bottom, they all had a story worth absorbing. I have always felt that it was important to listen to others, look them straight in their eyes, and never think I was too powerful or entitled to care about what they were saying.

Having spent half of my life in public service and the other half in the private sector, I do believe that if I have any gift at all it is to serve others. I must admit that there was far more excitement and challenge for me when I held political office, and I would be lying if I said I didn't miss it. But, I've tried to work on worthy causes to fill that void in my life, and one of the ways I've done that is to record, remember and cherish some of the most special and memorable moments with presidents, kings and convicts and everyone in between. Having had a front row seat all of my life to some of world's greatest individuals and events has taught me a thing or two. What I have seen and learned, I am honored to share with others.

Here are some of my most favorite stories laced with humor, sentiment and shear absurdity during my adventures with presidents, kings and convicts:

The Watch that Made an Impression on the Prime Minister of Israel

One of my first trips as a newly-elected member of Congress from Tennessee was to the State of Israel. It was a thrilling experience for me, and I decided that I wanted to share it with Mary. We visited with the Minster of Defense of Israel—Yitzhak Rabin—and Israel's top leaders. Mr. Rabin had been the commander of the troops during the Six-Day War with Egypt in 1967, which resulted in the expansion of Israel's borders; he was one of my heroes.

My father made his own visit to Israel years before the 1967 War, and he was invited there by the Prime Minister at the time, David Ben-Gurion, who was Israel's first Prime Minister. Dad talked to me about his trip many times, and was very proud that Ben-Gurion gave him a very special gift when he was there—a watch with the map of Israel on its face. That meant the world to Dad, and after Dad's passing, I inherited this wonderful piece of history. On the trip that Mary and I took to Israel, I decided that as a symbol of respect and admiration, I would wear the watch that David Ben-Gurion gave to Dad.

During our meetings in 1989 with Prime Minister Yitzhak Shamir, Defense Minister Yitzhak Rabin and Minister of Foreign Affairs, Simon Peres, I told them the story behind the watch I was wearing: "My father cherished this watch, and he and I always joked that if he only received it after the 1967 War, I would have a bigger watch." Everyone in the room laughed, and a photographer who was covering the meeting for a local newspaper thought the moment important enough to take a photo of the four of us together, with me showing them the watch and all of us laughing. Well, wouldn't you know it, that photo must have appeared in every newspaper all across Israel, because everywhere we traveled throughout the country people would come up to me and ask me if they could see the watch!

Towards the end of the trip we had a lovely farewell dinner hosted by the Israelis for our congressional delegation. Earlier in the day, Mary by chance overheard one of the wives of a Republican congressman say, "I'm sick and tired of hearing about that damn watch." I couldn't let that one get away. So here's what I did. During my remarks that evening, and with that congressman's wife in mind, I said: "I know a lot of you have commented about the watch I inherited from my father who visited Israel before the 1967 War and was given to him by David Ben-Gurion. But I assure you, the next time I come to Israel, I'm also going to bring the watch that Abraham and King David gave my ancestors." The room burst into laughter and applause. I'm sure I don't remember the congressman's wife even cracking a smile! Regardless, even though it was obvious that she thought what I said wasn't very funny; nonetheless, it brought the house down.

It was an unbelievable experience, though, during a very difficult time for Israel and the world in general. Not much different, I am sad to say, than what is happening right now. Mr. Rabin later became Israel's prime minister, and was awarded the Nobel Peace Prize in 1994. It sickened me that in 1995 during peace negotiations, Mr. Rabin was tragically assassinated by a crazed gunman. To this day, every time I put the watch on my wrist, I think about him. I have always said that we must stand with and protect the people of Israel from the terror that surrounds them, and keep them as the trusted friend and ally they have always been and will be forever.

The Congressmen, the Guinea Pig, and the Treadmill

It is true that members of Congress have never been so distrusted and despised by the American people. Matter of fact, the recent approval rating—or should I say disapproval rating, is a pathetic five percent. I'm not surprised because now as an educated observer, I too, am frustrated by the lack of partisanship and common ground. I long for the days when our collective goal was to make and pass meaningful legislation and work on behalf of the American people.

I have to say that even though we did work long hours, I or my staff always took the extra time to respond to every one of my constituent's calls or emails. Serving in Congress if you do it right—is one of the most demanding and challenging jobs a person could ever have. That's why as viewers tune in to C-SPAN to watch the U.S. House proceedings in real-time, rarely are members laughing or joking with their colleagues. Matter of fact, they are more likely to be yelling, yawning, or generally doing everything they can do to control their tempers.

I thought I would share some lighter moments about my fellow members from both sides of the aisle beginning with my friend, Congressman Barney Frank of Massachusetts.

For those who follow politics, Barney is known as a brilliant legislator, and among the few openly gay members of Congress. I always appreciated his wit and determination to stick to his guns regarding any issue he was involved. Not that we always agreed, but still, I had to admire him for his drive and tenacity.

One day when we were working out together on treadmills in the U.S. House gym, while walking at a brisk pace, I looked over at him and said, "Barney, do you mind if I ask you a question?" "Sure," he said. "Be my guest." "It's about homosexuality," I said. He replied, "Well, what do you want to know?" "I always wondered is homosexuality a product of heredity or environment?" The look on his face was priceless! "Bob that's a fair question. It's ninety-five percent hereditary," Barney said. He did go on to say, "For example, just like you. Nothing I can say or do could move you toward becoming a homosexual." We kept working out and I left appreciating Barney's candor.

U.S. Senator, David Pryor, from the state of Arkansas was a great friend of mine and had a wonderful career as a U.S. senator. At the time Nashville was an American Airlines hub. It turned out he was coming in from Arkansas and we were both flying from Nashville back to Washington, D.C. heading back to work for the week. Luckily, we were sitting right next to each other and I just had to tell him what I had in each pocket of my suit jacket. "David," I said, "You won't believe what I have in my pockets?" I explained to David that I wanted to bring something special back to my two girls—Elizabeth and Rachel. I very discreetly put my hands in each pocket and pulled out one of two live guinea pigs that were along for the ride. I didn't want anyone on the plane, especially the flight attendants, to see what I had brought along with me. At that time it was before 9/11 and things were much more casual and relaxed.

David burst out laughing and could hardly contain himself. It was obvious to me that this was the funniest thing he had ever seen in his life. He just couldn't fathom that I would do something like that. "David, remember I told you that as a kid I raised guinea pigs when Dad was governor and I started with just three and eventually had 150." Well, that made him laugh at me even more. As we both exited the plane, he kept looking over at my pockets with a big smile on his face. I'm sure he was secretly hoping one of my critters would make an escape. I kept thinking too, if I had gotten up out of my seat and one of my guinea pigs fell out of my pocket and ran down the isle of the plane, I would have been in big trouble.

The last time I spoke with David he said, "Bob, my friend, how are those guinea pigs?" I replied, "David, they lived a long and productive life. Not like some of our colleagues!"

Itsy, Bitsy, Witsie

I've always been a great believer in the notion that, "Things always happen for a reason." When Dad was governor, on occasion he toured the Tennessee State Penitentiary because of his interest in inmate rehabilitation. Another person who shared Dad's passion for redemption was the prison chaplain, Reverend L.H. Hardwick, Jr. who ministered to the inmates, offering them forgiveness and a chance to move on with a better life. So, it was no surprise that over the years Dad and the reverend would cross paths. As luck would have it, their friendship led me directly to meeting my wife of more than forty years—Mary Carson Crews, or as her family called her, Witsie. They called her Witsie because she was a very, very, tiny baby, and her parents would always say to her, "You are so itsy, bitsy, witsie." The name just stuck.

Reverend Hardwick, who was married to Mary's sister, Montelle, mentioned to me one day that he had a sister-in-law he wanted me to meet. Her name was Mary Carson Crews. She had beautiful big brown eyes, was independent, funny, and very interested in politics, though at the time Republican politics. So, one day after attending a service at Christ Church, where he was the pastor, we struck up a conversation, thanks to Reverend Hardwick's intervention. I really couldn't tell if she liked me or not. Witsie and I were both married before, so we knew if we ever got married again, we would both make a much more mature decision, and at least for me, one where I would enter with my eyes wide open. Still, I couldn't help my heart from fluttering when I saw her standing by the church door. I immediately asked her out on a date for the following week. Needless to say that date went very well, and over time I began to understand why Witsie became my best friend and closest confidant.

My early opinions about Witsie came from her interactions with her family, as well as how I related to them. They were a close-knit bunch and loved to spend time together doing anything and everything. Her parents, Noble and Maggie Carson, were the most wonderful people in the world. Around the kitchen table they had deep discussions about so many things from religion to personal issues. This is one reason I knew I wanted Mary to be my life partner. I knew that Witsie's life had been shaped by her parents deep faith. But her greatest strength was her keen ability to listen to others, and actually care about what they had to say. After dating for two years, I got up the courage and proposed. Then, to my surprise, she looked me square in the eyes and said: "That sure is a big decision; I can't give you an answer right now." I couldn't believe what I was hearing, but thought that if I were going to spend the rest of my life with this woman then the least I could do was give her some more time to make her decision. Years later, after we were married, she let the cat out of the bag. "Bob, I really didn't need a week to decide, but since I was married before I was a little scared, she said."

Our journey began together. And what a ride it has been. We had our two daughters—Elizabeth and Rachel. We were a team through seemingly endless political campaigns, moves from Nashville to D.C. and back, and traveled together around the world when I was a member of Congress. There were hundreds of visits to all ninety-five counties in Tennessee, chicken dinners in rotary clubs, bake sales at churches, and speeches at American Legion halls. Many White House visits, too. In fact, one year at the White House Christmas party, President Ronald Reagan—who was one of Witsie's biggest fans-whispered in her ear, "Mary, is there anything you can do to convince Bob to become a Republican?" And Witsie did all this while having a significant career of her own. Among the senior positions she held in both federal and state governments, was director of consumer affairs for the State of Tennessee. She was appointed by Governor Phil Bredesen in 2003. I am very proud of the work she did to protect the citizens of the state from a wide range of scams, product malfunctions, and so much more.

As anyone who has ever been married knows all too well—marriage is like politics. Compromise goes a long way to get through the moments when one spouse or the other has a different point of view and just won't give in. Compromise is why we are still together after forty years. I guess things do happen for a reason, after all.

The Triple Threat

Like most people, I consider myself to be an accomplished actor, dancer and singer—well at least in the shower or standing in front of a large mirror in my bedroom! Though throughout my life I have been in the presence of entertainment legends, their talent never really did seem to rub off on me. Politics was my Oscar and about the only singing I ever did in front of a crowd was at home crooning the words, Twinkle, twinkle, little star to my children before they went to bed.

Imagine my surprise when I received a telephone call from a theatrical producer, asking me to participate in the revival of the Broadway patriotic musical, *1776*.

"Congressman, we think you would be the perfect for the role of Dr. Lyman Hall from Georgia, because we need someone with a deep Southern accent," the producer told me. "Are you sure?" I said, full well knowing that I didn't have a lick of acting talent, and have never even been in a high school play let alone be considered for a Broadway-type production. "Congressman, don't worry, we are doing this play as a fundraiser for the Washington Symphony Orchestra, and I promise you, we will have professional actors on the stage with you as well as professional coaches to help you with stage presence." "Well, that was reassuring," I thought to myself at the time; I was never one to retreat from a challenge.

Once we had our first rehearsal I knew I got in over my head. The role also required me to sing, dance and express all manner of emotions and facial expressions. But, since my character was one of the original signers of the Declaration of Independence, I was more comfortable knowing that I was going to play him and not one of the big-wigs like John Adams whom most people would readily recognize. It helped that my fellow members from Tennessee—U.S. Senator Fred Thompson who was a professional actor, and Congressman John Tanner, who clearly wasn't, were there with me to calm my pre-play jitters.

Every Friday we would rehearse with the cast, and I was also joined by eight other members of Congress from both parties; I never really felt that out of place. To my surprise, when I did have to sing, I wasn't that bad, and it certainly helped that my voice was only one in a chorus of dozens. Over the month that we practiced the play I was feeling more and more at ease. For one short moment, I truly believed that if I hadn't become a member of Congress I might have had a successful career on Broadway. Well, not really.

Then, it was show time. On February, 24, 1996, a packed audience of 5,000 people attended the one and only performance of *1776* at Washington's D.A.R. Constitution Hall. It was an exhilarating feeling to look out at the audience and know that I accomplished something that I would have never dreamed possible. I was a triple threat, a song and dance man ready to give it my all for charity. As the last scene ended, and we took our curtain call, it brought tears to my eyes. We live in the greatest country in the world, and even though I was a *1776* cast member for only one night, I was most proud to join the Founding Fathers, even if it was just on the stage.

The Astronaut and the Actor

While situations in my political career were sometimes trying, others were clearly out of this world! I am specifically talking about U.S. Senator John Glenn. Not only was he a senator and presidential candidate but also an astronaut. I got to know him while he was on the campaign trail. I always admired him for his intellect, courage, military service and friendliness. John Glenn was one of my all-time heroes, not in small part for being among the team of astronauts to participate in Project Mercury. He was also the first person to orbit the earth and the fifth person in space overall. But imagine my surprise when I learned that I was invited to be a witness as the seventy-seven-year-old Senator Glenn became the oldest living person alive to fly in space in NASA's history. Matter of fact, there was quite a controversy surrounding the mission, because some people believed that if something went wrong it would reflect poorly on the U.S. space program. But Senator Glenn lobbied NASA for two years convincing them to have him be a human guinea pig for geriatric study. While it was great risk for NASA, I was one of many people who encouraged them to accept his flight because he was one of the most exceptional people I have ever met.

The date was October 29, 1998, and myself, Mary, and the girls got to fly on the NASA plane from Washington, D.C. to Florida where the launch was going to take place. We were so excited to be there, not only because he was my friend, but a true national American hero. As we sat on the bleachers with a majestic view of the ocean and the Kennedy Space Center Complex, we were mesmerized by what was about to happen. As the rocket left the launch pad I was just so proud of Senator Glenn. This was history in the making and I knew that I would never forget this experience in my entire life. But all of a sudden Elizabeth and Rachel turned their heads away from the spacecraft for what reason I wasn't sure. As the rocket zoomed toward outer space all of a sudden I saw what the girls were looking at. It was the actor, Leonardo DiCaprio, walking in front of the bleachers. They were distracted from the main attraction, which was John Glenn. So, as any good father would do, I took them from the stands and raced down the beach to corner Mr. DiCaprio for an autograph. The girls were thrilled and he was most gracious in spending a moment talking to them and signing their programs. I was their hero after that for sure. I guess you could say that these were two very different yet significant emotional events in my life.

After the flight went well and returned to earth safely, I had many occasions to tell Senator Glenn how proud I was of him and what his flight meant to the country and the world. It also reinforced my commitment to NASA and our space exploration to Mars and beyond.

Clement's Contemplations

"Democrats love donkeys; Republicans love elephants; but what political party would tolerate Guinea Pigs?"

"Watches can be more than just timepieces. They keep time in check, and on the offace it, preserve eternity."

"Treadmills are for working out, not deep discussions. And like Starbucks, customers just want their cup of Jo."

"When the President of the United States whispers in your ear, you can count on one thing: he's not serious about secrecy."

"Acting is a talent, and most politicians, sadly, do it only too well."

Bob and U.S. Representative Jim Coyne of Pennsylvania during their trip to speak at Oxford University as members of the U.S. Association of Former Members of Congress' "Congress to Campus Program."

CLEMENT RAILROAD HOTEL MUSEUM

Birthplace of Governor Frank G. Clement

The Clement Railroad Hotel Museum, housed in the Hotel Halbrook State Historic Site, is one of the few authentic railroad hotels located in historic downtown Dickson, Tennessee. Since opening on June 2, 2009, the hotel has hosted thousands of visitors locally, regionally, and internationally and is the birthplace of my father Governor Frank G. Clement.

*Congressman Roy Blount of Missouri, who is now a
U.S. Senator, Congressman Ray Thornton of Arkansas,
and me—the only three former college presidents in
the U.S. Congress at the time—formed the Education
Caucus in the U.S. House of Representatives.*

*Bob and his fellow Members of Congress were asked to
sponsor the building of a Habitat for Humanity home. Bob
wanted to do more and made history in the process. Bob's
team built the house in a record four hours, thirty-nine
minutes and eight seconds and broke the world record!*

Governor Phil Bredesen and Mary in February, 2003, when she was appointed the Director of Tennessee's Division of Consumer Affairs where she served for eight years.

Cast members for the play 1776, the non-profit fundraiser comprised of U.S. House and Senate members and professional actors performed at Constitution Hall in Washington, D. C.

Tennessee Governor Phil Bredesen, U.S. Senator John Glenn
(former astronaut), Congressman Jim Cooper, Former
Senator and Secretary of State, John Kerry, Congressman
Bart Gordon, Nashville Mayor Bill Purcell, and Bob at
a rally for John Kerry's presidential campaign in 2004.

Bob and Drue Smith enjoyed many fun times together.
She was truly one of a kind. As an experienced journalist
in Nashville, she eventually went to work for Gary
Cunningham—who owned the Green Hills News, and
a number of other community newspapers, where she
wrote a popular column called, "Drue's Views."

Bob and John Seigenthaler in 1998 when John was editor of the The Tennessean. He was a reporter for The Tennessean when my father ran for Governor.

Veronica Seigenthaler, Mary Clement, Ambassador Jean Kennedy Smith, Bob, and Tom Seigenthaler at the Ambassador's residence in Dublin, Ireland – June 4, 1994.

*Senator Ted Kennedy with my daughters, Elizabeth
and Rachel. During one visit to Nashville, Tennessee
he gave a speech at the home of John Seigenthaler.
John was administrative assistant to Bobby Kennedy
when Bobby headed the U.S. Justice Department.*

Our Congressional mission trip to Bosnia, Kosovo, Croatia, and Macedonia. (Left to Right) Congressman Sylvester Reyes (Texas), Congressman Ike Skelton (Missouri), General Wesley Clark, Congressman Gene Taylor (Mississippi), and me. General Wesley Clark was Commander of the U.S. troops in Bosnia, and Kosovo and other hot-spots around the world.

Vice President Al Gore and Tipper Gore had a reception at the vice president's residence for several of Bart Gordon's closest friends to celebrate Bart and Leslie's wedding in1998.

President Obama arriving for his annual State of the Union address. Mary and I were in Washington, D. C. to attend a reception for the 100th Congress which I was a member.

The Congressional Art's Caucus was meeting in Hollywood and was hosted by Congressman Henry Waxman of California. The acclaimed actress, Jodie Foster, allowed us to visit her on the set of her upcoming film at the time, "The Maverick."

Bob, Jeannette Rudy, Jack Gregory, and the great Opera singer, Luciano Pavarotti, greeting each other at the U.S. Capitol House Dining Room. Jeannette Rudy has one of the largest duck stamp collections in the world and donated her entire collection to the Smithsonian Museum.

Elizabeth, Mary, Jay Leno, Rachel and Bob in Los Angeles to see Jay host the "Tonight Show." After the show Jay made a special point to greet us and welcome us to the show.

Hank Aaron, the world-famous left-fielder and all time major league home run hitter for the Milwaukee and then the Atlanta Braves visits Washington. Hank and Claire Aaron were at the U.S. Capitol where we were honoring them for their service and achievement.

Boxing Legend Muhammad Ali and Bob share a laugh when Ali made a visit to the U.S. Capitol. The boxing legend was honored in Washington for his role as one of the greatest professional boxers of all time.

Queen Elizabeth at the U. S. Capitol attending a reception in her honor. I was honored to shake her hand knowing she was wearing her iconic gloves.

Steve McNair, the popular quarterback for the Tennessee
Titans attending a political event in Nashville for
me. Steve was a leader on and off the field.

Epilogue

Over the years, I've learned quite a lot about what makes the world go round. From the time I was born, I was up close and personal with greatness, beginning with my family all the way through my career where I got to know major world leaders and all manner of celebrities and people from all walks of life.

The lessons I learned from all of them were not lost on me. Matter of fact, there is a little piece of presidents, kings and convicts within me each and every day. Their words guide me, and their presence, while not physical, gives me great comfort in times of trouble and despair.

I hear Dad's voice the clearest, always telling me to do my best and not be afraid of failure. Mother's words of love and encouragement gave me a sense of confidence and self-worth which I am grateful for each and every day. Without her pushing me to join the debate team and learning the art of public speaking, I may never have pursued a career in politics. Aunt Anna Belle's love of politics and her intrinsic sense of civic responsibility helped me forge ahead throughout my many campaigns—both successful ones and disappointments. I have learned just as much from adversity as success, such as the losses I experienced running for the U.S. Senate and later mayor of Nashville. I did not run in vain because I knew in my heart my motives were honest and issue-driven rather than ego-driven. I truly offered myself to public service to make a difference in people's lives. I can certainly attest to that from the wonderful things that have come into my life that otherwise could not have found their way in. Witsie's deep faith and emotional intelligence have given me strength and taught me the power of love and redemption. Without my daughters, Elizabeth and Rachel in my life, my two stepsons, Greg, Jeff and his family, and my five grandchildren— Tennysen, Selah Grace, Clement, Mary Carson, and Savannah Burke, I would have never fully appreciated the depth of love between a parent and a child. Having two outstanding sons-in-law—Trael Webb and Josh Raymond, bring the family experience full circle.

The prisoners who were my boyhood best friends taught me that forgiveness was possible, and a person's past need not determine their future. My colleagues in Congress helped me listen to differences of opinion and learn the art of compromise. Serving in the military for thirty-one years was the ultimate lesson in teamwork, discipline and service that has made me the man I am today. I will always hear the words and sounds that have made Nashville Music City U.S.A.

My sincerest hope is that our future generations will embrace service for all of their lives. They can join the military, run for elected office, volunteer for a local charity, or simply reach out to another person in need. The greatest gift we can leave behind is the gift of service. Those whom we help will never forget.

When it's all said and done, it's not fame or fortune that will sustain us; it is the love of the people we love, and those who love us back that makes this life worth living. No matter if someone is a president, king or convict, each in their own way shares one common denominator—they are all human beings placed on this earth by God. What they do when they are here is up to them. What I have done in my life is to carry with me all the lessons I have learned, and impart that wisdom to the people I've been blessed to get to know and love.

I'm hoping my story resounds with readers. I hope that my words touch a nerve, inspire, or at least stimulate a conversation. We live in the greatest country on earth, and our most precious natural resource is our citizens. All of us can be part of the American dream.

About the Authors

U.S. Congressman Bob Clement

Bob Clement is president of Clement & Associates LLC, a public affairs firm. Mr. Clement served as a distinguished leader in government, business and education, including eight terms in the U.S. Congress from the Fifth District of Tennessee representing Nashville (Davidson County and Robertson County).

As a consultant, Mr. Clement has traveled internationally working with businesses, humanitarian groups, and non-government organizations. He also advises clients in the U.S. on business development and government relations issues.

Mr. Clement's leadership covers a wide-range of professional experience including: a military officer; public service commissioner; Tennessee Valley Authority director; college president; U.S. Congressman; and business consultant. Through his years in public service Mr. Clement gained expertise in the areas of international relations, transportation, healthcare, energy and education.

As the youngest Tennessean ever elected to a statewide position at the age of twenty-nine, Mr. Clement stepped into public service when he chose to run for political office as a Public Service Commissioner. His father, Governor Frank G. Clement, was a three-term governor in the 1950s and 1960s. He was recognized for his progressive leadership, including: integrating the first public school in the South; providing free textbooks for all students; creating the first department of mental health; initiating state government reforms; and promoting industrial development.

Upon Bob Clement's election to Congress in 1988, Mr. Clement knew his committee work would be crucial to his constituents. He chose committees which would have major economic impact in his state, as well as across the nation. During his fifteen years in congress, he served on the House Transportation Committee, improving infrastructure projects such as highways, public and mass transit, airport improvements and preserving waterways. One of Mr. Clement's landmark initiatives was co-authoring legislation on funding and establishing a nationwide system of greenways and bicycle paths. He was also a strong advocate of rail transportation. He supported more passenger rail service in Tennessee and around the country, and he launched Tennessee's first commuter rail line—the Music City Star. The successful run between Nashville and Lebanon, Tennessee significantly increased ridership.

While in Congress, Mr. Clement also served on the Foreign Affairs, Budget, and the Veteran's Affairs Committees and then he assisted Gulf War veterans suffering from illnesses after the first Gulf War. He's also responsible for major upgrades to the Veteran's Affairs Hospitals in Middle Tennessee and improvements in healthcare for veterans.

In addition to his committee assignments, Mr. Clement founded and co-chaired the Education Caucus promoting and supporting more federal funds for public education. He helped found the New Democrat Caucus that concentrated on high-tech and trade issues. As an active member of the Tourism Caucus, he promoted trade and tourism for the United States.

Mr. Clement was one of only three former college presidents during his tenure in Congress. He served as president of Cumberland University in Lebanon, Tennessee. During his tenure, he revitalized the struggling junior college, raising it to the level of a four-year accredited college with full university status. He also tripled the school's private donations and doubled its educational income which saved the historic college from closing.

Mr. Clement earned a Bachelor of Science Degree from the University of Tennessee at Knoxville. After obtaining a Master's Degree in Business (MBA) from the University of Memphis, Mr. Clement joined the U.S. Army, serving for two years. He then joined the Tennessee Army National Guard and served another twenty-nine years before retiring as colonel.

Dava Guerin

Dava Guerin is the author of *Unbreakable Bonds: The Mighty Moms and Wounded Warriors of Walter Reed.* It was released to critical acclaim on November 14, 2014, and is published by Skyhorse Publishing. Guerin is also a freelance writer with more than forty-five stories published in regional and national periodicals, newspapers and social media outlets. She is also the co-author of *Keep Chopping Wood*, along with Churchill Mortgage CEO, Mike Hardwick. She was also founder and president of Guerin Public Relations, Inc. where she managed major communications programs for Fortune One Hundred companies, as well as government agencies, political figures and non-profit organizations. She has extensive media relations experience having worked on major national and international events including: the Bicentennial of the U.S. Constitution; Live8; the 2000 Republican National Convention; the Liberty Medal; Welcome America; Mrs. Bush's Story Time, The President's Summit for America's Future, and many others. She has also managed dignitary appearances for major celebrities, U.S. presidents and world leaders, and also serves as communications director for the U.S. Association of Former Members of Congress. She holds a Bachelor of Arts Degree in English and Literature from Goddard College and a Master's Degree in Organizational Behavior from Temple University where she graduated Summa Cum Laude. She also spent a summer abroad attending the University of London. She volunteers her time helping wounded warriors and their families. She resides in Berlin, Maryland with her husband, Terry.

Peter Weichlein

Peter Weichlein is CEO of the U.S. Association of Former Members of Congress (www.usafmc.org) and he is managing partner of AWP Strategic Consulting (www.awpstrategies.com) and is a freelance writer. For the past fifteen years he has revitalized FMC, growing it from a purely social organization to one of the most respected non-profit organizations in the nation. Under his watch, FMC has instituted major national and international programs that serve to increase bipartisanship, dialog, and service, promote civic education, and bring the benefits of representative democracy to emerging democracies around the world.

Born and raised in Munich, Germany, Weichlein is the product of an American mother and a German father. His family moved to Princeton, New Jersey, in 1984, where he completed high school. He holds two Bachelor of Arts Degrees from the Pennsylvania State University and proudly cheers on his Nittany Lions every football Saturday. He attended law school at the Freie Universität in Berlin, Germany, where he spent four semesters studying European and German civil and public law. Weichlein completed his legal studies in Washington, D.C., graduating from the Catholic University of America, and the Columbus School of Law, *cum laude* in 1998. After law school and passing the Maryland Bar Examination, he worked for a number of years as an assistant counsel for the Senate Judiciary Subcommittee on Administrative Oversight and the Courts. He first joined the U.S. Association of Former Members of Congress as international programs director and has been its CEO since 2003. He lives in the Virginia suburbs of Washington, D.C. (the same neighborhood as Bob Clement lived in during his congressional career), with his wife Annette and their three daughters Julia, Emily and Anna.

Printed in the United States
By Bookmasters